Self Beyond Self

Judaism's Dynamic Ascent to the Infinite

FELDHEIM PUBLISHERS
Jerusalem
5755/1994

ISBN 0-87306-674-X
Published 5755/1994
First edition, 5755/1994

Copyright © by the author

All rights reserved, including translation rights.
No part of this publication (except sections of Part Seven) may be translated, reproduced, stored in a retrieval system or transmitted in any form or by any means, electronic, mechanical, photocopying, recording or otherwise, without the prior permission, in writing, of the copyright owner.
All the charts, continuums and dichotomies in Part Seven may be reproduced or photocopied so long as the following is clearly printed on each copy: "Taken from *Self Beyond Self: Judaism's Dynamic Ascent to the Infinite*, Feldheim Publishers, Jerusalem, 5755/1994, p. (cite the applicable page), with the author's permission."

Edited by: Shalom Kaplan
Computer-typeset: Sarah Kramer
Typesetting & Layout: Akiva Atwood
Cover art: Yaakov Kaszemacher
Cover design: Harvey Klineman
Graphics: Rafi Shachar

Distributed by:
Feldheim Publishers
POB 35002
Jerusalem, Israel

Feldheim Publishers
200 Airport Executive Park
Nanuet, NY 10954

Printed in Israel

Library of Congress Cataloging-in-Publication Data
Hurwitz, Y.S.
    Self beyond self: Judaism's dynamic ascent to the infinite/ by Y. S. Hurwitz.
       p. cm.
    Includes bibliographical references and index.
    ISBN 0-87306-674-X
       1. Judaism—Essence, genius, nature. I. Title
BM582.H87   1994
296—dc20   94-28449

RABBI MOISHE STERNBUCH	משה שטרנבוך
Vice President "Eda Hacharedis"	סגן נשיא העדה החרדית בעיה"ק
and Dayan Jerusalem Beth-Din	מח"ס מועדים וזמנים ועוד
Head Torah Centre Communities	ראב"ד דק"ק חרדים ביוהנסבורג
Johannesburg S.A.	

S.A. Address: 63 Fortesque Rd.	הכתובת בירושלים:
Yeoville Johannesburg	רח' מישקלוב 13, הר-נוף, ירושלים
Tel: 271-1- 648-5374 Fax: 271-1-648-5456	טל: 435780 פקס: 529610

בעזהי"ת, יום ט"ז שבט תשנ"י

הן בא לפני המופלג הרב י.ש. הורביץ שליט"א עם תכריך כתבים, בספר שמוציא לאור בשפה האנגלית Self Beyond Self, וכוונתו בזה לחזק האמונה. וכבר אתמחי בספריו הקודמין שקיבל עליהם הסכמות מגאוני ישראל לרבות הגאון הגדול רבי משה פיינשטיין זצ"ל. ובודאי גם עכשיו ממשיך בדרך הזה לזכות הרבים, והספר דבר טוב ומועיל בעהשי"ת. והנני בזה מצרף ברכתי שהספר יביא תועלת מרובה לחזק האמונה כרצונו ולהחזיר תועים למקור מחצבתם לאבינו שבשמים. ויהיה לו בזה זכות הרבים בעזהשי"ת.

הנני מצפה בכליון לישועת ה' ורחמי שמים

[signature]

Translation:

R' Y. S. Hurwitz has shown me his new book in English, *Self Beyond Self*, written with the intention of strengthening Jewish commitment. He has already demonstrated his competence in his prior works, which have received the approbation of leading Torah authorities, including Hagaon Rabbi Moshe Feinstein, z"l. Undoubtedly, his current work continues this effort to enlighten the Jewish public, for it is indeed both a worthwhile and, with Hashem's help, effective book.

I wish to add my blessing that this work be influential in enhancing our adherence to Judaism, as the author intended, and in helping those who err to return to their Source, our Father in Heaven. And in this way, may the author earn a portion among those who bring merit to the Jewish People.

Anticipating daily Hashem's salvation and compassion,

Moishe Sternbuch

בס"ד

KIRYAT NACHLIEL · קרית נחליאל

RABBI NACHMAN BULMAN   הרב נחמן בולמן

בעייה ג' לסי "אם בחוקותי תלכו" תשנ"ב

For both the Torah-observant Jew and the Jew who is not committed to Torah, the question that is fundamental is: Are our basic personality traits in harmony or disharmony with the requirements of a Torah life? Must I "break" myself to live in accord with Torah, or will my basic nature be fulfilled and "enlarged" through Torah observance?

The present work of Y. S. Hurwitz is a remarkable exposition of the structure of personality in classic Torah sources (both "revealed" and based on *Kabbalah*), of the biological, affective, and rational aspects of life. In contemporary idiom, the author focuses his primal portrait on the realization of *Am Yisroel*'s life-goals, on our "special" calendar days, and on the eternity for which this life is preparation and vestibule.

In a world of so much ignorant distortion, but of ever greater need for the redemptive powers of Torah, such works as Y. S. Hurwitz's book, *Self Beyond Self*, deserve rich commendation.

Dedicated
to the sacred memory
of those who lost their
lives because they
were Jewish

הי״ד

לעילוי נשמת
שלום הרצל
בן
חיים חנן
נ.ל.ב.ע. ז' תמוז תשנ"ב
ת. נ. צ. ב. ה.

For comments, questions or
criticisms, please contact:
Y. S. Hurwitz
POB 5964
Jerusalem, Israel 91057

*To my devoted
and patient wife*

A Word of Gratitude

Everyone who writes a book knows that many people and a huge amount of effort go into writing, editing and publishing the final product. But there are two participants, besides the author, who are absolutely essential in the creation of a book.

Number One is, obviously, the Creator Himself. The thoughts, the words, the sources, the organization, the entire manuscript depend on Him blessing the author with insight, ingenuity and perseverance. I thank Hashem with all my heart for how, on countless occasions, He helped me with an important idea, a well-expressed phrase or a hard-to-find source. Whatever has been achieved — indeed, that this book has seen the light of day at all — has been because of His abundant kindness in making it happen. And how can I say enough to thank Him?

Number two is my wife, together with our children. She allowed me to pursue this project, though the time and effort involved severely limited my activities in the home. For this whole book has been on overtime, leaving practically no extra minute for anything else. She deserves so much credit for her love and patience, and, again, words do not suffice to express my indebtedness and gratefulness to her.

And our children also were so accepting and considerate of a father who was always so busy and preoccupied. Without a doubt, they are certainly part of the sacrifice that went into making this book, and as such they deserve my deepest gratitude for being such special children, diligent and steadfast in their performance despite my curtailed involvement. May Hashem bless my wife and them to grow in their joyful and faithful service of their Creator.

So many other people are part of this book that I must mention them in order to properly express my appreciation:

My parents, may they be in health and comfort, for all they have done to make me an aspiring, persevering and positive Jew.

My father-in-law ז"ל, and mother-in-law להבחל"ח, for their concern and close support.

My rebbe, my *Roshei Yeshivos* and all my other *rebbeim*, for their efforts to inspire me to reach my highest potential.

My learning partners and colleagues, for sharing their talents and exemplary qualities.

My students, for prompting me to give them as much clarity as I could.

My editor, Reb Shalom Kaplan, together with Mrs. Sarah Kramer, who computer-typeset the book, for their diligence and patience in helping to produce as polished a result as possible.

Mr. Yaakov Feldheim and his highly professional staff, for their persistence in demanding a quality product, and for their help in bringing this book to the Jewish world.

Reb Akiva Atwood, Mr. Harvey Klineman and Rafi Shachar for their very competent work on the page layouts, cover typography and graphics.

Reb Yaakov Kaszemacher, for agreeing to the use of his artistry on this book's cover.

Additionally, I want to thank Reb Menachem Rudman, Mrs. Sarah Chavah Mizrachi, Mrs. Nechama Berg and the many others who made important contributions to the completion of this book.

And, finally, I am particularly grateful to the rabbis who encouraged me as I tried to produce not just a book, but rather the summation of my life's work: the expression of my Jewishness in its most dynamic and fulfilled dimension — the process of persistently and joyously going beyond self.

Yerushalayim
22 Teves 5754

Y.S.H.

Footnote Key

TB: Talmud Bavli — the Babylonian Talmud

TY: Talmud Yerushalmi — the Jerusalem Talmud

Pirkei Avos: Different editions have different numbering systems. We have used the Eshkol Publishers' *Mishnayos* and the Tiferes Yisroel *Mishnayos*, with some references in parentheses to the Artscroll *Siddur* numbering system.

Rambam: refers to the Rambam's *Mishnah Torah*, his 14-volume codification of the Oral Law

Michtav: Rabbi Eliyahu E. Dessler, *Michtav MeEliyahu*, B'nei Brak, 5734. (English translation by Rabbi Aryeh Carmell, *Strive for Truth!*, Feldheim Publishers, Jerusalem, 1978)

Discovery Sourcebook: the *Discovery Seminar Sourcebook,* Pathways to the Torah, Arachim Seminars, Avraham Sutton (ed.), Aleynu, Old City, Jerusalem, 1992

* : indicates that the quotation was taken from the *Discovery Sourcebook*

Yated: Yated Ne'eman (English edition), weekly English language newspaper printed in Israel and distributed in the United States and England

Contents

Part One: In the Beginning
- I   What's in It for Me? 2
- II   The Basic Thesis: The Threefold Key 5

Part Two: The Fundamentals of Jewish Identity
- III   The Genealogy of the Jew 16
- IV   Genetic Qualities 26
- V   Signs of a Unique Identity 34
- VI   The Subtle Power of the Jewish Woman 53

Part Three: A System Vital for Life
- VII   Living for a Purpose 64
- VIII   Achieving Unification 68
- IX   Identity Savers 82
- X   The Pillars of the World 90
- XI   Three within the Three 93

Part Four: Exemplary Celebrations
- XII   A Profound Beginning 106
- XIII   Holidays of Ascent 114

XIV	Food for Thought at the *Seder* Table	119
XV	Meaningful Frivolity	127

Part Five: Keys to Eternity

XVI	An All-Pervading Theme	138
XVII	Very Rewarding Meals	150
XVIII	Only in Heaven's Hands	160
XIX	Effort-Filled Presents	169
XX	The Final Resolution	178

Part Six: From Theory to Actualization

XXI	Practical Applications for Torah-aware Jews	194
XXII	Practical Applications for Jews Unfamiliar with Torah	204
XXIII	Conclusion for Torah-aware Jews	216
XXIV	Conclusion for Jews Unfamiliar with Torah	220
	Epilogue: Success!	222
	Postscript	226

Part Seven: Internalizing Mechanisms

Chart A	The Self—Beyond-Self Continuum	231
Chart B	The Integrated Dynamic of the Self—Beyond-Self Continuum	232
Chart C	Basic Dichotomies of Life	236
Chart D	Summary Review of *Self Beyond Self* in Chart Form: The Threefold Key to Being Jewish	238
Appendix A:	Special Prayer	241
Appendix B:	Love Your Neighbor	243
Appendix C:	The Fourth Component	247
	Glossary	251
	Index	259

Part One:
In the Beginning

   I What's in It for Me?
  II The Basic Thesis

I
What's in It for Me?

The obvious first question for any person who picks up a book to read is, "What's in it for me?" In other words, "What does the book offer, and how can it help me understand what I don't already know?"

Concerning this book, *Self Beyond Self*, the answers to these questions depend on who you are.

If you're already quite familiar with Torah Judaism, then this book will give you — perhaps for the first time — a clear, all-encompassing, and practical explanation of very many of Judaism's laws and traditions. You will discover that there is a simple, threefold key to being Jewish which helps to organize very much of what Judaism is saying. Putting together all the great wealth of Jewish ideology and practice into a straightforward and succinct system will be a very refreshing and enlightening experience. Moreover, we hope that this new key will help you maximize the clarity, effectiveness and enjoyment of all that you do as a Jew.

If you are somewhat familiar with Torah Judaism, then this book will give you an insider's explanation of what makes classic Judaism tick. In other words, what is the goal behind all these ancient Jewish traditions and laws? What, for example, makes the Jewish Sabbath such a unique and special experience, even in an age which offers so much leisure time. Why is circumcision as important today as when we Jews started performing it over three millennia ago? With modern refrigeration and public health departments, why is kosher food still a vital consideration? In other words, what possible contemporary relevance do all the Biblical Jewish practices have? Isn't just being a good Jew all that is necessary, without all these details?

This book will help you see that there is far more at stake than you ever realized. A very precise and simple threefold key to Judaism explains the purpose of life and how to achieve it. Once you see this system, you'll be amazed at how your whole view of Judaism will change and how much more interested you'll be to start learning more about what you thought wasn't so relevant.

Finally, if you are fairly unaware of Torah Judaism, you're in for a big surprise. A system of thought and living that has been around for such a long time — 3800 years — obviously must have had something going for it. But you always assumed that it probably was nothing more than a sectarian, blind adherence. Now you will have an opportunity to open your mind to an entirely different perspective on the Jewish religion. This book will show you a simple threefold key to how Judaism works. This system will impress you not so much with its religiosity as with its practical, insightful approach to successful living techniques. Would you like to learn how to control your anger, your frustrations, your jealousies? Would you like to live in a society free of crime, selfishness and alienation? Would you like to promote more love in a world where people really care for each other and help each other? Making a better human being and a better world are precisely Judaism's goals, and the threefold key to being Jewish will show you clearly and succinctly how these ideals can be accomplished.

Approaching such a huge subject as Judaism requires a certain patience and perseverance. With these two qualities, the unfamiliar reader will gradually become knowledgeable and fluent with the main points presented in this book. To assist this process, we have prepared a special glossary near the end of the book where many of the unfamiliar names, concepts and expressions are explained.

We shall begin with an explanation of the basic thesis (next chapter). Then we shall proceed to show how this thesis interweaves so many of Judaism's ideas and traditions (Parts Two through Five). Then, finally, we shall give examples of how the theory can be practically applied (Part Six), plus internalizing mechanisms (Part Seven). It has always been Judaism's approach to use wisdom and knowledge to make a better world, achieving for everyone greater success, fulfillment and happiness in life. *"L'chaim"* — to life — is the classic Jewish toast, and with all its implications, we extend this toast to our readers.

II
The Basic Thesis: The Threefold Key

Studying Judaism even cursorily, one comes across many sets of threes. There are other significant numbers, but the number three noticeably abounds: the three Forefathers, the three signs of a Jew, the three pilgrimage festivals, the three pillars upon which the world stands, the three meals of Shabbos, the three daily prayers. The summary chart in Part Seven of this book (Chart D) lists forty such sets of threes, and there are quite a few more.

The prevalence of these threes is not coincidental. They reflect a precise and all-embracing system of human development in which the three "parts" comprising any individual are guided and trained to achieve a higher level of behavior and awareness.

These three parts, elements or components of a human being are easily observable and definable. We start at the top with the head and its brain which represent the intellect. Going further down, we reach the torso and the heart which represent the emotions. And finally, further down are the stomach and reproductive organs which represent the instincts. (See Diagram A.)

Intellect

Emotions

Instincts

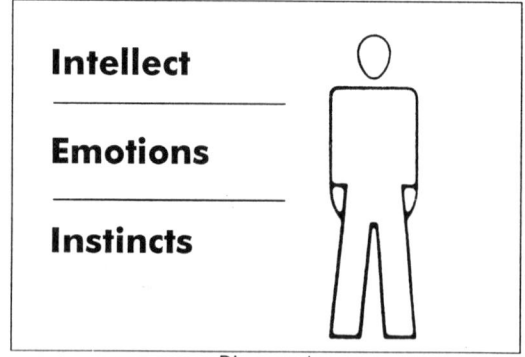

Diagram A

These are the three basic elements of all human beings. Although everyone possesses these three components in different proportions, they are the tools which we all use to build our world.[1]

Further, everyone shares a common and critical continuum regarding the *use* of these three elements. For although they are neutral in themselves, each person uses his components, to varying degrees, in one of two ways: for himself and

---

1. With the aid of the Vilna Gaon's explanation on the Scroll of *Esther* 3:13, we can compare these three human components to their metaphysical counterparts: mind — *neshamah*; emotions — *ruach*; instincts — *nefesh*. (Interestingly, *guf* is considered inextricably linked with *nefesh*.)

    We can also suggest that personality types revolve around these three basic components:
    - Those who are intellectual, philosophical, truth and purpose seeking, goal-oriented, articulate.
    - Those who are more emotional, sensitive, intuitive, aesthetic, eager to give love and help others, impulsive.
    - Those who are instinctual, physically active, work best with simple, straightforward instructions.

    The existence of a fourth component as a composite of all three elements is discussed briefly in App. C, p. 247.

his own interests, or for "beyond self" — beyond his own interests, for others. Everyone conducts his life somewhere in a range between these two polarities — totally for himself or totally beyond himself. (See Diagram B.)

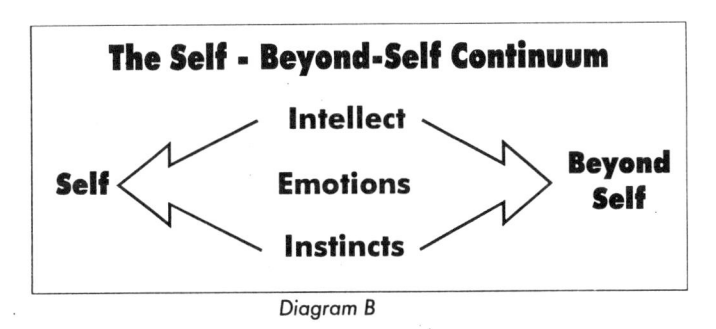

The Self - Beyond-Self Continuum

Self ⟷ Intellect / Emotions / Instincts ⟷ Beyond Self

Diagram B

Judaism's goal is to train each individual to move further in the direction of Beyond Self. Only then will the person achieve his greatest possible success and achievement.

Why? The answer is straightforward.

If we analyze the effect of directing the three basic human components towards the Self end of the continuum, we find the following:

To the degree that the intellect is used primarily for self, it continually promotes the person's perception of his self-importance and eventually leads to egocentricity and arrogance. Persistently, the person strives to rise above and dominate others and his environment. This behavior inevitably causes tension, anger and conflict, both with others and within himself.

To the degree that emotions are used primarily for the satisfaction of the individual, they result in selfishness, avarice and jealousy. The self-involved person has emotional needs which drive him to be concerned only with how he is being cared for and provided for. He can become so preoccupied with taking for himself that he has very little time for or interest in relating to others, inevitably causing loneliness, alienation and even enmity.

To the degree that instincts are used primarily to fulfill one's bodily cravings, they promote self-indulgence, lust and promiscuity. The physical drives can become an end in themselves, devoid of any ultimate purpose. The human allows himself to sink to the level of mere animal behavior, in effect undermining the very bases of civilized society — self-restraint, the family unit, morality. See Diagram C, which depicts what we just have described.

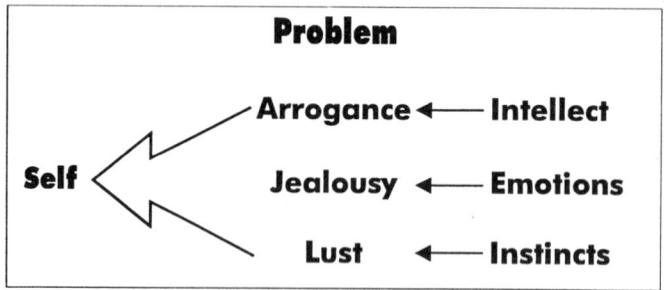

```
                    Problem

                 Arrogance  ←——  Intellect

        Self  <  Jealousy   ←——  Emotions

                 Lust       ←——  Instincts
```

Diagram C

In summary, we may say that many of life's problems occur when the person directs his three basic elements to the Self end of the continuum.[2]

---

2. See *Pirkei Avos* 4:21(28), Tiferes Yisroel, note 108; Eitz Yosef.

Throughout the ages, Torah literature has stressed the importance of avoiding these three pitfalls of arrogance, jealousy and lust: Rambam, *Hilchos Deos* 2:7; Rabbi Moshe Chaim Luzzato, *Mesillas Yesharim/Path of the Just*, end of Chap. 11; Rabbi Shlomo Volbe, *Aley Shor*, Be'er Yaakov, Israel, 5732, p. 102; Rabbi Aharon Feldman, *The River, the Kettle and the Bird*, CSB Publishers, Jerusalem, 1987, pp. 19,30. The Vilna Gaon in *Even Sh'laymah* 2:1 also discusses these basic deficiencies in an arrangement different than that presented here. Also, Rabbi Eliyahu E. Dessler states openly that the root of all evil is "love of self," which we have here simply broken down into its three components (*Michtav*, Vol. 1, p. 32).

In contrast, when these components are directed beyond the self, we find the following:

The intellect develops humility and self-effacement because since its perspective is focused beyond itself, it does not become lost in its own importance. Instead, the person sees a vastly larger picture, which immediately forces him to appreciate his own insignificance and the accompanying requirement of humility. Further, using this power beyond the self to benefit others rather than merely to promote himself, he helps to build a world of mutual understanding and cooperation.

The emotions are trained more and more to feel love for others and, consequently, to suffer less and less the insecurity that leads to seeking approval, attention and acquisitions. By giving of himself to others, he builds relationships in which sincere concern and altruism create wholeness and unification.

By going beyond self, the instincts learn control and restraint, for the person is no longer the arbiter of how he uses his instincts. Instead, a system of rules and discipline *beyond himself* guides and trains the person to control his physical drives and self-indulgent inclinations. Once he is self-controlled, his body then becomes a means to an end rather than an end in itself and, as such, can actually assist him to reach higher and higher levels of meaning and purpose. See Diagram D, which illustrates what we have just explained. We see that to counter the major problems that result from focusing on self, we contend that the solutions come when the person goes in the opposite direction and moves his same three components beyond self.[3]

---

3. See *Pirkei Avos* 1:2, Tiferes Yisroel, note 10. These three solutions will be described, in other terms, as the pillars upon which the world stands: Torah, Lovingkindness and *Avodah*. (See Chap. X and Chap. III, fn. 11).

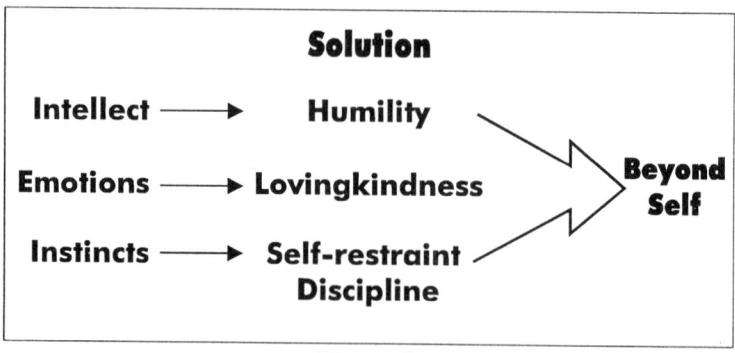

```
              Solution
   Intellect ──▶  Humility          ╲
                                     ╲  Beyond
   Emotions ──▶  Lovingkindness  ────▶  Self
                                     ╱
   Instincts ──▶  Self-restraint    ╱
                  Discipline
```

Diagram D

The advantages gained in going from self to beyond-self are quite amazing. For example, everyone is familiar with the description of the normal maturation process: As an infant and a young child, a person is totally preoccupied with himself; as he grows older, he develops beyond himself, becomes involved with and takes an interest in others and in his environment. However, this secular developmental process lacks any significant continuation at the adult level; the grownup just does whatever he feels like doing, with practically no system to help him continue growing.

Torah Judaism, in contrast, has a system, a system which constantly trains the individual to move on the continuum further and further beyond self, with the goal of creating a totally humble, giving and controlled human being.[4] In Jewish

---

4. To clarify a possible misunderstanding: It is a given that each individual has unique qualities, talents and personality traits. "Further and further beyond self" does not mean that he must sacrifice these abilities. On the contrary, each person takes those capacities which have been specially given him and uses them to go beyond his particular self in his own unique way. So, for example, if he is particularly gregarious, instead of capitalizing on this attribute for private gain, he can employ it selflessly in influencing others to reach a higher Jewish dimension.

terms, this person is called a *tzaddik*, a righteous one, and to attain such a high level of behavior, the world and, indeed, the universe were created.

Since Judaism's central goal is just this — for *every Jew* to become a *tzaddik*,[5] it contains precisely this triadic system, one which is intentionally designed to train and perfect the three components of each human being. We call this process of human development and problem-solving the "Threefold Key" to being Jewish, and through properly using this system, we can all become *tzaddikim*.

Having outlined our basic thesis, we want to begin by applying it to a fundamental dilemma of life, and in this way, the reader will see the practical usefulness of our approach. With the Threefold Key, we can translate even the most profound issues of Judaism into very pragmatic terms of personal action and growth. We will then go on to look at many variations of the Key in more detail.

The dilemma is this: Given that God is Infinite and, therefore, Omnipresent, how does the finite world exist? Where is there any room for us?

The *Kabbalah* explains that the Creator contracted His existence in order to make a place for the physical universe to exist.[6] However, even so, an imbalance still persists, since the finite has no real or ultimate meaning vis-à-vis the Infinite. In other words, since the finite comes to an end, by definition it

---

5. See Rabbi Aryeh Kaplan's lucid and thorough *Handbook of Jewish Thought*, Vol. 1, Moznaim Publishing Corp., New York/Jerusalem, 1979, p. 26, para. 3:23, which states: "It is thus taught that for the sake of the righteous the world was created," citing sources in fn. 31.
6. *Ibid.*, p. 15, fn. 46. This concept is termed *tzimtzum* in Hebrew, meaning *constriction* or *contraction*.

can have no essential or lasting meaning compared to the Infinite. This deficiency forces the next both poignant and obvious question: Is there any way that the finite can gain real and permanent meaning?

Judaism answers that the only possibility is for the finite to strive to become *like* the Infinite.[7] Fortunately, since the finite derives from the Infinite, it contains a spark of the Infinite and, consequently, has the potential to reach even further toward the Infinite. Yet how does one accomplish such a challenge? This huge task actually becomes more manageable with the Key which we have described. The goal of the human is to take his finite self with its three component parts and move it beyond self. By definition, the "self" is finite, and therefore "going beyond self" means going beyond the finite. "Going beyond the finite" is, in effect, the same as moving towards the Infinite, which, from the Jewish perspective, is the one and only way that finite existence can have any ultimate meaning.

Judaism usually explains this "imbalance" between the finite and the Infinite from the opposite direction. Since Hashem withdrew Himself in order for the physical world to exist, the task of humankind is to do all that it can to bring Him back into this world.[8] But how? The answer is direct and to the

---

7. *Ibid.*, p. 24, para. 3:17. The purpose, then, of creation was to give humankind the opportunity to achieve eternity through its own effort. For a full discussion of this subject, see Rabbi Moshe Chaim Luzzatto, *Derech Hashem/The Way of God*, Feldheim Publishers, Jerusalem/New York, 1988, Part I, Chap. 2.

8. On this point, we want to make it very clear for now and throughout the book that we are speaking only metaphorically. All that a person can do is to endeavor to bring the *qualities* of Hashem into this world. He Himself always exists completely independent of creation. However, in a world that is physical, we have the opportunity to reveal and make manifest this spiritual Force which, in actuality, permeates

point: by doing His will, for by doing what He wants, it is as if He were here.

Fundamental to the whole plan of creation is the power of free choice which human beings have. With this power, we can either block Hashem from being in the world, so to speak, simply by doing what *we* want, or we can promote Hashem's being in this world by doing what *He* says. It would make sense for us to choose to go along with what Hashem wants, for without a connection to the Source of our existence, a vital part of our significance is missing. The situation would be analogous to a computer terminal disconnected from the main body of the computer. Would the terminal alone serve any real purpose? Certainly not. And likewise, we lose our purpose unless we maintain our connection to our Source. Hashem expressed in the Torah and its commandments the means of maintaining this connection, and by our sincerely following His will as delineated in the Torah, it is as if we actually made Hashem an intimate part of our world. At the same time, we are also making our finite selves like the Infinite, resolving the essential imbalance of existence.

These two explanations resolving the imbalance actually describe the purpose of creation, a purpose which resembles two sides of one coin. On one side, the goal is to bring Hashem back into His creation by precisely following His will — Torah and *mitzvos*. On the other side, the purpose is to strive to become like Hashem (the Infinite), giving, in effect, each and every person the opportunity to earn his own infinity. Or, in the terminology which we are using in this book: to go from self —

---

and controls everything. This basic contradiction is classically described as the difference between Hashem's immanence (His presence) and transcendence (His absence). *Ibid.*, p. 15, fn. 46.

the finite — to beyond self — the infinite.

This approach to life applies to both the sublime *and* the mundane. For example, the simple cobbler who is banging nails into shoes can also be connecting to Hashem. How? By intending his work for the benefit of his customer and not for the money he is profiting.[9] By going beyond self, he is, in effect, performing an infinite-like act, emulating the Infinite's selfless giving and thereby connecting to Him, i.e., His qualities.

Having elucidated our basic thesis and its relevance, we will now show how so many of Judaism's concepts, values, laws and traditions designedly reflect this Threefold Key, all in order to help us build ourselves into fully actualized, infinitely successful Jews.

---

9. *Cf. Bereishis* 5:22; *Michtav*, Vol. 1, pp. 34-5 (*Strive for Truth!*, Vol. 1, pp. 123-4).

Part Two:

The Fundamentals of Jewish Identity

III The Genealogy of the Jew
IV Genetic Qualities
V Signs of a Unique Identity
VI The Subtle Power of the Jewish Woman

III
The Genealogy of the Jew

As we unravel the threads that comprise the rich fabric of Judaism, the first step must be to understand where we Jews come from, our background, our lineage. For a person is not born in a void. He is the product of that which preceded him — his parents, their parents, and so on. The science of genetics tells us how important our ancestors are to us biologically, but for the Jew, this fact is just the beginning of the story.

Who, then, were our ancestors?

The great, great, great-grandfathers of the Jews were the *Avos*, Avraham, Yitzchak and Yaakov. Each one of them implanted in us a major character trait that teaches us something about ourselves.[10] Avraham implanted lovingkindness.[11]

---

10. As will be seen in Chap. VI, our great Jewish Matriarchs, Sarah, Rivkah, Rachel and Leah, made the same contribution from the feminine side, with the necessary addition of their subtle, unpretentious, but all-important modesty. Together their names contain thirteen Hebrew letters, which when added to the equivalent number of letters in the Patriarchs' names, equal the numerical value of Hashem's name: 13 + 13 = 26. This indicates that, in Judaism, only together do the male and female roles achieve completion and wholeness.

Yitzchak implanted strict self-control.[12] Yaakov implanted love of truth.[13] With these three characteristics, we Jews were given the means to correct the three main problems of life — jealousy, lust, and arrogance — which result from using the basic human components primarily for self. Our forefathers' lives established the foundation of the Jewish People, and we owe our entire existence and character as a nation to their successful injection of these fundamental traits into our collective personalities.

Avraham was famous for giving food and drink to all travelers, and indeed, we find that his tent was open on all four sides, a striking statement and symbol to the world that the person inside is not concerned with his own needs, but only with the needs of others.[14] Avraham actively sought to bring in

---

11. *Micah* 7:20. Avraham, like the other *Avos*, possessed all three qualities (see Chap. XVI, page 140). Indeed, throughout our discussion, there will be many instances where an example of one category has within it the other two as well. See Chaps. XI, XIII, XVII, XIX, fn. 259.

    As the reader will understand as the book progresses, our forefathers represent the foundations of the world's construction, i.e., the purpose of the human's creation. Indeed, the Maharal specifically relates the *Avos* to the three pillars of the world: Avraham — Acts of Lovingkindness; Yitzchak — *Avodah*; Yaakov — Torah (*Derech Chaim*, Yerushalayim, 5731, pp. 28-9). Further, in a speech given in 1960, Rabbi Aharon Kotler explained the following:

    "Each of the *Avos* was master of a specific pillar of life: Avraham — *chesed*; Yitzchak — Hashem's service; Yaakov — Torah. This does not mean that the other *Avos* did not encompass all these traits, rather that each of the *Avos* was the prototype of the specific trait attributed to him; his prime task was to construct that pillar."

    Rabbi Aharon Kotler, *How to Teach Torah* (pamphlet), Light Publishing Co., Jerusalem, 1978, p. 13. The article cited *The Eight Gates* by Chaim Vital and the *Sefer Ha'bahir* (On the lovingkindness of Avraham). See also the *Chofetz Chaim on the Torah (Bereishis* 32:25-6) and Chap. X, herein.

12. *Sefer Ha'bahir*, Sec. 135, Ohr Haganuz.
13. *Ibid.*; *Micah* 7:20.

guests, showering munificence and love upon them. In fact, his love extended even to the seemingly undeserving, for goodness has the power to overturn all evil.[15] Essentially, he was working to bring Hashem totally into the world. As a result, this Ultimate Good would automatically dispel all that was undesirable.

Further, Avraham's capacity for being truly concerned about others derived from a profound awareness that everything is One and that therefore, each of us is really interconnected and part of this Oneness. With such a perspective, jealousy and envy — forces which divide and separate us — can be uprooted. No longer do we have to worry that others are getting ahead of us, that we are falling behind, that our "piece of the pie" is getting smaller or theirs, larger. By giving and sharing, we are training to see others not as our competitors, but rather as our brothers. Avraham strove to make this ideal a reality, using lovingkindness as a powerful tool to unify humankind.

This awareness includes not just giving money, food or clothes, but also time, concern and support. For example, by speaking with one who is lonely, we actualize the basic Jewish ideology that our lives are inextricably intertwined and that it is our common task to work together. An isolated person's feelings of separateness and inadequacy are immediately supplanted by love and wholeness. No longer is he alone in his own world, for we have actively shown him that what looks like so many disconnected parts is really an illusion. The real Oneness unifies and unites us all, impelling us to care for and help each other.

---

14. *Bereishis* 18:1-8; *Matanos Kehunah*, *Bereishis Rabba* 48:9, compares it with *Avos d'Rebbi Nossan* 7:1; *Midrash Shochar Tov*, *Mizmor* 110.

15. See *Bereishis* 18:23, where Avraham tried to save the inhabitants of Sodom and Amorah, cities of great evil.

The conclusion is clear: Avraham's tent of lovingkindness symbolizes a very crucial aspect of our Jewish lineage and graphically represents the first component of our Threefold Key to being Jewish.

Moving to Yitzchak, we see how Avraham's son was totally prepared at the *Akeidah* (binding on the altar) to give his life to serve Hashem, using absolute self-control to offer himself for the ultimate sacrifice.[16] This great test actually came at the prime of his life, when he was thirty-seven years old.[17] Whereas his father, Avraham, had worked *externally* to make Hashem manifest, Yitzchak used the same powers to work on himself *internally* for the same purpose. The awesome presence of Hashem dominated his being so thoroughly that not one of his thoughts or movements deviated from the exact will of the Creator. In other words, his human perspective never lost sight of his spiritual objective, a goal which necessarily required total control over his physical nature. Yitzchak succeeded so completely in this life task that he was fully prepared to give up his physical existence if Hashem so decreed.

---

16. *Bereishis* 22:7-10. The *Akeidah* shows the connection between *Avodah* (service), prayer and self-control. The service in the *Beis Hamikdosh* demonstrated our single-minded intention to bring the physical close to Hashem, in which the "animal" (i.e., all physicality) was placed on the altar and symbolically raised to a higher dimension. Prayer is exactly this same focusing of intention to raise the physical to a more elevated plane. If a person is seriously beseeching Hashem, he must necessarily direct his "wish list" to some more profound purpose. The result of both activities (*Avodah* and prayer) is increased self-control over one's instincts and appetites, reaching the ultimate level when Yitzchak overcame his instinct for self-preservation when specifically requested to from Above. See also fn. 18; Chap. X, p. 90; Chap. XX, p. 178.

17. *Bereishis* 25:20, Rashi.

From this extraordinary example of self-control, we Jews find within ourselves a latent ability to master our own physical desires and lusts. As a result, we stand diametrically opposed to the underlying philosophy of Western culture: eat, drink and be merry. Without question, we should always be happy, but it is a completely different type of happiness. We do not define happiness by how much pleasure our bodies receive. Instead, our test is constantly to realize that the physical is a *means* to achieve the spiritual, rather than an end in itself. Through this approach, we attain our true and ultimate happiness because we are using the physical for a higher goal.

Most people, though, assume that life is solely for the purpose of having a good time. The more ways their physical senses can be stimulated and satisfied, the more they feel that they have succeeded in life. The more money they have, the more enjoyment and comfort they can buy: a fancy sports car, a yacht, a sauna bath, a mountain summer home or a beach house close to the surf. If anyone suggests abstention or control, he is pounced on for being inhibited, abnormal or prudish. Indeed, this preoccupation with the corporeality of the transient material world extends so far that when one's physical realization inevitably falls short, the imagination starts taking over. With ease, one's mind constructs worlds where all physical fantasies are realities. And he can always rationalize to himself, "After all, nothing could possibly be wrong with just *thinking* my desires. I haven't hurt a soul!"

But, in truth, he and all of us who adopt his way of thinking have hurt ourselves, for this craving for more physical satisfaction only drives us to try and indulge our imaginations, which in turn are never satiated. There are always more things to have, more things to buy, more things in which to revel. And since there are very few controls or limits in the ever-spiraling system of sensual gratification, we find people actually harming themselves with excessive food, alcoholic beverages, drugs and illicit sexual relationships, not to mention the "workaholics" who literally kill themselves working an inordinate amount in order to afford all these things.

However, by learning to control our desires, we could behave in an entirely different manner. We could feel content with what we have, being satisfied with what is necessary without looking for additional, unnecessary indulgences. Instead of working so hard to have so many things, we could have time to study the deeper aspects of life. Instead of primarily catering to our bodies, we can experience dimensions beyond the physical.

The secret lies in learning from our forefather Yitzchak that the clearest possible recognition of the Infinite Creator allows us the best perspective on our finite, physical natures.[18] With this awareness, we can then appreciate the need for a system of self-control which will discipline and reign in our shortsighted, fleeting impulses. As a result of the *Akeidah*'s powerful image of a man's placing himself on the altar, we have been given the potential for elevating our earthly nature to a far higher plane, even reaching a transcendental dimension.

Now we consider the last of the *Avos*, Yaakov. This Jewish forefather is famous for having a dream in which he saw a

---

18. Prayer is precisely this deep concentration that helps us feel intimately close to Hashem through the necessary divestiture of some part of our physical nature. See *Shulchan Aruch, Orach Chaim* 98:1, which describes the highest level of prayer preparation when the person has actually stripped himself of his physicality.

ladder standing on the earth and reaching to Heaven, with spiritual forces interacting between the two.[19]

If we were to think about life seriously and in depth, we would come to understand the vital connection between all that happens on this earth and its Source. Although the vicissitudes of life sometimes confuse us, with proper guidance we Jews would be able to find our way through the maze.

But what do we do instead? We secretly imagine that we more or less know it all. How do we arrive at such a conclusion? Blessed with better than average intelligence, we are a fairly secure and self-confident people. Diligent use of our abilities gains for us a fairly high level of achievement.[20] Such success, in turn, builds our egos and feeds our pride until finally we feel as if we were on top of everything. Whatever we do not know is conveniently overlooked, ignored or even dismissed as non-existent.

The image of Yaakov's ladder reminds us that man's real "dream" (i.e., aspiration) is to go beyond, to understand the totality of life, to achieve ultimate knowledge, to learn how this world of relative, vacillating transience can be connected to a far greater dimension of absolute reality and truth.[21]

Is such a connection possible? The ladder in the dream dramatically proclaims: Yes, there definitely is a connection between this world and a world beyond.

---

19. *Bereishis* 28:12 These spiritual forces are called in Hebrew *mal'achim*, which means *messengers* or, as often translated, *angels*, i.e., agents of Hashem.
20. See Chap. V, fn. 47.
21. The *gematria* of the Hebrew word for ladder, *sulam*, equals the numerical equivalent of the Hebrew word *Sinai* (130), the place where we directly experienced the absolute truth of Hashem. *Bereishis Rabba* 68:12; *Bereishis* 28:12, *Da'as Zekanim MeBa'aley Hatosephos*.

By what means is this connection to be made? Through the metaphysical forces (i.e., *mal'achim*) interacting between the two realms. Although the Creator is essentially completely beyond man's understanding, He has put into the world special forces (i.e., ideas, concepts, awarenesses) which humans *can* comprehend and use, in order to perceive the full reality. These messages from Heaven are called Torah, and they are the definitive means of understanding how humankind can link up with the Ultimate.[22]

How can we gain access to these special forces? First, we must be humble and truthful enough to admit the need to deal with our innermost aspirations, as represented by the dream, which typifies the deep introspection and self-analysis with which every person must grapple.

Second, we must realize that, though earth-bound and finite, we have been given a step-by-step system of reaching towards the Infinite, as symbolized by the ladder reaching to Heaven.

And third, we must diligently study, master and integrate the clearly-defined means which have been provided for our elevation, as represented by the spiritual forces that move up and down, for we must contribute from our side as well as receive from Above.

We should be aware how really crucial it is that we appreciate the significance of Yaakov's dream and act on it, for even

---

22. *Cf.* Rabbi S.R. Hirsch, *Bereishis* 28:12, who explains the symbolism of the *mal'achim* as follows:

"These messengers of God ascend the ladder in order to obtain above the image of what, ideally, this man should be like. They then descend and set this ideal image against the character of the man as he is in reality, so that they can 'stand against him' as a friend or as a foe, depending on how his actual character compares with the [Divinely-set] ideal."

though our intellectual abilities give us many advantages, they can also cause us many problems. To be specific, strangely enough, exactly that success which we gain can make us arrogant and prideful, ultimately meaning that we have failed. For with ease, we can blow ourselves out of our true minuscule proportion relative to the larger, absolute Reality. After all, is man's life even a split second in the face of eternity? Moreover, perched comfortably in our fairly impregnable parapet, we can often become condescending and aloof, despotic and exploitative. We can also become impatient (whether overtly or not) with those less competent than ourselves, and we can even lose our equanimity at affronts to our superior position.

But our forefather Yaakov engendered in us the truth-seeking potential that can correct all these negative traits. For the awesomeness and power of Hashem must inevitably humble us, gradually eliminating even the slightest traces of arrogance. The spiritual forces — Torah — which Hashem put in the world continually help us to know and feel Him, gradually reducing all vestiges of overblown self-importance. Working tirelessly to climb the ladder of truth, we must stay humble, for the more we know, the more we realize how much more we still need to know. Further, how can we lord ourselves over anyone else when every rung up the ladder teaches us Who is the *real* Lord and Master!

A concluding note: Where did Yaakov have his dream? On *Har Hamoriah*, the place:

- where later would stand the *Beis Hamikdosh*, the spiritual/physical linkup between Heaven and earth.
- where all the holiness of *Har Sinai* would be transferred to,[23] a holiness which would clarify for every human

---

23. See *Bereishis Rabba* 99:1, Maharzu; *Midrash Shachar Tov, Mizmor* 87.

the precise means to reach the Infinite—Torah and *mitzvos*.

– where Hashem formed the first man/woman,[24] fusing into their very being the purpose of existence — to climb the ladder to Eternity.

In summary, our three forefathers permanently implanted in their progeny three essential character traits: lovingkindness, self-restraint, truth-seeking. Grasping these images of the tent, altar and ladder, we are constantly reminded that as Jews we each contain within us the Key to solve the basic problems of life — jealousy, lust, and arrogance — and thereby to achieve the very highest plane of human existence.

---

24. *Bereishis* 2:7, *Targum Yonason*, Rashi.

We note that the basic problems of arrogance, lust and envy began with creation, long before the *Avos*. When the earth and moon disagreed with Hashem's arrangement of nature, they showed a misplaced pride in their own judgment. *Bereishis* 1:11-12, 16; *Bereishis Rabba* 5:9; *TB Chullin* 60b. When Adom and Chava ate of the forbidden fruit, they failed to control their physical desires (*Bereishis* 3:6). When Kayin killed Hevel, jealousy achieved its most tragic consequence (*Bereishis* 4:8).

According to the Eitz Yosef (*Pirkei Avos* 4:28, fn. 1), the three dominant problems unfolded historically as follows:

1. Kayin's killing of Hevel — jealousy (murder)
2. The Generation of the Flood — lust (sexual offenses)
3. The Generation of the Dispersion — arrogance (idol worship)

(See also our discussion in Chap. VII concerning the three major crimes.)

The *Avos* understood all these paradigms and implanted in their offspring the capacity to rectify the essential problems of life.

IV
Genetic Qualities

Now that we have learned about our ancestors and their historical input into our basic national character, it will come as no surprise that the Talmud teaches that there are three fundamental traits which epitomize a Jew.[25] If a person claims to be Jewish but has absolutely none of these traits, a question exists whether or not he is a Jew.[26]

Today's world might prefer a blood test or an examination of cellular tissue, chromosomes, genes or the like. It is symptomatic of the Jewish approach to life that we look to see how the person actually behaves in order to test his claims. Indeed, we are well aware of the genetic transference of physical traits. What people may not be so well aware of is the extent of the familial transference of character traits. Popularly, people accept that "an apple doesn't fall very far from the tree." But in Jewish thinking, the principle goes all the way back to a tree over 3,800 years old.[27]

---

25. *TB Yevamos* 79a.
26. *Shulchan Aruch, Even Ha'ezer* 2:2, Be'er Haitev.

What, then, are these three internal indicators of Jewish identity? We are taught that:

1) the person does acts of lovingkindness;
2) he is shamefaced (has a conscience); and
3) he is compassionate.

As a result, we can deduce that if a person does not act in accordance with these qualities, he is not behaving Jewishly or, at the very least, has grown estranged from Jewish behavior patterns for whatever reason. For the purpose of our discussion here however, as will now be explained, this statement in the Talmud means that we Jews have been blessed through our ancestors with exactly those characteristics which enable a person not only to avoid life's basic pitfalls, but also to achieve a much greater reality.

The first trait, performing acts of lovingkindness, is precisely the first part of our Threefold Key. Through the example of our forefather Avraham, we can appreciate that the more we learn to give, the less we feel jealousy and envy.

Why? First, because giving helps change our desire to receive. We may be upset by another person's receiving things because really, we also want to be on the receiving end. But if we learn to be always giving, then we reduce our inclination to take. By mentality switching from a "having" to a "giving" mode, we are less affected by what others receive, because this need to have has now become the opposite of our goal in life.[28]

Second, as mentioned before,[29] by giving to others we relate

---

27. Avraham was born in the year 1948 of the **Jewish** calendar.
28. See *Michtav*, Vol. 1, pp. 32-51 (*Strive for Truth!*, Vol. 1, pp. 118-58). Many of the ideas concerning lovingkindness expressed herein come from this source.
29. See p. 30.

and identify more with them and cease to see them as a threat to our existence and success. In fact, their success becomes our success, for we have contributed our efforts to their advancement. Jealousy begins because we feel threatened by another person, but by giving, we come close to him and see that we really are all partners in a common enterprise, rather than competitors. Our true success is to help everyone else succeed.

Third, we are jealous because we are afraid that there will be less for us, and we are insecure about whether or not we will get our portion. But what prompted Avraham in the first place to be such a giver? He realized that the Creator is the One Who is giving everything, all the time. What each of us receives is intentionally determined by Him, and so we do not have to worry that our present situation — the result of His decisions — is unfair. We can relax with the understanding that each is receiving exactly what he deserves or needs in order to complete his special mission in life. The Ultimate Giver and Planner has a precise accounting sheet for each individual, and we never lose as a result of another's gain.

With this awareness, one can give freely as Avraham did and not feel insecure that somehow he will be missing or lacking anything.

This approach is based on our molding ourselves more into the image of Hashem by becoming constant givers. Elevating our behavior to a beneficent mode dissipates the natural tendency to lowliness and pettiness within each of us. Largess and generosity dispel our narrow perspective of jealousy and envy. Self-centeredness and selfishness atrophy when we become a constant conduit of concern for others. Working in this way to become more like Hashem transforms our whole mentality away from "What am I getting?" to "How can I help others receive more?" Jealousy will not even enter our thoughts. And when others are doing a better job at giving than we, we obviously cannot be jealous. On the contrary, we are happy that there is more giving in the world and are eager to learn from those who are more successful.

The second quality mentioned in the Talmud is, in actuality, the same as the second part of the Threefold Key. Being shamefaced means that, yes, there is right and wrong, and that when a person sometimes does wrong, he feels pangs of conscience as a result.[30]

A brazen person scoffs at the notion of his doing anything wrong and ignores the alarm that rings inside of him. A shamefaced person, on the other hand, realizes that he can fall prey to his weaker, lowly impulses. Furthermore — and more important — he does not feel good about its happening. Strangely enough, no matter how many times he does a particular wrong, he still feels pangs of guilt. True, he may persistently try to offer excuses to salve his conscience, but deep down he is well aware that what he did was not right.

This Jewish conscience has been implanted in the Jewish People by our forefather Yitzchak. His exact adherence to rule and discipline achieved success for him in the absolute test: the ability to give one's own life when required. In the same way, through clearly contemplating the reality of the human situation, any Jew can understand that before the will of the Ultimate, he stands completely subservient. If Hashem decrees,

---

30. Our enemies can sometimes give us important insights about ourselves. Hitler said: "Conscience is a Jewish invention. It is a blemish, like circumcision." Herman Rauschning, *The Voice of Destruction*, G.P. Putnam, New York, 1940, p. 223.*

what can he say? That which is finite cannot claim parity before the Infinite. He who is created cannot challenge his Creator. Instead, the only sensible option is to yield totally to the Absolute, aware that His will brooks no abridgment, tolerates no deviation and permits no abstention. Just as anyone would be silly to attempt to defy Hashem's laws of nature (gravity, for example), so, too, no one should logically rebel against Hashem's laws in other areas. And failing in this obedience, the Jew automatically feels a sense of guilt, for he innately knows that there is an absolute right and wrong which he must follow.

This quality of being shamefaced emerges even more strongly during prayer[31] and introspection. At those times, we delve into our innermost mind and ask the most penetrating questions:

Am I so sure that I'm right?

Are there things that I'm doing wrong that should be corrected?

Am I fooling myself when I say it doesn't matter and give endless excuses for not improving?

When I know it's wrong, why do I still do it?

When I justify and condone the wrongs of others, am I not just preparing my own defense?

When others bend the rules too far, don't I feel like objecting? So why am I not honest enough to see that I also bend the rules and should object to myself?

Yes, without question, there are rules, and a Jew's conscience will not allow him to forget totally this reality.

On what issue does this feeling of shame most particularly touch our behavior? When it comes to matters of lust and

---

31. The literal meaning of the Hebrew word for praying, *l'hispalel*, is "to judge oneself."

physical desires. For how does the world term a person who restrains his physical desires? Inhibited — "hung-up," in the vernacular. Why? Because something inside him is holding him back from indulging himself. The group does not like this type of people because they are "wet blankets," "spoilsports," "killjoys" — blatant reminders that absolute standards actually exist which should not be dismissed under the label of "antiquated morality."

But the Jew who feels modesty and restraint has the means to buck the unbridled crowd, for it means that he is still able to hear his conscience telling him that something is wrong. The more he thinks deeply about life, the more he can energize these internal conscience batteries, particularly if he is shown a clear standard. For indeed, how can the facts be falsified when the person is standing before his Creator? Can he think for a moment that he can fool God, Who knows everything he is doing and even everything he is thinking? All the rationalizations, all the excuses, all the little games people play disintegrate before the "laser beam" of Absolute Right.

Just imagine for a moment: You are sitting before a banana split, three hefty scoops of ice cream — all different flavors — with a whipped-cream, crushed almond, hot chocolate syrup and maraschino cherry topping. Your mouth is watering like the garden sprinklers at the Versailles Palace. Then someone tells you that there is a question of whether the chocolate syrup is made from animal fats. You stare blankly at your informant and then gaze longingly back at your banana split. As a Jew, you are not allowed to eat milk and meat together. You know it; God knows it. No matter about your internal roars of anguish, your conscience will not let you squirm out of the right thing to do. You have controlled your physical desires through your awareness that you cannot escape following the rules. Cognizant of your Creator's presence, you cannot pretend that no one knows, for your shame and guilt confirm that there is no other real alternative than obedience. Banana split — into the trash can!

The third Jewish character trait is being compassionate and is derived from Yaakov, who strove for truth.

When we see our true position in creation, we are humbled by our smallness and insignificance. In relation to the Creator, how can we raise our heads in pride, in intelligence, in strength? Where is there room for haughtiness, condescension, domination? How long will our sovereignty reign? What will be the ultimate end of our empire? Moreover, can we say — even with all our power and might — that tomorrow will not take them away, that all our plans could not go easily astray, that even our best efforts will not fail?

Truth gives us this awareness that our power and control are limited and that a Force beyond controls and directs our lives. In such a position, we should realize that we have only one hope: that Hashem — this Force — will have compassion on us and exercise a light and kindly hand. Then, appreciating our own need for merciful consideration, we learn that we ourselves must be compassionate.[32] For how can we expect sympathetic treatment if we ourselves have acted unsympathetically? Indeed, the more we internalize how much we really are dependent on Hashem's mercy, the more compassionate we can become.

Moreover, what is the quintessence of compassion?—Em-

---

32. The principle involved is termed *mida k'negid mida*, measure for measure, and is basic to the Jewish understanding of how Hashem constructed life. See further, p. 161.

pathy, putting ourselves in the shoes of the other person, really feeling for him in his predicament and dilemma. By removing ourselves as the center of the universe and firmly realizing that Hashem is the only Center, we can thereby reduce our egos which usually promote an interest only in ourselves and our own concerns. Effacing our self-importance, we can purge any haughty aloofness and can, instead, behave with a humility which would equate us with our neighbor. It is no longer merely his problem, but *our* problem. It is not *his* struggle, but *our* struggle. It is not *his* suffering, but *our* suffering.

This quality implanted by Yaakov is so embedded that Jews have compassion even on their enemies. Jewish soldiers have behaved mercifully to their captives, sometimes to their own detriment. Even murderers of Jews (e.g., Arab terrorists) are considered with forbearance. Further, in any cause to aid the oppressed or disadvantaged, Jews are involved far beyond their percentage in the population.

The presence of this trait in the Jewish personality promotes humility and counteracts arrogance. Allowing ourselves to be moved by this natural empathy, we Jews are less likely to lord over others. On the contrary, we feel badly if we try to dominate or impose our will. Further, through constantly appreciating the greatness of Hashem as we study His Torah, we can continually increase our humility and realize how much we depend on His compassion, for a humble person realizes how much he is receiving. At the same time, this increased humility will foster a populace where ever greater levels of compassionate behavior become the societal norm. This quality and the traits of lovingkindness and shamefacedness are not just admirable; they are the inner essence of being Jewish.

V
Signs of a Unique Identity

Ask a Jew what makes him Jewish. If he is familiar with Jewish Law, he will answer that he is Jewish because he has a Jewish mother or he was converted under Torah rules. If he does not know the Jewish legal system, he will give various other answers. Perhaps he will tell you that he is Jewish because he feels Jewish, and he may mean that he senses in his being some of the qualities which we discussed in the previous chapter: that he is a giving person, that he has a sense of right and wrong, that he is concerned for his fellow man. Or maybe he defines himself as Jewish because of cultural or social factors: by living in a Jewish neighborhood, supporting Jewish organizations, enjoying Jewish food and Jewish jokes. Or perhaps he is a strong advocate of Jewish causes: the State of Israel, freeing Jews trapped inside repressive regimes, memorials to the Holocaust, opposing anti-Semitism.

The behavior traits typical of the Jew can be shared by other nations of the world to various degrees. As we said in the previous chapter, only if a person lacks the three main qualities is there a question of his being a Jew. Obviously, having these

Signs of a Unique Identity / 35

qualities in itself does not prove the person is Jewish. Jewish cultural and social activities are not true indicators of a unique identity. After all, even if the labels are different, they may actually be about the same as non-Jewish customs and behavior. The Irish prefer beer and Jews prefer Scotch whiskey; the Italians like pasta and the Jews like bagels; non-Jews attend the Grand Lodge and the Ladies' Auxiliary, Jews, the B'nai B'rith, Sisterhoods and Hadassahs; non-Jews have their religious holidays and ceremonies and so do Jews.

Given these similarities, we still lack a definitive handle on what makes a Jew unique — which things he does that no one else does. Non-Jews can support Jewish causes, participate in Jewish cultural activities and enjoy Jewish food, and all these activities would not make them Jewish. So what we want to discover is what *does* the Jew show to the world that proves he *is* different from everyone else? These activities will be a sure sign that he is unmistakably Jewish. At the same time, not only will these signs externally prove that he is a Jew, but they will also most likely reflect a fundamental uniqueness at a deeper level.

As perhaps expected, there are three signs, three identifying factors that demonstrate without question that the person is a Jew. Even a non-Jewish bystander, upon seeing these three signs, would say, "That's a Jew!"

What are these three signs?
1) *Shabbos*[33]
2) *Bris milah*[34]
3) *Tefillin*[35]

---

33. *Shemos* 31:13,17.
34. *Bereishis* 17:11.
35. *Shemos* 13:9,16.

How do these three signs together demonstrate our uniqueness?

Shabbos is a day of rest, yet it is actually quite unusual in the way that the Torah defines it. For example, a person is permitted to move around and rearrange his heavy living room furniture,[36] but he is not allowed to carry a sewing needle from his house to the public domain. Turning on an electric light, driving a car, writing a poem are all prohibited on the Jewish day of rest. Also, only Jews are allowed to "rest" in this fashion, for only we feel that full commitment to totally cease creative work in order to prove that, in actuality, there is only one creative power — Hashem.

Bris milah is performed on a healthy, eight-day-old Jewish boy. The procedure both removes the foreskin and completely uncovers the crown. Some might ask: "Since God created man with a foreskin, why should He tell Jews to cut it off?"[37] The answer is that in order to show that He is involved in all aspects of life — even the physical — Hashem commanded that we willingly mark on our bodies an indelible sign that He controls everything.

Tefillin are the little black "houses" (that look like cubes or boxes) which we strap onto our heads and our arms. The Torah envisioned that we Jews would wear our *tefillin* all day, constantly showing to ourselves and the world our special relationship with the Creator, binding ourselves to His sovereignty and control.

---

36. In order to preserve the specialness of *Shabbos*, the rabbis hold that a person should not do such toilsome activities. See *Aruch Hashulchan, Hilchos Shabbos* 333:4.

37. See the famous discussion on this subject between Rabbi Akivah and Turnas Rufus, *Midrash Tanchumah, Parshas Tazriah*, Sec. 5.

Signs of a Unique Identity / 37

These three quite unique external signs — described here only briefly — also reveal the Threefold Key to being Jewish. To see this connection, we have only to focus on a main theme expressed in each sign.

Shabbos is a sign of Hashem's profound and extraordinary love for His creation. The word for "love" in Hebrew is derived from the word "to give."[38] For in Torah Judaism, love is not just an emotion; it is an action, it is real giving. And on *Shabbos*, we experience Hashem's giving. When we take the time on *Shabbos* to realize how much Hashem is giving us, we truly feel His love. Indeed, on this day He specifically tells us, "Today, I am your Host, you are My guests, and everything is on My expense account."[39] Something very special and completely wonderful!

Think of a traveler, weary and worn from his long journey, finally reaching an inn. The innkeeper welcomes him with open arms, carries in his bags and ushers him into a spacious room replete with a fully-prepared meal, a warm bath and a comfortable bed. Imagine the traveler's delight, happiness and gratitude for the care with which his needs have been amply provided for. Where else on the lonely road would he have found such a welcome reception and such gracious hospitality?

Shabbos tells us that throughout life, Hashem is the Innkeeper and we are His guests. And as a consequence of strongly sensing this relationship, we want others also to feel this joy and lovingkindness. Naturally, therefore, a central activity on *Shabbos* is entertaining guests.[40] In fact, it is *the* day of the week where hospitality reigns supreme. Perceiving Hashem's love, we acti-

---

38. *Cf. Devorim* 6:5, Rabbi S.R. Hirsch. Compare *Bereishis* 29:21, 30:1.
39. We are taught that our expenditures for *Shabbos* and *Yom Tov* are given us from Heaven apart from our yearly income. *TB Betzah* 16a.
40. See, further, Chap. XVII, pp. 151-3.

vate our own potential to give by opening our homes to relatives, friends, acquaintances and strangers — people whom we never even met before. Moreover, we take the time to be with our families to make certain that they never become strangers to us. We see clearly, then, how *Shabbos* epitomizes the essential solution-key of lovingkindness.

Through giving, as we have said, we learn to correct jealousy and envy. A giver is not looking for what he will receive but for how much he can give to others. By consistently doing acts of lovingkindness, we learn to become less self-centered, less self-concerned and necessarily less upset when others are seemingly getting ahead of us. Our job is to keep giving and not to be worried by how much is coming back to us.

Keeping *Shabbos* teaches us to correct our jealousy in yet another way. The whole atmosphere of *Shabbos* — the enchanting candles, the delicious food, the warmth of family together, accompanied by singing and lively Torah discussions — makes us feel directly Hashem's overwhelming love as we enjoy all the blessings He has given us in life. Once we sense our own happiness, security and tranquility, we are less insecure about what others have. People who are concerned with their own security needs are more worried by the advancement of others. "Maybe his success proves that I'm not as good, maybe even a failure." Appreciating the bounty which we are receiving, we feel secure because we sense the tangible love being bestowed upon us. There is really no room or time to be jealous of what others have, for we are filled to overflowing by all that we are already receiving.

Indeed, as a result of the *Shabbos* experience, our only true response is to want to help others feel this boundless love. We want to give them all that we can until they too realize how much Hashem is blessing them, until they too learn to look for opportunities to be givers.

We may add further here that since on *Shabbos* both master and servant, employer and employee are forbidden to work,[41] this day becomes the great equalizer. For one day, at least, the effect of competition, the force that so easily causes jealousy and envy, is muted. Commerce and weekday pursuits are held in abeyance. Even the conversation on *Shabbos* avoids business, money, politics, sports teams, bargain purchases . . . . Instead, on *Shabbos*, every Jew — from the rich to the poor — is king and queen for a day, seated in his most regal clothes before a festive table bedecked with the finest food and drink. Ease and comfort pervade, enabling everyone to feel elevated from the usual physical bounds to a higher spiritual plane. For this day celebrates Hashem's "personal" creation of both the world and each one of us, as well as our collective selection as the Chosen People. Perceiving these unifying factors, we Jews sense our solidarity and learn how nonsensical it is to feel any jealousy of one another. On the contrary, our bond is immutable; our interrelationship is congenital; our love for our Creator and for each other is integral to our very existence. It is no wonder, then, that *Shabbos* is so joyfully welcomed each week. Look how profoundly it expresses our lovingkindness, how completely it dispels all competitiveness and envy!

The second unique sign of a Jew is the *bris milah*.

The often-dominating physical desires of the body are most typified by the sexual impulse. A lion-hearted warrior can become like a cuddly kitten when caught in the wiles of the

---

41. *Devorim* 5:14.

"feminine mystique." Why? Because what has been implanted in the human as an instinct essential for the continuation of the species is easily converted into simply a means of personal pleasure. Indeed, most of the world sees no behavioral difference between an animal and a human in this basic life function.

But the Jew comes with the sign of his *bris milah* dramatically to proclaim the world's error: an animal cannot control his instincts, but man — the Torah Jew — can.

The *bris milah* is an overt physical sign that the Jew's body is under the supervision of Hashem. From the beginning of his life, the Jew carries on himself this permanent reminder that what everyone else thinks is strictly his own business, he, the Jew, marks as an instrument in the service of the Creator.

Imagine a brand on the hide of a sturdy bull. If it goes onto someone else's property, it can be immediately brought back to its proper field. At a glance, we can know who its owner is — the one who has control over this animal and decides how it will be used.

The *bris milah* actually lowers the degree of one's physical pleasure, and some oppose circumcision precisely for this reason. But through this sign, the Jew learns that this most excitable of all instincts is under the control of the Owner of the world. He is allowed to use it only according to the instructions of the Owner. And if for any moment he goes off the path, he is in trouble and can expect a variety of adverse consequences.

Obviously, in dealing with an instinct so easily misused, the Creator must have fashioned many guidelines to guard against foreseeable errors and pitfalls.

For example, a Jew is not allowed to be with his wife during the period of her menstrual flow and until she has immersed in a special ritual bath. As a by-product of this abstention, the sexual urge between them is kept fresh within a cycle of control, anticipation, and expression.

Another example is that the Jew is not permitted to have relations with any woman outside the boundaries of a Torah marriage. As a result, the sexual instinct is given structure and parameters that restrain it from being merely an animal drive. Also, a Jewish man is not allowed to be alone with any woman other than his wife[42] in a place where the unexpected entrance of others is unlikely. Through these rules, compromising situations which can be so tempting are avoided. Yet another example is that a Jew is not permitted to see any parts of a woman's body that could lead to provocative thoughts. Consequently, even the mind is protected from sinking to an animalistic level.

A whole book could be written on this subject, but by now the reader can see that the sign of *bris milah* also represents a detailed system geared to teach control over a basic physical desire, promoting, in the process, the development of a mature and truly loving relationship between husband and wife.

At the same time, this sign clearly represents the whole category of instincts, for if one of the strongest instincts is under Hashem's control, certainly the lesser ones are also under His control. For example, the word *kosher* signals how exact and complete are Hashem's rules regarding food. They encompass what you can eat, when you can eat, how you can eat, where you can eat, what you have to do before and after you eat. Indeed, the list of what to know covers every item on the menu, from chicken *chow mein* to zucchini *kugel*, from cheese *blintzes* to eggplant Parmesan.

---

42. Or mother, grandmother, daughter, granddaughter, or (temporarily) sister.

And why all these rules? So that we Jews can learn to control our appetites rather than having our appetites control us. Man can so easily be corrupted by his sensuality that every bit of available restraint is essential to help him perceive the spiritual within the physical, the Infinite within the finite.

Indeed, even an already temperate person can use this sign of *bris milah* to learn how to gain even greater mastery over his instincts *and* how to elevate them to a higher plane. We do not mean that he should abstain or fast every other day, for restraint in itself is not the goal. Rather, the deeper goal is to realize that *all* of the physical world is only a means to an end. In other words, we should focus on our instincts not of and for themselves, but for what they were given to achieve, and *this* purpose should guide our usage of them. For example, our drive to eat comes in order for us to have the energy and health necessary for our intellect and emotions to grow beyond self. For each part of our corporeality the Creator has defined its purpose and exactly how this purpose can be attained. We have only to learn the instructions and follow them whole-heartedly, and then we can elevate our physical natures to a higher reality.

Finally, we must note that *bris milah* graphically demonstrates that through a system of strict adherence to Hashem's rules, we Jews can control those very instincts which empires and civilizations have used hedonistically and immorally. By faithfully fulfilling this second part of the Key to being Jewish, our People continue forever, replacing lust with discipline and self-indulgence with a higher service.

And the third sign?

Signs of a Unique Identity / 43

Nothing more epitomizes the uniqueness of the Jew than his intelligence. It is well known that the proportion of Jewish contributions to Western civilization far exceeds the percentage we occupy in the world population. Not only in quantity but also in breadth and depth, Jewish achievements are astounding. In the realm of secular endeavors, the lists of notable contributors are studded with Jewish names, particularly in the fields of science[43] and economics.[44] Jewish wealth and influence are also clearly demonstrable, alas, contributing to the scourge of anti-Semitism.[45]

In other realms, Western religions and philosophies, humanism, democracy, capitalism — all stem from the Torah which Jews have directly or indirectly spread throughout the world.[46]

---

43. In December, 1984, the *Science Digest* (pp. 36-71) reported a survey of America's 100 brightest scientists under 40. Among the sciences included were: mathematics, physics, biology, chemistry, astrophysics, computer science, environmental science, psychology. These young scientists achieved their distinction by advancing the knowledge in their particular specialties one step ahead. Approximately thirty of these top hundred are Jewish.

44. The Nobel Prize in economics was initiated in 1969. From that date until 1991, 33% of the laureates have been Jewish. See sources in fn. 47 below.

45. Dennis Prager and Joseph Telushkin, *Why the Jews?*, Simon and Shuster, Inc., New York, 1983, pp. 56-7.

46. Count Leo Nikolayevitch Tolstoy (author of *War and Peace, Anna Karenina*, etc.) described the Jewish influence succinctly: "The Jew is that sacred being who has brought down from heaven the everlasting fire and has illumined with it the entire world. **He is the religious source, spring and fountain out of which all the rest of the peoples have drawn their beliefs and their religions.**" "What is a Jew?", *Jewish World*, London, 1908.*

Similarly enlightening is the following observation by John Adams, the second President of the United States:

"**In spite of Bolingbroke and Voltaire, I will insist that the Hebrews have done more to civilize men than any other nation. If I were an atheist and believed in blind eternal fate, I should still believe that fate

From the percentage ratio of Jews who have received the Nobel Prize and from the percentage ratio who are doctors, lawyers, scientists, engineers, economists, "think-tank" policy advisors, financiers, business executives, psychologists, professors, teachers, journalists, writers, . . . , the conclusion is inescapable: Hashem has blessed the Jew with exceptional

---

had ordained the Jews to be the most essential instrument for civilizing the nations. If I were an atheist of the other sect, who believed or pretended to believe that all is ordered by chance, I should believe that chance had ordered the Jews to preserve and propagate to all mankind the doctrine of a supreme, intelligent, wise, almighty Sovereign of the universe, which I believe to be the great essential principal of all morality, and consequently of all civilization.

"I have read this last fall half a dozen volumes of this last wonderful Genius's Ribaldry against the Bible. How is it possible this old fellow should represent the Hebrews in such contemptible light? **They are the most glorious Nation that ever inhabited this Earth**. The Romans and their Empire were but a bauble in comparison of the Jews. **They have given religion to three-quarters of the Globe and have influenced the affairs of Mankind more, and more happily than any other Nation, ancient or modern**." Letter to F.A.Van der Kemp (1808), Pennsylvania Historical Society.*

Finally, the assessment of a non-Jewish, secular historian should remove any doubt concerning the vital contribution of the Jewish People to world history:

" . . . Certainly the world without the Jews would have been a radically different place. Humanity might eventually have stumbled upon all the Jewish insights. But we cannot be sure. All the great conceptual discoveries of the intellect seem obvious and inescapable once they have been revealed, but it requires a special genius to formulate them for the first time. The Jews had this gift. **To them we owe the idea of equality before the law, both divine and human; of the sanctity of life and the dignity of the human person; of the individual conscience and so of personal redemption; of the collective conscience and so of social responsibility; of peace as an abstract ideal and love as the foundation of justice, and many other items which constitute the basic moral furniture of the human mind. Without the Jews it might have been a much emptier place**." Paul Johnson, *History of the Jews*, Harper and Row Publishers, Inc., New York, 1987, p. 585.

abilities.[47] But the crucial question we hope to resolve here is:

---

47. In the modern era, the piquant observation of Mark Twain quite graphically summarizes the Jew's success story:
 "If the statistics are right, the Jews constitute but one per cent of the human race. It suggests a nebulous dim puff of star dust lost in the blaze of the Milky Way. Properly the Jew ought hardly to be heard of, but he is heard of, has always been heard of. He is as prominent on the planet as any other people, and **his commercial importance is extravagantly out of proportion to the smallness of his bulk. His contributions to the world's list of great names in literature, science, art, music, finance, medicine, and abstruse learning are also away out of proportion to the weakness of his numbers.** He has made a marvelous fight in this world, in all the ages, and has done it with his hands tied behind him. He could be vain of himself, and be excused for it . . . ." "Concerning the Jews," *Harpers Monthly*, September 1898, in *The Complete Essays of Mark Twain*, Doubleday, New York, 1963, p. 249.*
 One wonders what this sagacious non-Jew's reaction would have been, were he still alive, had he seen the up-to-date statistics:
 Approximately 25% of the top 400 richest Americans are Jewish. The three most prominent business families in Canada are all Jewish. Edward S. Shapiro, "Jews with Money," *Judaism, a Quarterly Journal*, Winter 1987, pp. 7-8. Jews make up 33% of Australia's top 200 wealthiest magnates. *Business Review Weekly*, May 12, 1989, p. 64. And even in staid and aristocratic England, where the listing of its top 200 richest includes more than half (114) who inherited their fortunes, still, approximately 15% are Jewish. *The Sunday Times*, April 2, 1989, p. A1; *The Sunday Times Magazine* (same date), p. 35. (For proper comparison, the Jewish proportional population in these countries should be noted: United States — 2.5%; Australia — .43%; England — .73%.)
 Statistical studies have shown Jews ranking significantly higher over the general population in income, professional occupations and education. The United States Bureau of Census and the National Jewish Population Survey reported that Jews have the highest income of any ethnic group in the United States, earning 72% more than the national average, and 40% more than the Japanese, the second highest earning ethnic group. American Jews are over-represented in medicine by 231% in proportion to the general population, in psychiatry by 478%, in dentistry by 299%, in law by 265% and in mathematics by 238%. Further, they are twice as likely as non-Jews to go to college, and they are represented in Ivy League schools over five times their percentage in the population. See Dennis Prager and Joseph Telushkin, *Why the Jews?*,

46 / *Self Beyond Self*

for what purpose? And not merely to give the reader any shallow, false sense of superiority.

Given his obviously greater cerebral potential, what is the Jew *actually* meant to do with it? *Tefillin*, the third sign of the Jew, tell us.

The dictionary term for *tefillin* is phylacteries, derived from the Greek word, *phylakterion* — outpost, safeguard, amulet. They come as a pair of black cube-like "houses," one for the arm at the biceps muscle and one for the head above the hairline directly over the midpoint between the eyes. Inside these houses, which are held against the body with black leather straps, are four Torah inscriptions which convey one dominating theme: the mind and actions of the Jew are to be directed to the service of his Creator.

The four inscriptions actually represent the theme through two main ideas.[48] Two of the inscriptions speak to the Jew's inherent intuition and awareness that an Infinite Being exists

---

Simon and Schuster, Inc., New York, 1983, pp. 49-50, fns. 9-12, citing various sources. The following are the percentages of Jews at several top American universities (graduate and undergraduate): Harvard/Radcliff — 26%; Yale — 30%; Univeristy of Pennsylvania — 30%; Columbia/Barnard —39%. *The Hillel Guide to Jewish Life on Campus*, 1991/1992, B'nai B'rith Hillel Foundations, Washington, D.C.

Through 1991, Jews received approximately 18% of all Nobel Prizes awarded, hugely disproportional to their small percentage in the world population. *The World Almanac and Book of Facts* — 1993, *Encyclopedia Judaica* 1973-82 Decennial Book, p. 493. Of American Nobel Prize recipients, Jews make up approximately 33% of the total. *The 1987-88 Jewish Almanac*, p. 97. By the way, a huge segment of Jewish acumen never registers on these statistics simply because it has been and is dedicated to the study of Torah.

48. The word for *tefillin* in the Torah is *totafos*, which means "frontlets." *Shemos* 13:16. Rashi explains that the word derives from two foreign words, each meaning *two* or *pair*. In other words, the four inscriptions are really two pairs, two main ideas.

and interacts with humankind.[49] The other two remind him of his objective, historical attachment to Hashem, Who liberated him from the bonds of human masters, the Egyptians, and placed him, instead, directly under His sovereignty. The latter idea naturally leads the Jew to want to learn what his Master wants him to do, while the former reminds him continually to strive to reach ever closer to this Source of his existence.

After this brief explanation of their content, we can now explore how the sign of *tefillin* relates to the Jewish People's above-average mental aptitude.

Quite clearly, our minds are our greatest assets. With them, we build our own little empires wherein we try to become as important and as powerful as we can. Our mental talent gives us a certain advantage which can then gain for us money, which can in turn buy for us whatever we want. Pretty soon, we can become almost independent forces — mini-gods — certain that our success grants us the right to do whatever we want. And since, in truth, we have been granted substantial intellectual prowess, a process of ever-increasing preeminence can intensify until we pridefully deny the existence of any force greater than ourselves.

However, to correct this error, we are commanded to put on *tefillin* every morning to tell us just the opposite:

Hold on a second! Are you sure you're the boss? Isn't there Someone else above you Who gave you your brains? Or, in your pride, do you imagine that you were responsible, deftly snatching

---

49. The disproportionately high participation of Jews in groups that seek to find a deeper reality to life, awareness beyond self, transcendental experiences, etc., is well known. The source of this involvement is the need to relate to Super-Reality, the inherent connection between the human and his or her Creator. See Rabbi Dov Aharoni Fisch, *Jews for Nothing*, Feldheim Publishers, Jerusalem, 1984, pp. 90, 155.

them up at the Brains Counter before the others in line?[50] *Furthermore, doesn't this Benefactor have a historical claim on your services since He freed you from slavery and guided your destiny over these hundreds and hundreds of years?*[51] *And maybe, just maybe, you're not using your brains for the purpose for which they were given?*

So what, then, is the purpose of all this brain power? *Tefillin* tell us that the true reason for providing this extra cerebral facility is this: Jews are to take this above-average gift and use it to create an above-average world! The word "average" refers to the physical, finite world we see, no matter how high above the earth we build the skyscrapers. "Above-average," on the other hand, means a world that is "above itself," i.e., a world where the Infinite is manifest.

For Hashem really exists everywhere, as we discussed in the beginning.[52] But He created the physical world where He does not appear to be present, and then gave us Jews the hardest job in the world: to bring Him fully into His creation. This is such a demanding task that only with the help of extraordinary talent can it be done. We Jews have been blessed with this capacity, but with ease our powers can be misused

---

50. *Cf. Devorim* 8:17-18: "And you said in your heart, 'My power and the strength of my own hand made for me this wealth.' But you should remember Hashem, your God, for it is He Who gave you the power to obtain wealth in order to fulfill His covenant which He swore to your forefathers as it is this day."

51. For a masterful description of the Jewish People's supernatural existence, see the quotation from Mark Twain in Chap. XV, fn. 165. Historians have echoed Twain's amazement over how the Jews could still be here and still exercise such influence. However, anyone who understands the purpose of life according to Judaism could correctly resolve this enigma. See further Chap. XV, pp. 129-30.

52. See Chap. II, p. 23 and fn. 8.

and misdirected for personal goals and aggrandizement. *Tefillin* come to remind us: "No, you're not here to be the boss. You're here to succeed in making *Me* the Boss of the world!"

The message is even more specific:

You might have thought, says Hashem, *that I gave you special skills in order for you to build a better physical world, advanced medical research, political reform movements, even huge, modern synagogues, not to mention all the personal wealth and luxuries your considerable talents can help you to accumulate.*

But this was not My intention, for then why would I have favored you, the Jew, over all the other nations of the world? If your job were simply to compete in the physical world, to become doctors, lawyers, engineers, there would have been no need or logic in giving you advantages over other peoples. In fact, it would have been very unfair.

My intention, says Hashem, *was, rather, that by using your superior abilities, you would build a superior (i.e., supernatural) world, a world much harder to achieve.*[53] *For it requires a superior head and a very sharp mind's eye to see deeper than everyone else, to understand the purpose of life better than everyone else, to put your ideals into practice better than everyone else. Your qualities are to help you go far beyond what the rest of the world is able to achieve, not to glorify yourselves, but to bring Me, i.e., the Infinite, as totally as possible into My creation.*

---

53. Even while we Jews are occupied with this elevated activity, we also have to deal responsibly with the physical world's requirements (e.g., livelihood) — a double test of our acuity. See *Pirkei Avos* 2:2; *TB Kiddushin* 82a; *Shulchan Aruch, Orach Chaim* 156:1; compare further *Mishnah Berurah, op. cit., Bi'ur Halacha,* "*Sofa b'taylah* . . . ."

And your tefillin? Day in and day out, they are My reminders to you that you are supposed to think, to concentrate, to use your superior gray matter to the utmost to comprehend the greater Reality of life and to integrate this Reality into your existence.[54]

If we use *tefillin* the way in which they were intended, they will check our misplaced desires to become independent power sources. For by binding ourselves, literally, to thinking and acting according to Hashem's will, we are actually humbling ourselves to serve the real Power Source. His instructions to us are called Torah, and they channel our great abilities toward achieving the purpose of creation.

Alas, how we Jews, with our prominent egos and brains, can obstruct and bend this purpose! True, we may certainly use our brains also to make money, just as long as we spend this money within Torah guidelines. But *tefillin*, the third essential sign of being Jewish, remind us daily of the real reason our great talent was given to us. Indeed, one of the inscriptions inside specifically explains that this sign is "in order that the Torah of Hashem will be in your mouth," constantly studying it and speaking of it.[55]

As an interesting by-product of *tefillin*, the Torah states that when the nations of the world see us wearing them, they will

---

54. Note that the basic Hebrew root of the world *tefillin* is *pilel*, which means *think, judge, decide, entreat, pray*. Every Jew, no matter what his level of intelligence (except, of course, mentally uneducable), can direct his cerebral capacities to the Highest Goal. The Torah was designed to be learned by both simple people and geniuses.

55. *Shemos* 13:9. See also, Rambam, *Hilchos Tefillin* 4:25: "The sanctity of *tefillin* is great, for as long as the *tefillin* are on a man's head and arm, he is humble and fears Heaven. He is not drawn to levity and idle talk, nor does he entertain evil thoughts, but rather he opens his heart to the words of truth and righteousness."

fear us.[56] And as a matter of fact, we actually do see that people are wary and suspicious of us because of our intellectual skills which *tefillin* represent. Indeed, dictionaries even list the word "Jew" as a verb: "To bargain sharply; to beat down in price." Although popular usage of the word is derogatory, a fast mind and a quick tongue *are* valuable assets in law, business, finance, securities, investments, real estate, insurance, advertising. And just look at how many Jews are involved in these fields!

But what would be if, instead of using our acumen for personal goals, we turned that same intellectual talent to the service of the Creator — seriously studying the Torah and meaningfully fulfilling the *mitzvos*? Then all the negative aspects of our superiority would be obviated.[57] The world would

---

56. *Devorim* 28:10; *TB Menachos* 35b. We should mention here that up to this point our discussion has focused on the *tefillin shel rosh* as symbolic of using the intellect to serve Hashem. While it is certainly true that the *tefillin shel yad* — representing action — is equally important, for several reasons the *shel rosh* more definitively projects the image of *tefillin*:

1) It is openly observable, whereas the *shel yad* should be covered (*Orach Chaim* 27:11, *Mishnah Berurah* 47).

2) The *shel rosh* and its straps have a higher sanctity, which is prohibited from being reduced to the lower sanctity-level of the *shel yad* (*Orach Chaim* 42:1).

3) The *shel rosh* represents four of the human senses, whereas the *shel yad*, only one (*Orach Chaim* 25:5, Eliyahu Rabba 8).

4) Thought and learning should logically precede action and are, therefore, primary. See *TB Kiddushin* 40b, which discusses study as being greater because it leads to action.

5) The *shel rosh* is emphasized more, for example:
   a) as the cause for the nations fearing us (*TB Menachos* 36b).
   b) the knot of Hashem's *tefillin* which Hashem let Moshe see (*Shemos* 33:23, Rashi).
   c) as specifically representing the Crown of the Torah (*TB Menachos* 35b, Maharsha, "*Kesher shel tefillin*").

57. Many lament how jealousy is a major cause of anti-Semitism. But no one would suggest that we cease producing to the fullest extent of our

look at us not as self-serving entrepreneurs but as awe-inspiring reflections of Hashem's overwhelming presence. No wonder that the nations are supposed to fear us, not the *us* that we are now, but the *us* that fully manifests the Eternal to humankind!

In sum then, the three distinctive, external signs of Jewish identity — *Shabbos*, *bris milah*, and *tefillin* — demonstrate how our emotions, instincts and intellects are persistently being trained to move from self to beyond-self, from the finite towards the Infinite.

---

abilities. So, in other words, given our likely success, are we not admitting that envy and anti-Jewish behavior are inevitable phenomena — a completely self-defeating situation? The straightforward answer given in the text (using our mental prowess for Hashem), therefore, seems the only way out of this irreconcilable dilemma.

VI
The Subtle Power of the Jewish Woman

Everyone knows the axiom that great men happen only because they have great women as wives. In Judaism, this principle is no platitude; it is a self-evident reality, as can be seen by anyone who visits the Jewish home and observes in action its chief architect, the mother. While some may be trying gently to move her away from this vital position, 150 generations attest to her importance and are not likely to be undone, for without her, there is no home. And without the home, there is no Jewish People.

Our history and life experience prove her crucial significance. We were saved from the bondage of Egypt because of our righteous women,[58] and in every generation they are the builders of the Jewish People from within. The inclinations which are uniquely Jewish come from the mother. She, in her very being, inculcates compassion, emotional warmth, generosity, modesty, humility, loyalty, gentleness and, most of all,

---

58. *TB Sotah* 11b; *Shemos Rabba* 1:12. See Chap. III, fn. 10; Chap. IX, fn. 100.

54 / *Self Beyond Self*

happiness and a cheerful certainty of Hashem's love. A building that is established on a proper foundation will stand, and with their mothers' qualities built into their basic structure, Jewish children are assured success in their life's mission. It is no wonder that, under Torah law, it is the mother who determines whether a child is Jewish.[59]

The Jewish woman has her qualities because of her mother, and her mother because of her mother, and her mother because of her mother, from time immemorial. And if we trace back to the beginning of our People, we find that our Matriarchs established the pattern that all subsequent generations have successfully followed. And again, not surprisingly, we find our Threefold Key to being Jewish.

We are taught that when our matriarch Sarah passed away, three miracles which she had brought to the home ceased. However, when our matriarch Rivkah later married Yitzchak, Sarah's son, and moved into the home, these miracles returned.[60] What were these special achievements of our Matriarchs?

First of all, the *Shabbos* lights stayed lit from one *erev Shabbos* to the next.

In Judaism, light symbolizes Torah education, for the wisdom given to us by Hashem dispels the darkness (i.e., constraints) of the physical world and brings light (i.e., expansion and understanding) into our everyday lives.[61] Women must study the laws and knowledge within the scope of their respon-

---

59. *Devorim* 7:3; TB *Kiddushin* 68b.
60. *Bereishis* 27:67, Rashi, Sifsei Chachomim, Gur Aryeh. Compare *Mishnah Shabbos* 2:6.
61. See *Mishlei* 6:23: "For the commandment is a lamp and Torah is light."

sibilities, but otherwise they have no general requirement to learn Torah. So why do *they* light the *Shabbos* candles?

Life is very often more profound than what meets the eye. The subtle nuances can be missed, but simple, unnoticed factors can make all the difference. The famous parable, slightly adapted, can remind us of a universally-accepted truth: "For want of someone to attach the nail, the horse's shoe was lost; for want of the horse's shoe, the horse was lost; for want of the horse, the horseman was lost; for want of the horseman, the battle was lost." Today, it is not uncommon to be confused about the role of the Jewish woman. But those who look more deeply will discern that her power and influence are subtle, unobserved and as essential as that person attaching the nail. For want of the Jewish woman, the Jewish People would be lost.

When the mother lights the *Shabbos* candles, she is demonstrating her commitment that there be light in the home, the light of Torah wisdom.[62] With a subtlety that defies the superficial glance, the Torah light in each home depends mostly on the inclinations and efforts of the Jewish woman. Her power is such that, though she has no requirement to learn Torah herself, her husband and children's success in their Torah education depends completely on her. For example, the more things she wants in life, a fancy dress, a gold necklace, the house decorated again, the more income is needed to satisfy these wants. If the husband is working more, he will have less time to learn Torah. Even if she just wants him around the house for companionship or home activities, he will have less or even no time left to learn. Indeed, in a case where he is noncommittal about his learning, her encouragement can make all the difference.

---

62. See *TB Shabbos* 23b, Rashi: "*Banim*"; *Shulchan Aruch, Orach Chaim* 263:1, *Mishnah Berurah* 2.

Further, her whole inner system of belief and values is constantly being tested, and the results manifest themselves in the entire family's experience of life. If she has less faith in Hashem, she will insist that her husband work full-time in order to have sufficient savings for whatever might happen. If she wants social advancement, she will push him for job promotions and prefer that her children concentrate on their secular education rather than their Torah studies. In brief, if her drives and needs are other than for Hashem and Torah, this spiritual light in her home will be considerably diminished.

One may ask how she has so much power. But as we explained, subtleties and hidden factors have greater influence than are generally appreciated, especially in the spiritual realm. Women are probably the best example of the truth of this statement. We can be infinitely grateful that the Torah-oriented woman has channeled her powers within the parameters of our matriarchal models. Having naturally absorbed a value system based on loyalty to the Creator, she senses with her whole being an abiding commitment to Torah learning, the key to maintaining this system. Every week for over 3,500 years, she has lit the *Shabbos* candles. And thanks to her, the reality of the spiritual light of the Jewish home remains eternal.

The second blessing that Rivkah brought back was a special cloud which was always tied above their home.

A cloud represents the Divine Presence, the *Shechinah*, the loving closeness which Hashem has with His creation. Today it can be felt in at least three places:

— at the *Kosel*, the Western Wall in Jerusalem

— in any place where Torah is being learned

— in a Torah home

The *Kosel* is the undestroyed remnant of the outer wall of the Temple Mount where the entire Jewish nation gathered to feel the presence of the Creator. This feeling to some degree is still perceptible. Indeed, to help remind us that we always have a latent potential to sense the Ultimate, the *Kosel* has miraculously remained standing since the time of its construction by King Solomon. Further, the prophecy promises that the *Kosel* will stand until the *Mashiach* and the rebuilding of the Third Temple.[63]

The *Shechinah* is also felt whenever and wherever Torah is studied.[64] Learning Torah is a direct link to the Creator, for Hashem communicated His ideas to humankind when He gave the Torah at *Har Sinai*. By studying these ideas, we actually come closer to Him, just as any book, article, letter or fax bridges the gap between the author and the reader. And since Torah is both an intellectual *and* an emotional experience, we can feel Hashem's presence and love as we learn.

The *Shechinah* is thirdly sensed in the Torah home. Our tradition refers to the Jewish home as a small Holy Temple and, as such, it has a special aura. Imagine walking into a dwelling where adornments of spirituality are located everywhere: *mezuzos* on every doorpost, pictures of righteous Jews for inspiration, remembrances of Jerusalem, Torah quotations and proverbs, the Jewish calendar with the times for candle lighting. Where the walls are lined with tomes of our sacred teachings, where objects of our Jewish life-style may be suitably displayed: the *Shabbos* candlesticks and *Kiddush* cups, the *Havdalah* set with

---

63. *Midrash Rabba, Shir Hashirim* II 9:4.
64. See *Pirkei Avos* 3:3,7.

spice box and multi-wicked candle holder, the Chanukah menorah, the *esrog* box. Little children may be playing on the floor, their toys scattered. The furnishings are pleasant, simple and unassuming. There is a feeling of wholeness and well-being. The frantic race of the outside world seemingly dissipates as one enters this world of Hashem's sovereignty and control. For here there is order, here there is rule, here there is an atmosphere of true love.

What is this feeling of true love?

We are taught that when a person wants something for himself in the love relationship, then it is not true love. Instead, it is merely giving in order to receive. When a person is giving with no thought of return, however, then it is true love.[65]

Imagine, for example, that you've decided to take care of a very elderly, dying man. He has almost no money and can barely function. Practically speaking, you have very little expectation of ever getting anything back for helping him. Now you are acting with true love for your fellow creature.

Under such a standard, marriage frequently seems very remote from true love since each partner often comes into the agreement only because he wants something back. To help promote true love, the Torah has certain rules concerning the husband/wife relationship. The cloud of the *Shechinah* brought by the Matriarchs over their homes symbolizes these rules, for their effect is to create a home of greater purity and refinement. These laws of *taharas hamishpacha* (family purity) train the married man and woman to become more givers and less takers even in the most physical aspects of their relationship.

Controlling these instincts is considered almost impossible

---

65. See *Pirkei Avos* 5:16, Tiferes Yisroel, note 115.

in the world at-large. From presidents to peasants, everyone wants whatever pleasure he can take for himself. Yet precisely where a Jewish couple could be most distant from Hashem, the Torah comes to provide guidelines to elevate marital behavior, actually bringing the participants closer to holiness (i.e., beyond the physical) and, thereby, closer to Hashem.[66]

And the person most responsible for these Torah rules is the woman. The complexity and meticulousness of the procedures reveal her commitment to serving Hashem to the highest measure. Her control, discipline and faithfulness again, just as with the *Shabbos* lights, dramatically influence the spiritual level of her husband and the purity/modesty level of the whole home.

Marriage is colloquially referred to as tying the knot, and now we can see an infinitely higher significance to the metaphor. The Jewish couple knots a permanent symbolic cloud representing sexual purity above their home. These laws of family purity help promote true love and control of physical desires — vital components for lasting marital success. Bound to a system that elevates the animal to the angelic, the Torah home emanates a spiritual tranquility wherein the Divine Presence can also feel at home. With such a "silent" Partner, no wonder the Torah-Jewish family is an enterprise that has yet to fail.

Aside from the blessings of the candles and the cloud, our

---

66. Obviously, we are touching just the surface of this topic. Further worthwhile reading can be found in *Waters of Eden* by Rabbi Aryeh Kaplan (NCSY Publication); *A Hedge of Roses* by Rabbi Dr. Norman Lamm (Feldheim Publishers) and *The Secret of Jewish Femininity* by Tehilla Abramov (Targum Press).

Matriarchs instilled yet a third blessing into the Jewish home. *Chazal* explain that because of them and all the righteous women who follow in their footsteps, there is also a blessing in the dough.

Dough symbolizes the physical substance of the home: food, clothing, shelter — in brief, livelihood. Because of the woman, the home is blessed with physical plenty. When we look at our situation objectively, there is always enough of what is *needed*, and generally even more.

What does she do to cause this blessing? In the days before large bakeries, bread — the staff of life — was made in the home. And before electrical appliances, the hardest work was kneading the dough, tough, arm-breaking and back-breaking effort. Who was it who exerted herself most to fill the table with this staple? The woman, with her love, her dedication, her selfless devotion. When guests came, who made it possible for them to enjoy a satisfying meal? The woman. More guests arrived, some from quite distant lands. Who made them feel right at home, providing fresh towels and bedding and, perhaps, even washing their clothes? Everyone in the house helps out, but the woman is the prime organizer and provider. Her tireless work and giving are the vital elements in the whole home atmosphere, and the feeling which is generated creates the greatest blessing, the blessing of selfless love.

But what is the secret of why, no matter how much money is earned, abundance in the home depends on the woman?

When the dough is made, Torah law requires that a small portion (called *challah*) be separated and given to the *kohanim*, the priests who served in the *Beis Hamikdosh*. (Today, *challah* cannot be given, and instead, once it is separated, it is burnt.)[67]

This action of separating and giving to others is the secret of the Jewish home's material blessings.[68] Through this constant procedure, which represents sharing one's material means,[69] the woman dramatizes her home's goal to provide for others beyond the needs of her own family. Achieving this selfless concern, she sets in motion the blessing that brings more abundance, since the more she is granted, the more she gives to others, and the more she gives to others, the more she is granted.

Moreover, by constantly giving rather than worrying solely about her family's needs, she proves her sincere and truthful reliance on Hashem. As a result, Hashem will want to bless her and her home, for He sees that there need be no concern that the physical plenty will corrupt her pure intentions.

In summary, it is our Matriarchs who implanted into Jewish womanhood the Threefold Key to being Jewish:

- a love and self-sacrifice for Torah learning
- a stalwart commitment to following the laws of family purity and modesty[70]
- selfless giving to others beyond the family unit.

Such is the subtle power of the woman that all the good that comes from the Jewish home will derive from her success

---

67. *Shulchan Aruch, Yoreh De'ah* 322:1,4.
68. See *TB Yevamos* 62b, where the wife is credited with bringing *beracha* into a man's life, with a proof from *Yechezkel* 44:30 which discusses the requirement of taking *challah*. When properly taken, it will cause a *beracha* to come on the home (Metzudos Dovid on *Yechezkel* 44:30).
69. See *Sefer Hachinuch, Mitzvah* 385. The concept behind *challah* still applies even if the actual piece of dough cannot technically be given to the *kohanim*.
70. See p. 86, where some of the rules of proper dress are discussed.

in these three areas. Indeed, whatever her husband and children imagine their achievements to be, they should know and understand that the true credit for their attainments rests upon her.[71] It is no wonder that we gratefully sing her praise every Friday night as our "Woman of Valor,"[72] for her valiant deeds are the basis for all our blessings.

A concluding note: While the primary focus of the Jewish woman is her family and home, there are women who, in addition, can successfully and with modesty use their talents outside the home. Just as with men, the determining factor of every activity is whether that activity and the intention behind it are directed to fulfilling the purpose of creation: namely, bringing Hashem into the world, converting the drive for self into a dynamic ascension beyond self.

---

71. As stated succinctly by the *Midrash*, "Everything depends on the woman" (*Bereishis Rabba* 17:7). By the way, this principle is so fixed that it applies to secular homes as well. See *Yalkut Shimoni*, Sec. 23, discussing the remarriage of righteous and unrighteous spouses.

72. *Mishlei* 31:1-31. This song of praise appears in every *siddur* just before the *Kiddush* of Friday night.

Part Three:

A System Vital for Life

    VII Living for a Purpose
   VIII Achieving Unification
     IX Identity Savers
      X The Pillars of the World
     XI Three within the Three

VII

Living for a Purpose

Now we come to the really difficult part of being Jewish — in fact, of being alive at all.

Is there anything for which we would be willing to give our lives?

The Western world has become such a physical Garden of Eden, it is hard to suggest to, much less convince, anybody that there is anything for which he should be prepared to give up his life. "What's the sense of it," he could say. "I'm going to say good-bye, and all the rest of you folks are going to stay alive and continue having your good time?! I'll stay back here and pack the ammunition, and *you* go out on the front lines. Or, if necessary, I'll just move to another country, or maybe to the South Pacific, with its palm trees, coconuts and surf."

Years ago, there used to be the slogan in America: "I'd rather be dead than Red." Now the approach is quite different: "I'd rather be alive, and we can bargain the Russians off, particularly now since communism has fallen apart. What could possibly be so serious between us that either one of us has to die? Let's both live, and join together in a toast to life: you —

vodka, and me — Scotch, gin, bourbon.... Nuclear war is obviously absurd; so let's make peace and get on with the rest of our eight-course banquet."

God forbid that there should ever be even a serious thought of a nuclear holocaust! But, living in such a milieu of accommodation, the reader could naturally think that this chapter is certainly a bit too extreme. Why should it be necessary to come to such a grave situation where one may have to die for something? But then, we all know how political events can sometimes rapidly deteriorate, and some power-hungry madman can start a war, threatening and endangering many people's lives.

The truth is that until a person is able to imagine under what circumstances he would be willing to sacrifice his life, he will not be able to understand what makes his life worth living for, or ultimately significant. For if there is nothing for which he is willing to give his life, then his life is in effect worth nothing. If he could be compromised on every value that he holds to be true, then in essence his life represents nothing of substance or enduring value.

For what, then, is the Jew supposed to surrender his life?
As you would anticipate, there are three major cases of Jewish self-sacrifice.[73] We must be prepared to die rather than
    1) commit murder
    2) commit adultery or other prohibited sexual offenses
    3) worship idolatry.
It might appear that today we have been spared such

---

73. *TB Sanhedrin* 74a; *Shulchan Aruch, Yoreh De'ah* 157:1.

extreme tests. The Roman persecutions, the Moslem massacres, the Spanish Inquisition, the Polish and Russian pogroms — all seem distant nightmares. But in actuality, this subject is also rather recent. Only a generation and a half ago in Europe, for example, Jews were faced with participating in the killing of others to save their own lives.

But without moving our discussion into broader questions of morality and ethics, we can still gain an appreciation of the relevance and fundamental importance of our threefold problem/solution analysis.

We have said that to train ourselves not to be jealous of others, we must strive constantly to give to them. This principle is so strong that we must be prepared to give everything we have, even our very lives, rather than take someone else's life — the first mortal issue in our list above.

We have explained that to inculcate control over our physical desires, we must discipline ourselves with a multitude of guidelines which maintain a spiritual perspective on our natural bodily instincts. And, ultimately, we must not give in to these desires, when they are prohibited, even if our lives are at stake — the second case on the list.

Finally, controlling our arrogance and egocentricity, we must learn Torah to appreciate our true position of humility in relation to Hashem. And when any other gods — including ourselves or our money — seek to replace Him, the third item on the list informs us that we must be willing to give up our lives rather than deny Hashem's absolute supremacy.

Of course, Hashem gives life in order that we have the opportunity to succeed in the normal, daily tests that He presents before us. But we should realize that there is no limit on how far we are to avoid jealousy, lust and pride. Long before any ultimate tests, we should be steadily and diligently developing our mastery of the threefold problem with its threefold solution.[74] *L'chaim* — "to life" — is the perpetual Jewish toast, and the Creator Himself concurred in this toast when He said, *"Vachai bahem."*[75] Still, He also determined the whole reason for which life was given in the first place: to become like the Infinite, to link up with the Ultimate Reality. And if we deny any one of these three essential ways of achieving this goal, then life itself has lost its meaning. We all want to live, but we should want to live so that our lives fulfill and justify the purpose of their creation.

---

74. See Chap. II, pp. 5-11, and Chart A: The Self—Beyond-Self Continuum, p. 231. We note that the first *Beis Hamikdash* was destroyed because of the failure to master these three issues. See Chap. XIX, p. 181.

75. Lit., "and he shall live in them," i.e., a person should live and do further *mitzvos* rather than die. *Vayikra* 18:5. For further study of this both serious and complex subject, see *TB Sanhedrin* 74a-75a; Rambam *Hilchos Yesodai HaTorah* 5:1-10.

VIII
Achieving Unification

When the average person looks around and asks himself what is his life worth, what is he living for, he might discover that he feels a bit empty.

Is he living for his country? Well . . . not really. Remember, he'd rather pack the ammunition than fight the wars.

Is he living for his work? Well . . . not really. He has to retire some day, and does that mean that the morning after his retirement party he might as well climb into the grave?[76]

Is he living for his family? Well . . . not really. They all grow up and go their diverse ways, and then what is he supposed to do?

And this question is more than just academic, for as sug-

---

76. Those who want to work until their dying day should ask themselves another question: "What would be my life goal if I were no longer able to work or no longer needed to work because I had sufficient income through pension plans, social security, dividends, interest on savings, etc.?"

Those whose work is their main life goal should ask themselves: "Am I absolutely certain that this activity is the main reason for my being placed on this planet?"

gested in the previous chapter, a person's life is worth what he would be willing to give it up for. So, what is he living for?

Judaism answers this question succinctly and to the point: **"Hear, O Israel, the Lord is our God, the Lord is One."**[77] This is the famous *Shema*, the sentence that
- epitomizes the Jewish way of life,
- is almost the first sentence a Jewish child is taught,[78]
- is said several times every day throughout a Jew's life and
- is the last words on his lips before he leaves this world.

This is what the Jew is living for.

Let's explain what we mean.

In brief, the Jew recognizes that there is only one Reality, and it is his opportunity and challenge to totally identify his life with this Reality — from the beginning of the day to the end, from the beginning of his life to its end. God's Oneness means that everything is really included within His Totality, but this physical world — with all its apparently independent parts — is a test to see how much we can achieve this unification on our own. As explained earlier, Hashem withdrew, so to speak, from His creation, and our life effort is to put Him back in. The *why* of such a task was mentioned briefly before.[79] Explaining *how* to achieve this unification is the purpose of this book. And how the *Shema* helps us in this process and goal of unification is the topic of this chapter.

---

77. *Devorim* 6:4.

78. The first sentence is "Moshe commanded us Torah, the inheritance of the congregation of Yaakov" (*Devorim* 33:4), for this is the fundamental starting point from which everything else in Judaism originates: Moshe conveying the Torah to the Jewish People. But the first principle we teach the child *from* the Torah is the *Shema*.

79. See p. 12 and fn. 7.

As it turns out, the very next sentence in the Torah after the *Shema Yisroel* actually tells us the details of how to attain this Oneness:

"You shall love the Lord, your God, with all your heart, and with all your being, and with all your substance."

First of all, what is meant by "love"?

On the surface, the idea of loving God seems so incomprehensible, so beyond reach. But we Jews are practical people, and our 3800-year-old life-style would not have succeeded if we had nothing more to work with than amorphisms.

As explained, the root of the Hebrew word for love means "to give."[80] In Judaism, the essence of loving is giving.

Once we understand this principle, we can appreciate what the Torah is endeavoring to teach us here: If we want to make Hashem One (i.e., make Him manifest in the world), we must *give* to Him three things: all our heart, all our being and all our substance.

What does it mean to give Hashem something? As the Source of everything, He is the Continual Giver and needs nothing from anyone!

The answer is that since we are the only ostensible forces which can seemingly "block" the Oneness of Hashem (animals, flowers and stones, for example, all perform exactly Hashem's will by doing nothing but what they were created to do), by our giving these three things to Hashem, the world *will* be One (totally Hashem, i.e., His will), for we will have given over all that could have ever blocked this Oneness. In other words, by exercising our free will consistent with His will, we are in effect giving Him the one thing (with its three components) that could

---

80. See p. 37 and fn. 38.

have possibly blocked Him from being totally manifest, totally One.

Why these three components particularly? Because essentially they represent our basic Threefold Key to being Jewish.[81]

All Our Heart:

Throughout our discussion, we have described ourselves as potential blockages in allowing Hashem to enter His world.[82] Yet if Hashem is everywhere and really all-dominating, how could anyone of us ignore Him or even attempt to block Him? Still, despite this awareness, we often do go about our business, blithely listening to our own viewpoint and disagreeing — sometimes respectfully and sometimes not so respectfully — with the Boss.

How could we be so audacious, so impudent, so *chutzpahdik*?!

Very simple. Hashem put a counterforce in the world which is *seemingly* capable of challenging Him. It is called the *sitra achra* — "the other side" — and it represents the forces felt within each of us pulling the heart and mind away from Hashem. For example, instead of concluding that Hashem is the Creator, we can choose to attribute our existence to other originators: the "Big-Bang," random evolution or "Mother Nature."[83] Instead of understanding that Hashem is solely

---

81. See *Devorim* 6:5, *Sifrei* and Ba'al HaTurim, who relate the *Avos* to these three parts of the *Shema*.
82. See Chaps. II, p. 13, and V, pp. 48-50.
83. The latest effort to replace Hashem is a new theory in evolution called "kin selection." No less than "the most important evolutionary biologist of the second half of this century," William D. Hamilton of Oxford University, has "discovered" this new force that caused life to evolve.
(cont.)

directing events, we can attribute it to "coincidence," or "luck," or "that's just the way things happen." Instead of sensing that Hashem is the Ultimate force with Whom to relate, we can decide to invest our lives in our careers, our money empires, our human ideals, our loved ones. A whole range of "other" ideas is easily available to block Hashem.

Why has Hashem created such a "scenario?" Because this is *the* test of life: to see if we with our own volition, insight and effort can achieve the truth — the 100% awareness that everything is really Hashem, that everything is only an emanation from Him in one form or another. And in order for us to have such a challenge, Hashem arranged this other force which we have to battle with, in order to reach the truth on our own. Indeed, we are alive precisely in order to understand that this counterforce is a direct agent of Hashem, placed there only to give us the opportunity of overcoming it and not letting it block our complete allegiance to Hashem. Therefore, when the *Shema* tells us to give to Him "all our heart," it is saying: give to Hashem this two-sided battle; i.e., in the two ways which the heart (i.e., our internal allegiance) can decide, make sure that it decides for Hashem.[84]

The following quote from *Time* magazine may not do justice to the theory, but it does show how far we humans will go to find any answer rather than one positing an actual Creator to whom we must relate:

"... Because nearby cells tended to be related, they shared genes, so increasing cooperation among them made evolutionary sense, and this trend eventually led to utterly cooperative communities of cells, such as ourselves.

"Hamilton, then, is the biologist who first clearly discerned the force that propelled life over the chasm between single-celled and multi-celled. And this force is a primary reason that the first little living specks were likely to beget big thinking, feeling machines. Kin selection is a vital link in the argument that the evolution of intelligent life was very probable all along." *Time*, "Science, God and Man," December 28, 1992, p. 44.

Avraham, the first Jew, is famous for having made the right decision in ten dramatic encounters, ten extremely difficult tests, thus proving that Hashem is the single and only Force.[85] We as his descendants have a certain residual potential to make the same decision — particularly if we have been or are given the education and environment which will help this potential come alive.

Furthermore, when the verse tells us that our hearts have to decide, why not simply say our brains, the normal decision-makers? The answer is that there are decisions which we make that really come from the heart, i.e., our emotional, feeling, subliminal network.[86] Down deep inside ourselves, at the very quintessence of our being, is where we feel — or do not feel — the complete commitment to whatever our brains may have decided on the surface.

We note that this differential between the heart and the mind is well exemplified by the issue of jealousy. Originating at the inner core of our personalities, this powerful emotion is consciously controllable only with great effort and internal development.[87] And it is precisely this emotional essence of

---

84. *Devorim* 6:5, Rashi on "all your heart"; *Mishnah Berachos* 9:5, M'leches Shlomo, "*B'yetzer tov* . . . ."

85. *Pirkei Avos* 5:3. These ten tests "show[ed] how much Avraham cherished Hashem."

86. As it says of Avraham in *Nechemiah* 9:8, "And You found his heart faithful before You." We note that three times a day, we Jews are reminded in the *Aleinu* prayer that we must not only have knowledge of Hashem's sovereignty, but we must also *internalize* this awareness into our hearts, i.e., our intrinsic natures (*Devorim* 4:39: "And you shall know . . . and place upon your heart").

87. See *Bemidbar* 15:39, " . . . and you shall not go after your heart and your eyes," where Rashi brings: "The eye sees, the heart covets, and the body does the transgression." *TY Berachos* 1:8; *Bemidbar Rabba* 17:6.

ourselves which we are bidden to give to Hashem.[88]

We learn from Avraham that we can overcome envy through a profound awareness and an internalized acceptance that Hashem is running everything. Every detail of life is His creation, His formation, His direction. Thus, if others have more intelligence, more money, more charm than we do, we will know as an absolute fact deep within ourselves that Hashem — not some "other" force, such as blind fate — specifically made it that way, and that there is nothing for us to feel insecure or afraid about. We can immediately diffuse our jealousy, realizing that other humans, who might look like independent forces, are really only manifestations of Hashem's power and manipulation.

If we get upset about their superiority, we have let our emotions decide against the total awareness of Hashem. This is exactly the mistake which He tells us not to make in the *Shema*: "Give Me your heart — your innermost, complete acceptance that I determine all reality." Through deeply internalizing this directive, we can remove even the slightest traces of insecurity and envy.

Moreover, by correcting these inner feelings, we are performing an act of lovingkindness.

Which lovingkindness?

We are doing, in a manner of speaking, a kindness to

---

88. *Rachmona leba ba'ei* — "The All-merciful One desires the heart (*cf. TB Sanhedrin* 106b). See also *Shemos* 4:14, where Hashem testified that Aharon's heart was happy, feeling no jealousy at his younger brother's success in supplanting him as the leader of the Jewish People. Rashi explains that as a result, Aharon merited to wear the Breastplate over his heart (*TB Shabbos* 139a). We are also taught in *Mishlei* (14:30) that if the heart is controlled, it can remove envy and its effects: "A sound heart is the life of the flesh, but envy is the rottenness of the bones." See also *Bi'ur HaGra, Pirkei Avos* 4:21(28).

Hashem. For without us deciding to be aware of Him, it is as if He is not in His world, as we discussed above. Because of the way that He created free choice, we have the opportunity to make Him manifest in our world or to ignore Him, causing Him, so to speak, to be less present. It depends on us whether we will give to Hashem our love and commitment by following His instructions — just as when we give to others our love and concern when we do for them acts of lovingkindness. Again, Hashem needs absolutely nothing from us. Yet He is certainly pleased when we make the right decisions, as we say three times daily in the first blessing of the *Amidah*: "He remembers the kindnesses of the *Avos*."[89]

How fortunate we are to be able to give something back to Hashem, for in so doing, we return the seemingly disparate parts of life to their whole Source and, thereby, complete the purpose of creation: unification. This is the theme of the *Shema*, and the process involved is to go beyond self. By giving Hashem "all our heart" (i.e., our total internal commitment), we are, in effect, directing our emotions beyond self, a very crucial element of our Threefold Key to being Jewish.

All Our Being:

We are taught that when we are told to give all our being to Hashem, it means that should He ask us to give our lives, we should do so willingly.[90]

Here too, if we would stop and think about it, we would realize that our bodies are really not our own possessions. They

---

89. See *Vayikra Rabba* 27:2, where Hashem recounts the kindnesses done to Him by the *Avos*.
90. *Devorim* 6:5, Rashi on "all your being."

are merely on loan from the Creator until such time as He wants them back. Otherwise, up until the time that it is clear that He is reclaiming His loan, Hashem has forbidden us to sacrifice our lives.[91] But once His intention is clear, then we have the opportunity to give our very lives to Him.

But how could we be giving something when the circumstances must necessarily be one of having no choice?

In such a situation, our gift is our willing *acceptance* of Hashem's decision to take back His loan. Instead, we could try to hold on to life. We could become very upset, angry, bitter at our plight, denying Hashem's love and concern for us, denying also that there is any good or ultimate purpose to our death, or any continuation after death.

On the other hand, there is also the opening for us to actually actively transfer our bodies back to their Source. How is this accomplished? By joyfully giving over those last moments in loving recognition of how much our whole life was simply a gift from Hashem; how much we appreciated the opportunity to use it; how grateful and eager we are to prove that it is the Creator Who gave us life, by trustingly giving it back to Him. Just as we saw the good emanating from His bestowal of life, we are certain that good will also emanate from His taking it from us.[92]

Now, since we have seen that Hashem is asking us to be prepared to give all of our being to Him, it follows that anything less than that "all" is also included in the request. In other words, since we must be willing to prove the point that Hashem is the Creator of our bodies in the ultimate test, all the more so

---

91. *Bereishis* 9:5, Rashi on "and also your blood"; *TB Baba Kama* 91b.
92. This potential derives from Yitzchak. See fn. 81; see also pp. 19-21.

in the day-to-day use of our bodies do we have countless opportunities to make choices to demonstrate our belief in His complete ownership.

When we wake up in the morning and open our eyes, we say "Thank You" to acknowledge another day's extension on our "lease." When our bodily needs function in their natural course, we say praise for His kindness. When we take in any nourishment, we say a blessing, appreciating that all food pleasures essentially represent the manifold ways through which Hashem keeps us alive. And we already saw how the *bris milah* shows Hashem's control over our reproductive powers.[93]

All these rules which Hashem has given us provide a complete system of discipline and restraint over our physicality and enable us to put into practice the second part of the Key to being Jewish: controlling lust and self-indulgence. For to give Hashem our lives means to give Him our bodies, our instincts. We may feel that our physical desires are strictly for our own enjoyment, but the *Shema* proclaims that these instincts should also be used to acknowledge and serve the Creator through faithfully following His instructions. Realizing Who really has claim over our bodies, we have the opportunity of turning a potential blockage into yet another means of expressing the Oneness of creation. And again, the *Shema* has directed us as to how to accomplish this goal by teaching us to go beyond self, this time in the category of our instincts, the second part of our Threefold Key.

All Our Substance:

Throughout all ages and practically all cultures, we find that wealth becomes a major obstacle in man's identification

---

93. See pp. 39-42.

and unification with Hashem.[94] So fixed is this principle that, in order to be a truly righteous person, a destitute existence would almost appear a prerequisite. The ego inflates so quickly and so much under the air compressor of economic self-sufficiency that, most often, the awareness of Hashem's presence is in inverse proportion to a person's level of affluence. The reason is very simple.

We are, in actuality, completely dependent on the Creator. Being born, staying alive and healthy, dying — all depend on Hashem, as well as all the details of each stage. But using our skills to earn money, we form an illusion of independence and self-sufficiency. Indeed, it is a rare individual who does not nestle ever so comfortably on top of his treasure chest, convinced that his prosperity is protecting him from life's vicissitudes. Money — and the power it brings — *appears* to obviate the necessity of any Creator. "Who needs Him?" says the stock-bond-real-estate-cash-reserve secure individual. "My assets are what keep me going. And very nicely, I might add." To say the least, we can allow abundance to form quite a blockage to letting Hashem into our lives. And even when we believe in the Creator, maybe even do His *mitzvos*, how easily we can come to feel secure and confident — not because we are close to Him, but because we are close to the six or seven figures in our aggregate assets account.

Then comes the third component of the *Shema*, precisely to address this point. "All our substance" reminds us that all our wealth is really Hashem's, and ultimately, we are bidden to give it back to him.[95] This means that we must live as if we have

---

94. Of course, there are many exceptions. For example, Rabbi Yehudah HaNasi was extremely wealthy but never made use of his affluence for personal indulgence. *TB Kesuvos* 104a.

nothing. In this way, we keep our close connection to Hashem, never being so tied to our physical support systems that we forget Who is running the show. Moreover, when we use the money that is at our disposal, every penny should be spent consistent with Torah parameters, a standard of accounting which even the tax authorities do not come close to matching!

Besides this issue of a person's support system, there is a fairly normal spin-off from the ego-inflation which money promotes: a burgeoning sense of self-centered dominion that brooks no abridgment. We really can become little kings over our mini-empires. And even if deviations from our will are sometimes tolerated, internally we feel slighted by any diminution of our sovereignty. In sum, we can become arrogant despots, notwithstanding *noblesse oblige*.

This facet of the problem is dealt with through a second implication of the Hebrew words *kol m'odechah*. Although these words are usually translated simply as "all your substance," the root word *m'ode* in *m'odechah* can also be compared to the Hebrew word *mida*, which means *measure*. In this context, *kol m'odechah* now instructs us that no matter what measure — good or bad — Hashem metes out to us, we should be very grateful and accept it with great happiness. In other words, as another check on our pride, Hashem intentionally manipulates events to undercut our self-created superiority. This helps us to realize that we are not kings here, but merely servants of a much higher Master. When things go wrong, it is precisely to teach us

---

95. Here we are describing the mentality involved when dealing with money. This approach derives from Yaakov — see fn. 81 above. Halachically, we Jews are required to give a minimum of 10% and a maximum of 20% of our incomes to the poor and Torah institutions. Anyone who is wealthy may give more (*Shulchan Aruch, Yoreh De'ah* 249:1).

the reality of our true position. Then, instead of using our minds to disagree with what the Ultimate Mind has determined, we must humbly accept that, quite obviously, He *must* know better.

In order to help train us to understand and internalize our subservient position, Hashem requires us to learn Torah, for it has a tremendous potential to engender humility.

How so? Learning Torah keeps us constantly on the alert, trying to grasp the Infinite Mind, and this activity should in turn make us realize that

a) no matter what superiority or power we possess, it is nothing compared to the Ultimate Intellect;

b) coming face-to-face with a total system of relating to Hashem, we will never be misled to adopt any false support systems, such as our intelligence or our money;

c) working to comprehend the clear truth written in the Torah, we develop an internalized truth-barometer that helps us avoid the pitfalls of all false systems — even our "self-made" mini-empires;

d) our capable minds are obviously best utilized in understanding the thoughts of Hashem, rather than in any other mental activity;

e) when learning Torah, we are most often forced to seek out the help of a teacher, a dependency which can help promote humility.[96] Indeed, we are consistently awed by the greatness of the *talmidei chochomim*, a greatness that clearly justifies their position as the leaders of every generation.

In summary, learning Torah checks the arrogance which

---

96. One of the many explanations for the Oral Law is its role in training humility through the requirement of needing a teacher. Who, for example, would even attempt to learn the Talmud without Rashi, the indispensable explicator?

our ability and money easily engender. For this reason also, the requirement is to learn Torah on a regular, daily basis, for day-in day-out we work hard to become masters in our own domains. With the key of Torah learning, we live in the domain of Hashem, placing the crown of self-sufficient sovereignty where it truly belongs.

We now understand that, having given our *emotions* ("heart") and *instincts* ("being") to Hashem, we must also give our *minds* and their concomitant powers ("substance"). For the goal of the *Shema* is unification, and our three essences — when properly directed beyond self — are the necessary means to this end.[97] Giving over everything we have to Hashem, we are contributing our maximum effort in making Him One, in making Him and His entire creation — including ourselves — truly one entity.

---

97. See Chap. II, pp. 12-14, where we discussed the goal of becoming like the Infinite, which is really synonymous with achieving unification. See Chart C, p. 236, which joins these terms and others in a list of basic dichotomies.

IX
Identity Savers

Before we attempt to show further how the task of the Jew in his threefold approach to moving from self to beyond-self is reflected in other Jewish concepts and practices, it is important to demonstrate that this task is not a side activity, avocation or hobby. It is *the* reason for the Jew being created and kept alive.

We have already considered its seriousness in regard to the three transgressions for which a Jew must give up his life to avoid.[98] Now, we will see that if the Jew wants to succeed in his life mission, he *must* be aware of and diligently working on this threefold problem/solution key.

To begin, let us examine an important fact in our early Jewish history.

We find that when the Jewish People were enslaved in Egypt and were close to total assimilation, only a percentage of Jews were saved. Twenty percent, to be exact. The other eighty percent of the nation did not leave Egypt. Eighty percent had

---

98. See Chap. VII.

Identity Savers / 83

no part in the great Exodus of the Jews.[99] How were the twenty percent different from the eighty percent? How did they deserve to be saved whereas the vast majority were lost?

Chazal give various reasons, including three primary ones:[100]

---

99. See *Shemos* 10:22, Rashi, who records that those Jews who did not want to leave Egypt were killed and buried during the plague of darkness. *Shemos Rabba* 14:3 explains that these Jews had Egyptian patrons. They were wealthy and honored and, therefore, did not want to leave.

   The *Midrash* cited in fn. 100 gives the various identity factors through which the remaining Jews merited to be saved, and our discussion here assumes that the ones who failed to be redeemed lacked these factors. However, it could be that they kept their identity indicators and still did not want to leave because of their money and position. On the other hand, their association with Egyptian patrons indicates a high measure of assimilation. Further, their internalization of the identity factors had certainly been deficient if they did not see the necessity of abandoning the negative Egyptian environment and following Moshe Rabbeinu to *Har Sinai* and *Eretz Yisroel*.

   Finally, the *Targum Yonason* (*Shemos* 10:23) juxtaposes the burial of the "evil ones" (during the plague of darkness) with precisely those worthy Jews who were busy with those *mitzvos* connected with light: Torah, *tzitzis*, *tefillin*, *k'rias Shema*, which again suggests strong differences in levels of Jewish commitment and observance.

100. *Vayikra Rabba* 32:5. A fourth reason — not speaking *loshon hara* — is also given, but this factor often derives from the other three, and indeed, we have specifically described it as an all-inclusive, fourth component. See App. C: The Fourth Component, p. 247. Compare our discussion concerning *sinas chinom*, pp. 182-3 and fn. 276.

   The *Midrash* cited mentions directly the issue of sexual modesty and not dress, but the Abarbanel specifically lists our Jewish clothing as being distinctive from the Egyptians (*Zevach Pesach*, cited in *Me'am Lo'ez, Shemos*, Vol. 1, p. 248). Compare also the B'nei Yissachar on *Bereishis* 33:18, where *shalaim* as an acronym represents name, language and dress.

   In passing, we note that when Yosef revealed his true identity to his brothers, he also used three means: his name, his *milah*, and his speaking Hebrew. *Bereishis* 45:3,4,12. (*Milah* represents the whole issue of sexual control, which modest dress also reflects.)   (cont.)

1. They did not change their Jewish names.
2. They did not change their Jewish dress.
3. They did not change their Jewish language.

Clearly, all three reasons demonstrate a strong commitment to one's Jewish identity. These people refused to abandon their uniqueness and assimilate into Egyptian culture. Only they could answer the call for an Exodus of Jews, for only they had sufficiently maintained their self-awareness to desire a path separate from the overwhelming mainstream.

Let's look at these three factors more closely.

First of all, these Jews kept their Jewish names. What does a name indicate? How does it affect one's life? A name distinguishes a person as being part of a certain group or category. Particular names used over enough time become fixed indicators of ethnic background and culture. Keeping his Jewish name, each individual identifies himself with his group, feeling a personal connection with others in the group. These unifying names, furthermore, continually engender a closeness and attachment that promote mutual concern and involvement. For a name is a direct link to one's personality and identity, and by using Jewish names, the group shows that each member is considered like a brother, rather than some stranger or nonentity.

Optimally, envy and jealousy are dispelled when each senses a closer tie to his neighbor. The success of one in the group can be felt as a success shared by the whole group. In this

---

See also *Shemos Rabba* 1:12, where it states that in the merit of our righteous Jewish women, we were redeemed; and the Yafeh To'ar there, who brings various other causes. However, to the degree that the Jewish People worked on *specific* character traits, the three listed in the text seem primary.

way, the Jewish name is a sign to all how each can feel part of and proud of the other. As soon as we know from the name that the person is a Jew, we identify with him and share in whatever is happening to him.

Further, the soul of a person is reflected in his name,[101] and referring to him by name bespeaks a personal concern and interest.[102] It's not, "Hey, you," but "Hey, Sid, Josh, Louie, Moish . . . ." The fellow is somebody to whom we are relating on a personal level. Such an approach fosters greater caring and lovingkindness between people, necessarily reducing selfishness and insularity.

To sum up, then, preserving the Jewish names strengthened our emotional, brother-to-brother connection and was, therefore, a positive force reinforcing the first part in the Threefold Key to being Jewish.

The second saving identity factor was their distinctly Jewish dress. Clearly, dressing in a uniquely Jewish fashion differentiated the Jewish population from its surrounding neighbors. Assimilation is just that much easier when everyone looks and dresses the same.

But on a deeper level, the way a Jew dresses represents the whole issue of physical modesty and restraint. People wear clothes to keep warm and protected, but garments also clothe the body in order that an observer's eye will not be readily stimulated. Judaism, however, takes this further and holds that the fullest development of the person's spiritual potential requires as much control over his carnal nature as possible. By

---

101. See Rabbi M. Glazerson's interesting discussion of the meaning of names in *Shem u'Neshamah*, Jerusalem, 5748, pp. 11-56.
102. See *TB Ta'anis* 20b and Ben Ish Chai on *"B'mah ha'arachta yamim,"* indicating the importance of using the individual's personal name.

following the rules of proper and modest dress, the Jew prevents overt arousals of lustful desires by himself and his entire community. (Indeed, any immodest display of the human form in any medium — including art, sculpture, photography, stage, movies, television, video, newspapers, magazines, advertising — is also completely inconsonant with a Torah-Jewish environment.)

"Proper and modest" is not merely a matter of changing forms of etiquette, style or what looks nice. In Judaism the standard is quite exact and straightforward: minimize the lure that the body connotes.[103] For women, no flashy, see-through or tight-fitting clothes; blouses up to the neck-line (front and back) and sleeves that cover at least the elbows; dresses or skirts only, modestly covering the knees and helping not to draw attention to the feminine form. Married women must cover their hair, engendering restraint. Men's clothes should also epitomize modesty; shirt sleeves, however, may reach the mid-biceps. Short pants without long stockings to cover bareness, as well as uncovered feet, are not preferred. The overall focus here is to reduce the allurement that human flesh and form can arouse.

It is common to be influenced by our surrounding culture, particularly on issues of fashion. But the Jew knows that if he accepts the prevailing non-Jewish customs, he will gradually lose his unique qualities and identity. Particularly in all issues related to physical desires, when he fails to keep to his People's standards, the Jew steadily reduces his level, until finally he would rather stay with the Egyptians than be set free as a Jew.

Remember: Eighty percent of the Jews in Egypt thought

---

103. See, in general, *Shulchan Aruch, Orach Chaim,* Sec. 75.

that they were right in dressing like Egyptians. Fortunately, the ancestors of those Jews alive today — *our* ancestors — realized that dressing Jewishly to reinforce control of our instincts helps to keep us Jewish.

The third identity factor which saved the Jew from assimilation was the Jewish language — Hebrew.

Hebrew is the language which Hashem used to create the world.[104] The Five Books of Moses — the Torah — are written in Hebrew, and of course, practically all the other books of the Prophets and the Writings are in Hebrew. Jewish prayer books are in Hebrew. The greater proportion of the *Gemora* is in Hebrew. The great halachic works are in Hebrew. The huge library of commentators is almost completely in Hebrew. Many works on Jewish philosophy, morals and ethics are in Hebrew.

How could one generation convey to the next the huge treasury of Jewish heritage and wisdom without knowing Hebrew? Without this vital tool, the Jew is lost. True, today there are enumerable translations of very many Torah books. However, moving from one language to another often misses the many nuances and interpretations that are in the original. And this axiom is particularly applicable to Torah texts, which are strikingly subtle and laden with many levels of explanation. Furthermore, the full clarity, power and inspiration of the Hebrew is almost completely lacking in translation, to the point that, sometimes, other languages make the Jewish Torah sound very un-Jewish and even uncomfortable to the Jewish ear. Also, the translation of the *Gemora* does not capture the complex thought process which the original succinctly expresses. And,

---

104. *Bereishis Rabba* 18:4; *Bereishis* 2:23, Rashi; *Shemos* 30:13, Ramban.

finally, whole worlds of understanding and fuller appreciation, such as *gematria* and the mind-boggling coded messages,[105] are available *only* in Hebrew.

Our history from Egypt until today has proven that those Jews who failed to maintain their Hebrew language assimilated into the surrounding culture. This essential means for understanding clearly what Hashem wants was abandoned as unnecessary for life. Subconsciously, perhaps, we would prefer to avoid relating to Hashem and listening to what He wants, for then our conception of our central position in the universe might have to be altered. Lacking interest in Hebrew may reflect a lack of serious involvement in our Jewish way of life, which would certainly explain why the eighty percent who had this attitude did not participate in the liberation of the Jews from Egypt. It takes diligence and concern to master the language which best facilitates understanding Hashem's message to humankind — the Torah.[106] It takes an interest in learning something beyond oneself. In brief, it takes humility to admit that this is very important information that we really must know.

Hopefully, the point is clear that the Jew is such a unique creation that he does not last very long if he starts to imitate his

---

105. See *Discovery Sourcebook*, Chap. 2, Codes in the Torah, p. 63.

106. With Hebrew language lessons very popular and plentiful today, the average learner can master a basic skill without great difficulty. One such program by Rabbi Joseph Freilich (The London Jewish Academy, London, England) offers twelve lessons where two hundred and thirty basic words cover 93% of the *Chumash*. Two of the many books which teach Hebrew are: *The First Hebrew Primer for Adults* (Biblical and Prayerbook Hebrew) (3rd ed.), Ethelyn Simon, et al., EKS Publishing Company, Oakland, California, 1993; *Hayesod — Fundamentals of Hebrew*, Uveeler and Bronznick, Feldheim Publishers, Jerusalem/New York, 1980.

non-Jewish neighbors. This assimilation attacks his threefold task of bringing Hashem into the world by undermining his dedication to acts of lovingkindness, bodily purity and humility. But for those who hold firm and do not compromise, their potential can be fulfilled, and their survival, assured.[107]

---

107. The following quotation from the well-known Jewish historian Cecil Roth concurs in our conclusion, even from a secularly-minded position:
"Our survey of three and a half millennia of Jewish history is closed. But the story which we have set ourselves to tell is unending. Today, the Jewish people has in it still those elements of strength and of endurance which enabled it to surmount all the crises of its past, surviving thus the most powerful empires of antiquity. **Throughout our history there have been weaker elements who have shirked the sacrifices which Judaism entailed. They have been swallowed up, long since, in the great majority; only the more stalwart have carried on the traditions of their ancestors, and can now look back with pride upon their superb heritage. Are we to be numbered with the weak majority, or with the stalwart minority? It is for ourselves to decide.** But, from a reading of Jewish history, one factor emerges which may perhaps help us in our decision. The preservation of the Jew was certainly not casual. He has endured through the power of a certain ideal, based upon the recognition of the influence of a higher Power in human affairs. Time after time in his history, moreover, he has been saved from disaster in a manner which cannot be described excepting as 'providential.' The author has deliberately attempted to write this work in a secular spirit; he does not think that his readers can fail to see in it, on every page, a higher immanence." *A History of the Jews*, Schocken Books, New York, 1961, pp. 423-4.*

X
The Pillars of the World

Lest the reader imagine that these three aspects of being Jewish are just to save Jews, he should know that these are actually the pillars upon which the entire world rests. *Chazal* tell us, "The world stands on three things: on Torah, on *Avodah*[108] and on acts of lovingkindness."[109] Indeed, we are taught

---

108. *Avodah* (service) refers originally to the offering of the *karbonos* in the *Beis Hamikdosh*. As will be mentioned in the text, *Avodah* today refers to prayer, and in Chap. III, fn. 16, we explained the conceptual connection between these two activities.

    We note in passing that on the outside Altar there were three fires, with a fourth added on the one day of *Yom Kippur*. *TB Yoma* 45a; Rambam, *Hilchos T'midim* 2:4, *Avodas Yom HaKippurim* 2:5. These three main fires hint to a further subdivision of *Avodah*. The largest one was for burning the sacrifices — physicality raised to its highest level. From the second, fire was taken to burn the twice-daily *ketores* on the inner Golden Altar — representing the Jewish People all together joyously serving Hashem. *Midrash Tanchuma*, *T'zaveh*, Section 15; *TB Kerisus* 6a; *TB Megillah* 25a, Rashi: "*Y'varchucha*." And the third was a constant fire, symbolic of the constant learning of Torah, for from this flame was taken the fire used to light the *Menorah*, symbolic of Torah wisdom and study. *Vayikra* 6:6, Rashi; *cf.* Rambam, *Hilchos T'midim* 2:4, 5; 3:13. But see *TB Yoma* 45b, Tosefos: "Tamid."

109. *Pirkei Avos* 1:2.

that each of the *Avos* were specifically responsible for constructing one column of this pedestal.[110]

These three world pillars once again represent the same Threefold Key of Jewish beyond-self realization. **Acts of lovingkindness** come to correct jealousy and envy by training constant giving. *Avodah*, in our time, refers to prayer and discipline, through which a person can learn control over his physical desires through concentrating on their spiritual purpose and following a precise rule system.[111] **Torah** means constantly learning and obeying the Torah — Hashem's will — which reduces arrogance and increases humility.[112]

Why does the whole world depend on the Jew doing his special job?

We explained at the beginning of our study that the world is in an imperfect state; it is missing, so to speak, a main participant: Hashem. He withdrew and gave the Jew the task of putting Him back into His creation.[113] Since, in any case, the

---

110. See Chap. III, fn. 11.
111. The *Gemora* describes prayer as the *avodah* (service) of the heart (*TB Ta'anis* 2a), clearly placing prayer under the category of emotions. While prayer does require the softening of the heart in order to *feel* one's closeness to the Creator, it still, quite obviously, includes all three parts of the person: emotions, intellect (*cf.* p. 30 and fn. 31) and instincts. As we have consistently explained, though one category may also have the other elements within it, in any particular threesome the category will be emphasizing one element. When we are using prayer in place of the *avodah* of the *karbonos*, we are talking about going beyond our instincts (i.e., the animal), raising them to a spiritual plane. See Chap. III, fn. 16.
112. We see, for example, that 24,000 students of Rabbi Akivah died because they failed to give proper respect to each other (*TB Yevamos* 62b). The greater the Torah scholar, the greater his requirement to behave humbly.
113. Hashem's choice was based on our choosing Him. See *Bereishis* 11:28 (Rashi) and *Bereishis Rabba* 38:13, where Avraham established the concept of the iconoclast and chose Hashem. Later, Hashem offered the

Origin of every person is this Force we call Hashem,[114] and all that blocks Him from "coming through" in a person's experience of life is the person himself, the solution is to convert the ambition for self into aspirations for beyond-self — the Ultimate.[115] Moreover, the finite self's best opportunity for the infinite is to go as totally beyond self as possible. So, for example, when a person gives to others, he resembles Hashem — the Infinite One — Who is a constant Giver. A consistent behavior pattern of giving moves the person beyond the needs of his finite self and inevitably in the direction of the infinite.

Through the Jew striving for this goal, the world has purpose, for it is being intentionally used to achieve its correction and completion. If the Jew was not working hard to do his job, then the world would lack its purpose and would, therefore, cease to justify its further existence. Thus, these three pillars keep the world standing because, with them, the Jew completes the destiny of humankind.[116]

Torah to all the nations of the world, but they refused (*Devorim* 33:2, Rashi; *Midrash Tanchumah, V' Zos Haberacha*, Sec. 4; *Yalkut Shimoni*, Sec. 951). Even so, any non-Jew who is sincerely interested can take on the task of the 613 *mitzvos* through a halachic conversion.

114. In other words, our inherent, natural condition is to sense our connection to the Source of our being. Compare *Devorim* 30:11-14.

It is interesting how children in their ingenuous, uninhibited state feel Hashem's existence. But as we become adults, our egos grow and we block Him out. Still, we do see young adults searching for a greater understanding of life and its ultimate meaning (see Chap. V, fn. 49). And there are also those who are older and fully involved in the physical world yet still perceive that there must be something more.

115. See pp. 12-4 and pp. 216-7 where this process is also discussed.

116. Relevant here is the triparted blessing we give to every newly circumcised Jewish baby: "Just as he entered into the *bris*, so may he enter into Torah, marriage and good deeds." We all want this fledgling Jew's successful participation in holding up the world's three pillars:

XI
Three within the Three

Not only can the task of the Jew be seen in these major world pillars, but also in each category the Threefold Key can be discerned.

Let's begin with *Chazal*'s dictum that in three ways, acts of lovingkindness are greater than *tzedoka* (money owed to the poor):[117]

1. *Tzedoka* is given with one's money alone, but acts of lovingkindness are performed with both one's body and one's money.

2. *Tzedoka* is for the poor, but acts of lovingkindness are for both the poor and the rich.

3. *Tzedoka* is for the living, but acts of lovingkindness are for the living and the dead.

From the first distinction, we can learn that working to

Torah and good deeds (i.e., acts of lovingkindness) are two of the pillars, and marriage, like *bris*, represents the category of *Avodah* (compare pp. 39-42, 56-9). Similarly, when a daughter is born, we bless the parents to raise her to Torah, marriage and good deeds.

117. *TB Succah* 49b.

correct one's selfishness is not just a matter of writing out a check for *tzedoka*. A person has to put his whole being into an active concern for others. To break down jealousy and envy, the total personality must be involved in the needs of others.

So, for example, to help someone come closer to Torah and *mitzvos*, we may have to be willing to give many hours for discussion and learning together.[118] True concern means giving of self, selflessly.

As for the second distinction, we might think that when the other fellow is at least financially well-off, we do not have to inconvenience ourselves with acts of lovingkindness. But the second difference comes to explain that we must exert ourselves to do kindness at the cost of our personal comfort, even if the other person is rolling in money, velvet upholstery and wall-to-wall carpets. Our job is to learn control over our own physical desires in every way possible — with no excuses that the other fellow is hardly limiting his physicality.

And, finally, we often do not mind doing acts of lovingkindness because we anticipate that the recipients will appreciate our righteousness and duly reciprocate when we need their help. For this reason, the third distinction teaches us that acts of lovingkindness should have truly humble motives and, where possible, be performed anonymously. We should learn to give to others without any expectation of return (even in-

---

118. Rabbi Moshe Feinstein, the great halachic scholar, determined a special requirement for our times: "As in charity, where one has an obligation to give a tenth of his income to the poor, so must one spend one tenth of his time working on behalf of others, bringing them close to Torah. If one is endowed with greater resources, he must correspondingly spend more of his time with others," "A Time for Action," *The Jewish Observer*, June, 1973, p. 6; reprinted in *Reaching Out*, Rabbi Aryeh Kaplan, NCSY Publication, New York, 1991 (3rd ed.), p. 65.

creased respect), just as the kindness of burying the dead can result in no return favor or even appreciation from the deceased.

Concerning the second pillar, *Avodah* (taken here to refer to prayer),[119] many may know that the Jew prays three times a day: morning, afternoon, and evening.[120] But you may not have known that these three prayers also teach us about our Threefold Key.

Morning represents a mini-re-creation every day: the crisp air, the brilliant rays of sun, the fresh, vibrant energy granted us for our day's activities. The lovingkindness of Hashem literally pours out over the whole world, bestowing new life and vigor. Sure, it takes a little while for the initial grogginess to wear off, but afterwards, off we go with a new eagerness and anticipation.

Before we go running after our own needs in the day, however, we do a simple kindness for Someone Else, first thing in the morning: we doven *Shacharis*, thanking Hashem for giving us life and a purpose to fulfill. A genuine feeling of gratitude sets in motion an entirely different viewpoint on the day and our activities. Taking special note of how much we are receiving from Hashem, we will want to do for Him in return. And since He Himself needs nothing, He asks instead that we do acts of lovingkindness for others. So, it is only natural that if we are truly grateful to Him, our day will be filled with deeds of giving.

The *Minchah* prayer is short but significant, since it is said

---

119. See p. 91 and fn. 111; Chap. III, fn. 16.
120. Each of the daily prayers was established by one of the *Avos*: Avraham — *Shacharis*; Yitzchak — *Minchah*; Yaakov — *Ma'ariv* (TB Berachos 26b).

in the afternoon when we are generally preoccupied with our working-day concerns. Right then, when our physical needs seem to be so pressing, we stop and regain our spiritual perspective. We "check in" again with Hashem, stepping out of the race for worldly success. Now we have a moment to contemplate: If our bodies are all we are concerned about, what will be in the end? Surely materialism alone is insufficient. Surely our goals must be lifted to a higher plane.

Finally, the day is over and we come home in the evening. Although we might believe there is nothing left to do but relax and entertain ourselves, the *Ma'ariv* prayer comes to remind Jews that Hashem wants us to use even these remaining hours of the day to learn His Torah.[121]

"Wait a minute!" we protest. "I'm tired, and I want some time for *myself.*" But this is precisely the point. A true, loving servant asks nothing for himself. Instead, in spite of his fatigue, he is willing to devote all his time to the will of his master since he has made this his own will.[122] And, so, we Jews use this last prayer of the day as a springboard into further understanding of Hashem's will (Torah), continually molding ourselves into humble, self-effacing individuals.

The remaining pillar mentioned in Chapter X — Torah learning — is also divided into three subdivisions. We are taught that in order to be a fully actualized Jew, three categories of Torah studies should be mastered:[123]

---

121. We say just before the evening *Shema*, "and on them [words of Torah] we will meditate day and night." See *Yehoshua* 1:8.

122. Of course, *necessary* relaxation is also the will of the Master, as it says, "And you must very much guard your bodies." *Devorim* 4:15.

123. *TB Baba Kama* 30a with the Maharsha, who relates these three categories to life's three basic relationships: with others, oneself and Hashem.

(cont.)

1. The laws of *nezikim* (damages)
2. *Pirkei Avos* (Ethics of the Fathers)
3. The laws of *berachos* (blessings)

A Jew should learn all areas of the Torah. So why were these three categories singled out for special attention? Once again, they indicate the Threefold Key to realizing and fulfilling our Jewish identity.

The first category deals with the laws concerning situations in which injury or monetary loss occurs between man and his fellow. Very often, we fail to appreciate our responsibilities to others, solely because we have never seriously investigated the subject. People assume that they know what is right and wrong, or, if it becomes necessary, they will just check with a lawyer. But under Jewish Law, we each need to be knowledgeable enough to act intelligently and responsibly, on the spot when necessary. For example, what are your responsibilities

- when you find a lost article?
- if you see a hazard that could potentially harm someone?
- if you see a driver side-swipe a parked car?

In passing, we note a possible triparted division of the *mitzvos* in the question of the wise son in the *Pesach Hagadah* (derived from a verse in the Torah, *Devorim* 6:20):

1)*Eidos*: the testimonies (e.g., historical events) which correspond to Avraham and show Hashem's intimate love for the Jewish People throughout history.

2)*Chukim*: the fixed rules (e.g., *kashrus*) which correspond to Yitzchak and indicate the necessity of a disciplined regime in order to control physicality.

3)*Mishpatim*: the judgements (e.g., theft) which correspond to Yaakov and highlight the importance of true reason and logic in the management of human affairs and behavior, with "true" connoting a necessary link to the Source of truth.

98 / *Self Beyond Self*

- if the check-out clerk forgot to ring up an article on the cash register, and you realize the mistake only once you've arrived home?
- if you, as an employee or partner, want to use corporation or partnership property for personal use?
- if you want to use a borrowed object beyond the purpose originally requested, or to lend it to someone else in the meantime?

The list is so diversified and all-encompassing that it covers endless possible life situations. Many conceive of religion as prayer and ritual, spiced with pious aphorisms. But Torah Judaism is *not* a religion. It is the complete guide to life itself and, as such, requires diligent study in order to know the proper Torah response to every possible facet of our multifarious day-to-day existence.

In the context of our discussion, this category of Torah learning concentrates on our concern for the other fellow. We are taught to consider his person and property like our own.[124] We cannot hide from our brother, saying that our world is separate from his, that what happens to him is not our concern. Passivity, disinterest, selfishness are uprooted by laws which force us to take responsibility where we have the ability and opportunity to help. Studying the laws of *nezikim* forces us to realize that we are in training to care for others and not to look at them as strangers, competitors or bothersome distractions from our normal schedule.

On a deeper level, all these rules dealing with external actions actually help us to eventually change our *internal* moti-

---

124. *Vayikra* 19:18: "And you shall love your neighbor as yourself." See Rambam, *Hilchos Deos* 6:3; *Sefer Hachinuch, Mitzvah* 243. See also App. B: Love Your Neighbor, p. 243.

vations. For just as we are not allowed to cause any damage to our fellow's property, we are not allowed to covet his property.[125] How can the Torah legislate feelings? Part of the answer is that practice makes perfect. The more we condition ourselves in how to behave properly, the more our inner being conforms to our external activity. It is hard work, but constant, deep drilling eventually achieves the goal, with Hashem's help.

The second category of Torah learning — *Pirkei Avos* — speaks directly to the inner psychology of the Jew. *Pirkei Avos* is a compendium of ethical maxims to improve behavior, attitudes, motivation. Through it, we are asked to look honestly at our self-portrait of perfection and invulnerability. Naturally biased in our own favor, we persistently refrain from examining ourselves under a magnifying glass. "Who, me?" we answer sheepishly. "You want *me* to be honest with myself inside? Well ... actually, I'm a bit busy right now. Maybe, next week, I'll have some time."

What happens when we do look closer at ourselves?

If a person would go behind the scenes of a play or a movie, he would be amazed to see that all the props are only stage fronts, very impressive on the outside but with no depth, no substance. Then he would see how all the actors, who appear bigger than life on stage, look and behave quite differently when they are being themselves. And finally, the whole production can be packed up in boxes and put in storage, perhaps to be restaged or perhaps never to be seen again. What looked so real was, in reality, so ephemeral.

The stunning thing about this analogy is that it can apply

---

125. *Shemos* 20:14; *Devorim* 5:18.

100 / *Self Beyond Self*

to all areas of life: politics, business, medicine, law, romance, athletics, cars — it just takes knowing the behind-the-scenes story, and we would be quickly disabused of our innocent admiration.

The question is: Which type of life is better to live? A life of stage fronts and make-up, or a life that strives to reach the truth of existence?

Comes *Pirkei Avos* to force us to look inside and examine truthfully our goals, our character, our desires, our motivations. In other words, we are being encouraged to scrutinize intensely our so-called "natural" behavior.

For example, one of our Sages, Hillel, says in *Pirkei Avos*: "If I am not for myself, who is for me? And when I am for myself, what am I? And if not now, when?"[126] One commentator explains this cryptic statement as a pithy attack on a person's inertia and complacency.[127] We have to goad ourselves to make certain that we are changing our bad habits and character traits. And even when we do so, we should realize that we still have more to correct. And we should not say tomorrow, but start now.

Purposely sharp and to the point, Hillel's maxim rings like the speed buzzer on a car's speedometer: "Wake up! Get with it! Don't be content thinking you're 'perfect enough.' Remember what your life is for. Don't be lethargic!"

But this Jewish Fort Knox of wisdom is not just universal ethical currency with a *Magen Dovid* stamped on it. We are taught that although it was transferred to us through our Sages, all of it comes directly from Hashem.[128] Suddenly we see that the Creator of the world is involved and interested in even our

---

126. *Pirkei Avos* 1:14.
127. Rabbeinu Yona, Commentary on *Pirkei Avos*.
128. *Pirkei Avos* 1:1, Harav m'Bertinoro; Tosefos Yom Tov.

most private thoughts and behavior. Ethics from such an outlook is an entirely different process when we see the Boss Himself, as it were, pointing His finger at us and saying, *"I want you!"*

"I want you to realize why you're alive.

"I want you to stop chasing your superficial physical desires and to start working seriously on your inner being.

"I want you to purify and raise up your behavior to the very highest level possible.

"In short, I want you to move your entire being towards the infinite. Every response, every desire, every instinct."

The last category of Torah learning, the laws of blessings, works directly on the humility which we Jews are supposed to epitomize.

Imagine walking along in the springtime and seeing the first fruit trees blossoming. Then, filled with appreciation, you say a special blessing to Hashem, thanking Him for such goodly trees that give benefit to humankind. Or, perhaps, you are bending down on a lovely June day to smell a fragrant rose or carnation, and before inhaling, you bless Him for creating such a fragrant scent. Or, when you wake up in the morning, you bless Hashem for granting you renewed strength.[129]

Or when you see the beginning of the new moon, or a rainbow, or lightning, or the ocean — all of these otherwise easily taken for granted experiences have special blessings to

---

129. The Hebrew word for "bless" comes from a basic root that means "outside," i.e., extends outward (see Dictionary, p. 154, in *The Seven Days of the Beginning*, Rabbi Eli Munk, Feldheim Publishers, Jerusalem, 1974). By making a blessing, we Jews extend Hashem into the world by publicly declaring that He is the One responsible for the particular event in question.

Hashem. When you have a new baby or buy a new home or eat a new fruit in its season — all are opportunities to praise the Almighty's munificence.

And don't think only of special events. For what is more commonplace than human beings placing a morsel of bread or any other food or drink, between their lips? This mundane essential of essentials could do nothing more than feed an attitude of matter-of-fact self-edification: "My money bought this savory toasted English muffin, this scrumptious crêpe suzette, this delectable cheese cake." But the Jew is trained from the day he starts putting sentences together that he should feel nothing more than humble praise and gratitude to Hashem for every feast and every crumb that the Creator has granted him to enjoy.

Learning about all these blessings — their complexity and pervasiveness — again teaches one of the aspects of the Key to Jewish perfection: humility. In reality, Hashem creates and sustains everything.[130] But it *looks* as if natural and human causes run the world — Mother Nature, in conjunction with General Motors, IBM, Mitsubishi and company.[131] The Jewish way of living, however, helps us Jews to never make this mistake. For, through learning the blessings, we remind ourselves what is really making things tick. In actuality, everything depends on Hashem directing the forces that sustain us, not on our own abilities and power. Thus educated, we can then eat that apple and, saying its blessings before and after, profoundly

---

130. See *Devorim* 4:35, 39; *Zechariah* 4:6.
131. The Hebrew word for "world" is *olam*, the root meaning of which is "hidden." The world is so constructed as to hide the presence of the Creator. For, indeed, *this* is the challenge: Hashem must be hidden so that we can make our own free-will decision in the face of the seeming options.

appreciate how really delicious it tastes. Why? Because we have comprehended and absorbed at a higher level precisely the lesson it was put in this world to teach us.

In conclusion, we have seen in Chapter X how the Three Pillars represent the Threefold Key to being Jewish. Now in this chapter we have learned how the same Threefold Key intertwines each pillar. This reoccurring theme is a program of human development which constantly trains our intellect, emotions and instincts to move from self to beyond-self, from a finite plane to a more and more infinite dimension.

Part Four:
Exemplary Celebrations

    XII A Profound Beginning

   XIII Holidays of Ascent

   XIV Food for Thought at the *Seder* Table

    XV Meaningful Frivolity

XII
A Profound Beginning

Just as the Threefold Key interweaves our daily Jewish existence, so also does it permeate the high points of the Jewish year: the holidays.

Actually, though little known, *Shabbos* is also termed a holiday.[132] Since it comes every week, however, its specialness is sometimes overlooked. As discussed in Chapter V, it is one of the three signs that prove we are living our Jewish potential, and as such, it is obviously very important.[133] Here, though, we will concentrate on some of the other holidays, beginning with *Rosh Hashanah*.

The Jewish New Year stands in stark contrast to the inebriated parties marking the end of the secular calendar year. Very many attend religious services (in some places, the overflow demands traffic police!) and prepare for the holiday by buying new clothes and cooking special meals, embellished with foods

---

132. *Shemos* 23:3.
133. See also Chap. XVII concerning the three meals of *Shabbos*.

symbolic of our prayers for the coming year, like honey cake for a sweet year. *Rosh Hashanah* is quite a serious holiday. After all, it is also called the Day of Judgment, and it begins the Ten Days of Repentance which culminate in the Day of Atonement — *Yom Kippur*. Hashem is judging the whole world for the coming year on *Rosh Hashanah*, and who is so sure of the future that he is not awed by the occasion?

There is a special prayer book for *Rosh Hashanah*, called the *Machzor*, in which the blowing of the shofar is centrally featured, for this is *the mitzvah* of the day. The many prayers before and after, interestingly enough, deal with three major themes:[134]

1. The kingship of Hashem — *Malchuyos*

2. Hashem's remembrance of humankind's righteousness — *Zichronos*

3. The shofar blasts themselves, which call the Jew to his Creator — *Shofaros*

By now, the reader is familiar with the significance of three and, in addition, its correlation to each of the *Avos*:

Providing the model for the *Malchuyos* prayer, Avraham loved Hashem and declared His absolute unity and kingship over the world. What looked like a variety of forces, the sun god, the rain god, the fertility god, this god and that god, Avraham denied and proclaimed instead that all was One — Hashem alone. As explained, if we would see and know that *everything* that happens is being controlled by Hashem, we would have no thoughts of jealousy or envy, for we would realize that the other person's success is also by Hashem's direction. Further, if we would truly give our full allegiance to That Which is beyond us, we would learn to be less concerned

---

134. *Machzor* (*Rosh Hashanah*), *Musaf* Prayer — the longest formal *davening* of the year.

about what we are receiving in return. For Hashem's kingship should so dominate our minds and behavior that we would gradually replace and abandon all petty concerns for self.

Regarding *Zichronos*, Yitzchak proved that a Jew can control himself even in the ultimate test of giving one's life. When Hashem remembers such total adherence to beyond-self, He is "encouraged" to keep the whole world going. For He sees that there are some who are fulfilling the purpose of man's creation: to transcend the physical and achieve the spiritual. Every time a Jew controls his physical nature — lusts, desires, appetites — he is justifying the world's existence and bringing a positive remembrance before the Creator.

Finally, when the Children of Yisroel stood at *Har Sinai* and heard the blasts of the shofar which heralded the giving of the Torah, the whole world hung in trembling trepidation. Still, the rest of the nations were disinterested in following Divine dictates.[135] Only we Jews had the humility to realize that if Hashem is asking us to do His commandments, there is no point in allowing our egos petulantly to deny His sovereignty. Similarly, the shofar wakes up only the one who is interested in being awakened; the listener himself has to appreciate the meaning behind this primordial call. Like Yaakov, we must be willing to search for the truth, opening our ears and minds to the Ultimate's wisdom. Once having activated this humility, we can resolve again, at the beginning of the new year, to learn and listen better in the coming year.

This underlying triparted theme of *Rosh Hashanah* is dramatized even further at the climax of the day's davening, the *Unesane-tokef*. This poignant prayer (repeated on *Yom Kip-*

---

135. See Chap. X, fn. 113. *Individuals* of the nations were interested, which fact helps explain non-Jews converting to Torah Judaism.

pur) speaks of Hashem, the King and Master of all, judging his creatures for the year as a shepherd counts his flock: Who will live, who will die, who will have comfort, who will be disturbed, who will become rich, who will become poor, who will be brought low and who will be raised. After all, the Absolute Power can do absolutely anything.

But the prayer reaches its crescendo with practical advice as to what to do in order to avert an adverse decree:

1. Repentance
2. Prayer
3. Giving *tzedoka*

Rosh Hashanah is the day that the first human was created[136] and, along with him, the purpose for his being created: to bring Hashem into the world. The mistakes[137] we make as Jews can block this purpose, but Hashem is not interested in punishment as retribution. He prefers that we simply improve, and by taking His practical advice as listed above, we can correct our errors and start now becoming a conduit for His presence.

We have given some attention to the second one of these three suggestions in Chapters X and XI. Prayer provides a spiritual perspective on our physical desires and aspirations. With discipline, contemplation and a rule system, we can learn control over the physical world so that it forms no contradiction

---

136. Judaism maintains that the first human with the full, moral, decision-making potential which we have today was formed as many years ago as the current Jewish year. This concept is confirmed in every reliable history book, for "historic man" (one who made an imprint on history and the world) begins approximately the same time that Judaism holds that the first human being was created.

137. The Hebrew word for sin — *chet* — comes from a basic root that means "to miss the mark." In other words, very often, we are simply making mistakes, and all we have to do is re-aim and shoot again more correctly at the target.

to Ultimate Spirit. From *Rosh Hashanah* through *Yom Kippur*, we achieve levels of introspection and soul-searching greater than at any other time of the year. At this crucial beginning, we focus intensely on purifying our motives and elevating our goals. Sincerely and honestly resolving to improve the quality of our behavior, we can more optimistically anticipate a more favorable decree for the coming year.

The giving of *tzedoka* is within the category of acts of lovingkindness, for clearly a person is giving of himself when he donates his money.[138] Indeed, the vast majority of us identify very strongly with our money, depending on it for our security base and ego-support. And should someone suggest that we share our wealth with those in need, we reveal our commitment to individualism and free enterprise over Jewish lovingkindness by insisting that they go out and work as we do. Or let them file for welfare benefits with the government or private agencies. And we think to ourselves self-righteously, "I need my money for me, for my own needs, for my investments, for my savings, for my retirement. And what about that 'rainy day'?!" The "I, me, my" are just a little bit dominant here, and, consequently, there is not much room for Hashem to fit in.

But on *Rosh Hashanah*, Hashem wants to see if we realize that He is King: one King and everyone else His servants. A King like He is leaves no room for anyone to be more than a simple subject, each and every one. But by acting selfishly and not sufficiently giving *tzedoka*, the individual has separated himself from his brothers, behaving with uninvolved aloofness. Having made himself a little king, he immediately blocks the

---

138. Even though acts of lovingkindness can be greater than *tzedoka* (see pp. 93-5), giving money certainly shows a concern for others whenever there is a true intention for beyond-self.

absolute kingship of Hashem.

By giving *tzedoka*, we actively demonstrate that every Jew is our brother and is on the same level as we are in relation to the King and Father of all. We and he (the recipient) are part of one fabric woven by Hashem, one mold fashioned by the Creator. Indeed, the King has given us our money precisely in order that we give a portion to him, just like one part of the body gives to another its needed assistance. The new year should start on the right foot, i.e., the right hand (an open one!) — caring for and helping each other.

The last piece of very important advice given in the *Unesane-tokef* prayer is repentance. However, "Repent! Repent!" is the well-known and easily ignored theme song of any street-corner would-be prophet. And who has not seen its cartoon depicture and smiled amusedly? "A simple solution to complex problems," we say to ourselves. "True, if I ever do anything particularly wrong, when *Rosh Hashanah* comes around, I suppose that I'll feel regret and resolve never to do it again."

The Jewish concept of repentance, however, is something else altogether.

"Repentance" is an English translation of the Hebrew word *teshuvah*, which actually means "return." "Repent" tells us to regret and change our ways. But the word "return" tells us about the step *beforehand* which clarifies tremendously how we practical Jews look at repentance.

> *"So, what is this 'step before'?"*
> *"Please answer first: What does 'return' mean?"*
> *"Well, I don't know."*
> *"Just think a minute. Return to what?"*
> *"What do you mean, 'what?'"*

"All it says is return. But what are we supposed to return to?"

"Yeah, you're right. Return to what?"

"Exactly. And that is the first and most important question, even before we get to the next step of 'repent.'"

For the Jew, there is no question of what "return" means. It means return to Hashem's Torah. Hashem Himself tells us: "Would that the Jews leave Me but still keep my Torah!"[139] The explanation of this unusual order of priorities is that through studying Torah seriously, we can master the many details of truthful living, and this truth will then automatically return us to Hashem, for truth and Hashem are synonymous.[140] This return to Torah helps us see more clearly what is right and wrong. And only after we *know* these specifics, can we go to the next step of fully *regretting* our mistakes and, then, to *resolving* to choose only the correct behavior.[141] This process of Jewish repentance is called *teshuvah*, a concept which includes an initial first step vital to its success — learning Torah.

In brief, we see once again that the advice for a successful *Rosh Hashanah* and *Yom Kippur* is our Threefold Key to being Jewish:

Teshuvah: Returning to learning Torah and then humbly

---

139. *TY Chagiga* 1:7(6b).

140. One definition of Hashem, not commonly known, is *truth*. As stated by the prophet Yirmeyahu (10:10), "And the Lord God is truth."

141. According to the Rambam, there is no separate *mitzvah* of *teshuvah*. Instead, inherent in every *mitzvah*, if violated, is the requirement not to repeat the error and to return to the proper path. See Rabbi Moshe Sternbuch, *Derech L'teshuvah*, B'nei Brak, 5738, p. 7. We see from this approach that *teshuvah* is a factor of first studying and knowing the *mitzvos* in order then to determine whether or not one has failed to fulfill them.

obeying what Hashem wants us to do.

Prayer: Discipline and contemplation, directing our physical desires to spiritual goals.

Tzedoka: An act of lovingkindness that particularly shows our non-competitive connection with every Jew as an equal subject under Hashem's kingship.

XIII
Holidays of Ascent

Everyone knows about *Pesach*, when Jews eat *matzah* and drink four cups of wine. Perhaps not so well known are the other two major holidays which join *Pesach* under the title of the Three Pilgrimages. At the time of the *Beis Hamikdosh*, the Jewish People left their homes and ascended the mountains to Jerusalem in order to celebrate *Pesach*, *Shavuos*, and *Succos*, festivals of convocation which strengthened the whole nation in the realization of its spiritual destiny. Today these holidays are still observed in all aspects, except for those details dependent on the *Beis Hamikdosh*.

We Jews received these profoundly elevating festivals in the merit of the *Avos*, Avraham, Yitzchak and Yaakov.[142] Indeed, the first day of each Jewish month was also intended to be a holiday in the merit of the twelve sons of Yaakov. But because the Jewish People erred by worshipping the Golden Calf, we lost these holidays.[143]

---

142. Tur, *Orach Chaim*, Sec. 417.
143. *Ibid.*

How do these Pilgrimages represent our Threefold Key to being Jewish?

Pesach is in the merit of Avraham. He so completely extended lovingkindness to the Creator and humankind that Hashem, in return, bestowed His lovingkindness upon his descendants by freeing them from an otherwise inescapable bondage. In expressing his uncompromising love for Hashem as the only Force in creation, Avraham set in motion the open revelation of this Force in his own life and in the history of his children. The Exodus from Egypt is an unparalleled historical event that proves how much the Creator is deeply and lovingly involved with His creation. He saved us then against impossible odds, and throughout Jewish history we see that a remnant has always miraculously survived and continued on.[144] For example, even after a Holocaust, we find the return to the Land of Israel and the incredible and vibrant rebirth of Torah Judaism in our ancient homeland, with even more students learning the Talmud than there were in Europe before World War II.

The explanation for this ever-present miracle is the Jew's desire to follow in Avraham's footsteps, to go beyond self and give to others — to his fellow human and to Hashem. The greater the giving by us, the greater the giving by Him. And very often, His giving is really just another term for miracle, i.e., extraordinary acts of intervention in history. Indeed, even the continued existence of creation itself is just one big gift, and the more we actively respond to this realization by giving to others, the more Hashem bestows His miraculous gifts upon us. *Pesach* represents this process: Avraham's love generating the ever-

---

144. See Rabbi Berel Wein, *Triumph of Survival*, The Story of the Jews in the Modern Era 1650 - 1990, Shaar Press, New York, 1990.

present miracle of Jewish history.

Shavous, which celebrates the giving of the Torah and its commandments, is in the merit of Yitzchak, for he was so willing to accept the total dominion of Hashem over his life that, at *Har Sinai*, the Jewish People were granted the opportunity of accepting the absolute sovereignty of Hashem over their lives. For the first and only time in world history, a whole people communicated with the Creator of the universe, proving that flesh and blood can transcend itself to reach the Ultimate.[145] But success can come only through complete obedience, discipline and control because as soon as the physical works according to its own rules, it supplants the spiritual and becomes an end in itself rather than a means to an end. The body and its instincts are mortal and finite and, therefore, cannot be the end goal but rather are only the means to achieve a greater goal — the infinite. But since the body can so easily be misused, it is essential that it be carefully controlled and properly directed.

We are not espousing asceticism. Our bodies were given us to use, but we must use them in a way that will not hinder or contradict the ultimate purpose of life. The powerful yoke of the 613 commandments is just the right prescription for keeping the body under control. Indeed, the 613 *mitzvos* correspond to the 248 limbs and 365 sinews of the body, clearly showing how *every* part of the human form can be integrated with a higher law and a loftier reality.[146] On *Shavous* we went totally beyond the physical, proving the point that the human has an ultimate destiny that defies all physical limitations. And every year on

---

145. The experience quite overwhelmed us. *Shemos Rabba* 29:3.
146. The step-by-step purification of the physical will eventually lead to *t'chias hameisim* — the revival of the dead (*TB Avodah Zara* 20b; *Mishnah Sotah* 9:16). See Rabbi Moshe Chaim Luzatto, *Mesilas Yesharim*, Chap. 26.

this holiday, we joyously give thanks for this extraordinary capacity which Yitzchak Avinu engendered within us of going beyond the physical aspects of self.

Succos is in the merit of Yaakov, for he strove to learn Torah throughout all his travels and travails.[147] He thereby bequeathed to his descendants an indefatigable ability to battle adversity with a mind striving for truth. The *succah* is a thatched-roof hut which dramatically illustrates the protection which Hashem gave the Jewish People when they left Egypt and went into the Sinai desert. It is a temporary dwelling, less comfortable and secure than our homes and, as such, symbolically represents exile, difficulties, vulnerability to the vicissitudes of life. But this humble, simple abode has a strength that has lasted 3300 years.[148] Amazingly, it is a mini-chamber where Hashem actually dwells. Inside its walls, all our thoughts, ideas, words, speech, conversation, activities are within His immediate presence. Indeed, it is almost like a small *Beis Hamikdosh*.

What makes this spiritual dimension possible in the *succah*? Very simple. The only preferred activities there, besides eating and sleeping, are learning, discussing, debating, thinking words of Torah. And since Torah is the direct communication of Hashem to humankind, when we totally occupy ourselves with His thoughts, He actually becomes part of our existence — right there in the *succah*!

---

147. See *Bereishis* 33:17, *Targum Yonason*, Rashi, *Torah T'mimah* (note 11), where the word *succos* is used the first time in the *Chumash* in the context of Yaakov's establishing a *beis midrash*.

148. The wandering Jew is historical fact. Still and in spite of it all, everywhere we have traveled, we have established *batei kenesses* and *midrash*, learning Torah and maintaining our distinction as the Eternal People. See *Bereishis* 46:28, Rashi.

Additionally, the transient *succah* with its temporary, vulnerable roof, shows clearly the ephemeral nature of our lives. Aren't we mortals very much the same — temporary and vulnerable? In such a humble environment which effaces our self-importance, we can ask ourselves what, then, is lasting and truly worthwhile? The answer comes from our ancestor, Yaakov: The search for truth and meaning will inevitably lead one to knowledge of Hashem, knowledge of the Ultimate. Torah learning lifts the transitory to the level of the permanent, and the *succah* serves as the perfect symbol of something quite insubstantial lasting forever. If we stay diligently focused on truth — which by definition is unchanging and eternal, we can actually become this truth, which is the closest we can achieve to becoming eternal ourselves.

In conclusion, we are taught that *Succos* is considered the happiest of all the holidays, and we can see here another reason why. When a person works hard and accomplishes something significant, he feels a great deal of pleasure and satisfaction. The permanence we gain by learning Torah gives us the greatest joy that our ephemeral lives can experience. In effect, through this process we are earning an intimate relationship with Hashem, by understanding to the best of our ability the ideas, concepts, reasoning which He put in His Torah.

Indeed, to climax the whole experience of *Succos*, we go right into the holiday of *Shemini Atzeres/Simchas Torah*, the high point of the year, when we express our total love and connection to Torah by dancing with all our energy, joy and appreciation. This dynamic accession, together with *Pesach* and *Shavous*, completes a cycle that yearly helps us move ever persistently beyond self, closer and closer to the Infinite.

XIV
Food for Thought at the *Seder* Table

Looking more closely at one of the major holidays we discussed in the previous chapter, we find a further intensification of our Threefold Key.

The *Pesach Hagadah* states that three major subjects must be discussed at the *Seder* table:[149]

1. *Pesach* — the Passover lamb
2. *Matzah* — the unleavened bread
3. *Maror* — the bitter herbs

How do these topics elucidate our basic theme?

The *Pesach* sacrifice (Passover lamb) represents Hashem's lovingkindness in skipping over the Jewish homes when He killed the firstborn of the Egyptians. Only hours before, the Jews had sacrificed the lamb, the idol of the Egyptians, and placed its blood on their doorposts and lintels.[150] By doing so they were following in the tradition of Avraham, who had also shown his love for Hashem by destroying the false gods of his time. In

---

149. See the section in the *Hagadah* a little after the *Dayeinu* song; also *Mishnah Pesachim* 10:5.
150. *Shemos* 12:3, 7, 21-3.

120 / *Self Beyond Self*

response, Hashem promised His eternal commitment to Avraham and his progeny. In Egypt, once we showed our total loyalty to Hashem by sacrificing the lamb, Hashem's love for us was aroused, and He saved us. Indeed, the name of the lamb offering — *pesach* (noun form) — is the same word as the action which Hashem performed by skipping over the Jewish homes — *pasach* (verb form),[151] for the two were and are interdependent.

As mentioned before,[152] lovingkindness can also be performed towards Hashem, so to speak. After all, if we do not give Him a place to exist in our lives, then how will He be there? Certainly, we appreciate how kindnesses to others are essential for a goodly life, but we sometimes forget that Hashem arranged the world such that it depends on us whether or not He will be manifest. To the degree that we act on our love for Him, so too is the degree to which His presence is felt in the world.

Because this crucial Jewish task is very far from being just an individual enterprise, the *Pesach* offering was a national demonstration of our love for Hashem, for in the first instance it was to be prepared in groups.[153] Each Jew was dependent upon others to cooperate and work together in the offering, roasting and eating.

This demonstration in Egypt of the interconnection between Jews underscores a basic corollary in loving Hashem, as we have explained before: If this feeling of love for God is truthful, then it should naturally promote selfless giving and sincere concern between human beings. If a person is really concerned for beyond-self, then he also will not be limited to thinking only of self when it comes to the needs of others. The

---

151. *Shemos* 12:27.
152. See pp. 74-5.
153. See *Shemos* 12:3-4; Rambam, *Hilchos Korban Pesach* 2:1-2.

Pesach offering shows the Jewish People's unified effort — in all its interactions — to act with selfless giving. In fact, if we look closely in the Torah, it says that Hashem skipped over the Jewish *homes* in Egypt, not over individual Jews.[154] For the People as a home, as a unit, deserved being saved. Seeing such brotherly love, Hashem responded with love.

In summary, the communal slaughtering of the Passover lamb clearly demonstrates our intense commitment to Hashem and His People. As a result, we can see how this component of the *Seder* night is really showing how our emotions were being directed beyond self, one of the essential parts of our Threefold Key to being Jewish.

Matzah is the unleavened bread which we were forced to eat in our hurried exit from Egypt. Not for one second longer could we withstand the temptations of the New York/London/Paris of its day. The taste of the puffy *dolce vita*, the sweet, easy life, threatened to sink us into a hedonistic existence with no spiritual purpose.[155] *Matzah*, which, by definition, is missing precisely this puff (*chametz* — leavening), represents control over our sensual desires. We Jews use them to survive but not to indulge in them for their own sake.[156]

Search throughout the entire globe. Where can you find a whole nation which would refrain from eating the staff of life — bread — and instead, consumes a dry, difficult-to-chew and harder-to-digest cracker? Unknowing observers are dumb-

---

154. *Shemos* 12:27.
155. *Me'am Lo'ez. Shemos*, Vol. 1, p. 235.
156. Although *chametz* generally symbolizes the *yetzer hara* in all its many facets, here we see that *matzah* is counteracting our propensity to pursue our physical cravings — a very prime preoccupation of the *yetzer hara*.

founded with such abstention: "A sophisticated, intelligent people eating the same bread of affliction which their forebears ate 3300 years ago! Come on. Today we're modern — nutrition, balanced diets, health foods. Enjoy life! Why make yourselves suffer this way?!"

For us Jews, the *real* suffering would be to live our lives with our bodies controlling us. *Matzah* teaches us self-restraint, satisfaction with simplicity, the ability to see beyond the momentary pleasures. Indeed, reflecting the rigorous discipline which *matzah* symbolizes, there are innumerable rules on how to prepare and eat the *matzah*, as well as how to remove non-*matzah* products from the home and personal property. Quite a bit of physical labor is involved in fulfilling some of these requirements, teaching us that we must work hard in order to become masters over our instincts.

Such adherence to a regime of control and discipline established a basic building block in the construction of the Jewish People, right from our very beginning. If it looks as if we Jews are suffering during *Pesach*, it is only because the casual observer assumes that physical enjoyments are *the* goal of life. Instead, we eat our *matzah* and learn that there is a pleasure greater than the sensual one, the pleasure of transcending the physical.

Maror — the bitter herbs — comes to remind us of the bitter bondage which we suffered at the hands of the Egyptians. But what caused it to become so unbearable?

One of the reasons given is that we ourselves began working voluntarily, and then, afterwards, forced labor was imposed. Pharaoh himself cunningly went out and started the construction, rallying all his citizens to follow his lead. Uncoerced, the Jews loyally and diligently joined the ranks, only to be woefully enslaved in the end. What was worse, the extra effort they exerted the first day established a quota which became the required quota every day. What could be more bitter than to know that your affliction came through your own hands?[157]

This poignant mistake was actually brought about by an even more basic error. Eleven of the Twelve Tribes of Yisroel answered the call to follow the country's leader and jump on the patriotic band wagon. One tribe, however, refused any involvement in the entire affair. The Tribe of Levi insisted that it would continue learning Torah without interruption, even for top priority, national causes. The humble call to Hashem and His Torah was stronger than the power of kings and social pressure. As it turned out, Pharaoh's later decree of bondage applied only to those who originally volunteered. Thus, because the Tribe of Levi was already bound to the service of Hashem and His Torah, it never was subjected to the 210 year Egyptian servitude.[158] And, when the other tribes saw that their bondage, in actuality, derived from loyalty to the wrong cause, no doubt the bitterness of their plight intellectually and emotionally intensified.

Here we see even more deeply that learning Torah is *the* way to avoid the errors of judgment and false values which inevitably lead to undesirable consequences. Without meaningful and committed Torah education, our people are suffering a decimating rate of intermarriage and assimilation.[159] The Phar-

---

157. *Shemos* 1:13; *TB Sotah* 11b; *Yalkut Shimoni*, Sec. 163. The vegetable most preferred for the *maror* is Romaine lettuce precisely because at first it tastes sweet and, then afterwards, bitter. *Shulchan Aruch, Orach Chaim* 473:5, *Mishnah Berurah* 42.
158. *Me'am Lo'ez, Shemos,* Vol. 1, p. 9. See, further, Chap. XVI, p. 145.

aohs of our day rally us with their whip: "Harvard, Oxford, Wall Street, Madison Avenue, Hard Work, Big Money, Big Spending, Keep up with the Joneses...." Jewish children's

---

159. According to a 1976 report by Elihu Bergman of the Harvard University Center for Population Studies, by the year 2076, instead of six million American Jews, there will be 900,000. And this figure is his most optimistic projection. Higher intermarriage rates would result in half this amount of Jews.

A recent study by City University of New York for the Council of Jewish Federations confirmed a huge rise in the intermarriage rate: from 9% in 1964 to 52% in 1985. Moreover, nearly three of every four children of intermarriages are being raised as Christians or with no religion at all. Further, of the approximately six million American Jews, only 4.3 million identify themselves as Jews. *Newsweek*, July 22, 1991, p. 54.

Moreover, if we consider what the normal population growth could have been, then already several million Jews have simply "disappeared." For example, one non-Jewish population study estimated that from a base of 17 million Jews throughout the world in 1980 (a very high figure according to Jewish calculations), the natural growth of the Jewish People would yield 20 million Jews by the year 2000. (*Time*, May 3, 1982, p. 42). Reliable Jewish population projections all predict a decrease in numbers, certainly no 17.6% increase, which apparently could have been a normally anticipated development.

Perhaps adding salt to the wound, we note that even *Newsweek* (in its article cited above) realized that the glaring lack of Jewish education was the cause of the high rate of assimilation. It concluded its report about intermarriage with this stinging rebuke:

"... The point of these programs is to help adults become knowledgeable and committed Jews. It's an overdue step: **most American Jews try to get through life with no more knowledge of Judaism than what a 13-year-old can master for his bar mitzvah. In today's America, that apparently is not enough wisdom or commitment to maintain a durable identity as a Jew.**"

This opinion of *Newsweek* has recently been validated by a study co-published by the Maurice and Marilyn Cohen Center for Modern Jewish Studies at Brandeis University and the Jewish Education Service of North America. The report confirmed that the more Jewish education, the less likelihood of intermarriage and, also significantly, the greater likelihood of belonging to Jewish groups and volunteering and giving money for Jewish causes. *Yated*, 26 Menachem Av 5753 (August 13, 1993), p. 24.

religious education a few afternoons a week at best is considered sufficient. And any investment of serious, mature, intellectual effort for Torah learning is considered unnecessary, irrelevant, or even a complete waste of time. As a consequence, the bondage to a system foreign to Judaism has spawned a generation generally apathetic, often positively disinterested, and sometimes, even hostile to its own Jewish spiritual identity.[160]

If we want to avoid the bitterness of losing our full personality and destiny, as well as our children's, all that is necessary is to switch our loyalty from "Pharaoh" to Hashem and His Torah. We taste the bitter herbs at the *Seder* table to remind us not to make the same mistake once again.[161]

In conclusion, *Pesach, matzah* and *maror* are so important to discuss on the *Seder* night because they graphically symbolize the threefold system that overcomes the intrinsic bondage of the finite world.[162] With love for Hashem and each other, con-

---

160. For example, modern Jewish high school students in the State of Israel were asked in a survey whether, if they had the choice, would they have decided to have been born Jewish or non-Jewish. Approximately 50% answered that they would have preferred to have been born non-Jewish. *The Jerusalem Post*, January 9, 1978, p. 3.

161. Even for observant Jews, the same problem can exist but more subtly. The American success story can become their secret dream as well. Luxuries that become necessities, lavish spending on "kosher" vacations and celebrations, insufficient financial support of Torah institutions — all are by-products of a deterioration in the Jewish value system. And the bitter results are steadily rolling in: increasing divorce rate; decreasing interest in Torah learning by the younger generation; affluence promoting more affluence, adversely affecting the highest aspirations of the Jewish People — to be "a light unto the nations" (*Yeshayahu* 42:6).

162. The combined numerical value (*gematria*) of the words *Pesach, matzah* and *maror* (729) equals the same value as the expression *kara soton* — destroy the hinderer. Rabbi M. Glazerson, *Hagadah of Pesach* (Hebrew),

trol over our instincts and an uncompromising loyalty to the truth of Torah, we have the means of being freed from this bondage because, in effect, we have moved from self to beyond-self, from the finite to the infinite.

Jerusalem, 5746, p. 78. This correlation shows that these three *mitzvos* together have the power to remove the basic obstacles that prevent us from being close to Hashem.

Midrash Rabba Shemos (15:12) actually connects these three Passover *mitzvos* to our ancestors:

The *Pesach* offering is roasted on the fire because of Avraham, who was saved from a fiery furnace. His total willingness to proclaim Hashem's Oneness and sovereignty, no matter what the authorities threatened, set in motion Hashem's loving and miraculous intervention, both in his life and in the lives of his children.

The *matzos* come because of Sarah, who kneaded the dough that was supposed to be *matzos* for the three angels who visited Avraham. At that moment, she returned to her feminine youth and was concerned that the dough had become *tamay* (spiritually impure). She walked away, the dough became *chametz*, and, since it was *Pesach*, none of it was offered to the guests. (This episode certainly depicts strict adherence to the rules of physicality-control.) (See *Bereishis* 18:8, Rashi, Sifsei Chachomim, note 7. See also the Maharzu, who says that Sarah actually did become *tamay* and thus disqualified the dough for use.)

The *maror* comes because of Yaakov, who was pursued by his brother Esav; so, too, the Jews in Egypt were plagued by their nemeses. Out-numbered and necessarily more vulnerable in hostile environments, we Jews end up using all our mental acuity to outmaneuver the opposition. Torah wisdom warns us about these dangers and instructs us on how to avoid them.

XV
Meaningful Frivolity

The holiday in the Jewish calendar most full of frolic and merriment is *Purim*. Wine, music, dancing, costumes, balloons, antics, fireworks, fancy food trays, palatial feasts — a day unsurpassable for pure joy and delight.

Yet while all this is true, like all other facets of Judaism, *Purim* too has its more intricate, profound side. For while *Purim* appears on the surface as a lighthearted escapade, underneath actually lies the perennial effort to bring the world and ourselves to perfection. And, not surprisingly, here we also find our Threefold Key to being Jewish.

The *mitzvos* of *Purim* are four in number, but these can quite logically be fitted into three categories:[163]

1. Reading the Scroll of *Esther*
2. Gifts to the poor AND Gifts to a friend

---

163. See the Gra, *Aderes Eliyahu*, *Devorim* 32:32. The Gra in *Esther* 3:13 lists gifts to the poor under the category of *kinyon* (acquisition/possessions) — a type of all-inclusive component (*cf.* App. C, p. 247). Our discussion has taken a more standard approach and included gifts to the poor under acts of lovingkindness (see below pp. 131-3).

3. The festive meal

Purim is the historical bridge between Hashem's direct prophetic leadership of the Jewish People and His seemingly indirect leadership through events.[164] This latter type of guidance is called *hester panim* — the "hidden face" of Hashem.

The Scroll of *Esther*, the first *mitzvah* here, recounts the story of *Purim* without once mentioning Hashem's Name. For us to see His hand in the events that unfolded, we would have to examine each occurrence with careful attention. Indeed, the public reading of the *Megillah* (scroll) is almost the only time in the year where every word has to be clearly heard, for every detail is essential if we are to grasp the underlying meaning. In other words, in principle, the way to understand reality is to study very carefully and diligently all the facts at hand, including their interconnection.

Almost everyone who picks up the newspaper reasonably concludes that the world is being run by big powers and big money interests. And every so often, smaller power forces interject their influence, trying to exercise control or grab what they can. The students of history, politics, economics, international relations, all delve deeply into the wisdoms of their social sciences in order to comprehend the implications of world events.

The student of Torah is studying reality and the rules of life, only he eschews human source material and learns, instead, Hashem-inspired wisdom, with a difference that is truly phenomenal. For if history is a reliable teacher, the blatant failure to take lesson from it is frightening. Moving into its so-called

---

164. See *TB Megillah* 15a. See also *Kuzari* 3:65; Rabbi Aryeh Kaplan, *Handbook of Jewish Thought*, Moznaim Publishing Corp., Vol. 1, 1979, para. 6:86, p. 111.

twenty-first century, the world has learned very little how to stop wars and bloodshed. On the contrary, it has improved its murderous capacity and can now make "star wars."

What is the reason?

Very simple. Who's running the show? If man is in charge, then as such, all his wisdom is no greater than human wisdom, limited and easily subject to human expediency. In such a system, law, politics and diplomacy become no more than convenient slide rules in which right and wrong simply shift around to meet the needs of the ruling power or powers. Since there is no source of power beyond man, who dares tell him that he is wrong?! Only the balance of power can possibly constrain him: Athens-Sparta, Rome-Carthage, Roman Empire-Visigoths, Spain-England, Triple Alliance-Triple Entente, Allies-Axis . . . until one overcomes the other.

However, none of this scenario is true for the Jew. In fact, all the great empires have come and gone, but we Jews are still here. To quote Mark Twain: "All things are mortal but the Jew; all other forces pass, but he remains. What is the secret of his immortality?"[165]

The short answer is: we are humble enough to accept a

---

165. Mark Twain's full introduction to this remarkable question is equally eye-opening:

" . . . The Egyptian, the Babylonian, and the Persian rose, filled the planet with sound and splendor, then faded to dream-stuff and passed away; the Greek and the Roman followed, and made a vast noise, and they are gone; other peoples have sprung up and held their torch high for a time, but it burned out, and they sit in twilight now, or have vanished. The Jew saw them all, beat them all, and is now what he always was, exhibiting no decadence, no infirmities of age, no weakening of his parts, no slowing of his energies, no dulling of his alert and aggressive mind. All things are mortal but the Jew; all other forces pass, but he remains. What is the secret of his immortality?" See Chap. V, fn. 47, for source reference.

Power above us and learn what He wants us to do.

So, for example, in the *Purim* story, because we realized Who was pulling the strings behind the scenes, we put ourselves back in line with the Stage Manager and, thereby, set in motion the safe resolution of the plot. For the danger comes when we ignore or forget Who is really running the show; in the end, we end up cutting off our own performance — including the encore!

The only way to correct man's egocentricity and resultant self-destruction[166] is to accept the real Power who is in control and to study assiduously how to act consonantly with this Force. It is no wonder that we Jews are immortal; we are continually learning how to stay close to the Eternal. Through this process which keeps us humble, we never forget that Hashem is guiding every single, solitary detail that transpires in our lives.[167]

It is, therefore, with total glee that during the *Megillah* reading, we clamor down the name of Haman, our nemesis. After all, he strove to proclaim that there is nobody behind the scenes. And we — with every fiber of our 3800-year existence — know and perceive just the opposite: Hashem is here, there, everywhere. And by learning Torah, we keep ourselves intimately aware of this fundamental truth, for every word is a link to understanding this Force.

Moreover, this key to Jewish survival is particularly illustrated in the *Megillah* and the whole *Purim* celebration since the

---

166. See Chap. XVII, pp. 155-9.
167. Free will is an absolutely essential element in the Jewish conception of life (see *Bereishis* 4:7). But the reality of Hashem's absolute control means that we have, in actuality, only one decision to make: either to accept or reject His will; or, as we described it in Chap. II: either to promote or block His presence. See *TB Berachos* 33b: "Everything is in the hands of Heaven except for the awe of Heaven."

holiday is entirely a rabbinic enactment. Hashem Himself ordered the Jews to accept humbly the wisdom and leadership of their great rabbis in each generation.[168] He entrusted them with the responsibility of passing on the Oral Tradition, which we can understand as a way of ensuring our humble submission, through having to listen to those wiser and more aware of the Source. In this way, we saw vividly on *Purim* that we lost nothing by giving up our supposed pre-eminence. On the contrary, by following those rabbis who were close to Hashem and His Torah, not only were we saved from destruction, but also we were blessed with a wonderful, new holiday, filled with light, happiness, joy and splendor.[169]

The second part of *Purim* is the giving of presents to the poor (money/food) and to a friend (food). These acts of lovingkindness bring out the brotherhood and solidarity that is really inherent in the Jewish People but is sometimes overlooked. When Haman tried to destroy us all, (even though he had only been angered by the actions of one Jew[170]), certainly

---

168. *Devorim* 17:11. And the rabbis remain humble through the intense challenge of their own Torah learning and the discerning approval of their alert, highly talented and learned adherents.

169. *Esther* 8:16; 9:23, 27-32.

170. Mordechai: see *Esther* 3:5. This is a perennial problem for us Jews, as contemporary history dramatically illustrates:

On November 7, 1938, Herschel Grynszpan, a Polish-Jewish youth, shot and severely wounded Ernst Vom Rath, a German official, in retaliation for his parents' deportation to the Polish border. Vom Rath died on November 9, setting off riots in Germany (actually organized by the Nazi government). One hundred and ninety-one synagogues were burned, thousands of Jews were arrested, hundreds wounded or killed. The tons of broken glass somehow inspired the name "Kristallnacht." [Quoted from *Yated*, 17 Cheshvon 5733 (November 13, 1992), p. 5.]

This tie-in of *Purim* with the Holocaust is only one of many

then we realized that we were inextricably one people. But without an external threat, perhaps we might forget our unity. The gifts of *Purim* remind us how really close and bound together we are. Truly feeling this love, concern and interconnection, we have the best weapon to undo pettiness, selfishness and jealousy. *Purim* has become the happy occasion for sharing closely with our fellow Jew because on this day, as one entity,[171] we had our fate dramatically changed from tragedy to triumph. Haman and his cohorts were all undone, and we Jews were all saved.

The double aspect of *Purim* giving underscores our point.

Gifts to the poor are essential components of every Jewish festival. The holidays are special opportunities to come closer to Hashem, and we would be very hypocritical if we were to make such a claim of holiness and then ignore our fellow Jews who were in need. Particularly on *Purim*, how could we be fully joyful with our Creator, knowing that others may be lacking the means to join in on this grand celebration? In fact, on *Purim*, *everyone* who puts out his hand for a donation is duly enriched, for on this day we go beyond ourselves to prove our interrelationship.

For this same reason it becomes evident why gifts are given to a friend. "But," you ask, "He has enough money to make his own *Purim* party. Moreover, most likely he will simply reciprocate by sending a gift back to me. So what is the point of this

---

comparisons. And even though Haman failed completely and Hitler appeared to have succeeded, the Third Reich was utterly destroyed, whereas the Jewish People have survived and have gone on to build thriving Torah communities not only in *Eretz Yisroel* but throughout the world.

171. "And the Jews undertook [singular Hebrew verb construction] to do as they had begun [i.e., to make the Purim holiday]." *Esther* 9:23, the Gra.

exchange ceremony?"

Unmistakably, we are showing that we are one, inseparable bond. On *Purim*, what some Jews did wrong affected the entire people, even those very far away.[172] The death sentence hung on all of us, with no exceptions. We must never forget how much mutual responsibility we have for each other.

This concept reaches even practical considerations as shown through the gifts we give our friend: food, two types of ready-to-eat food. Why are we giving food when it is practically certain that our friend has enough food of his own?

Eating food prepared in the home of a friend tangibly demonstrates a central idea: we are truly brothers. It is not such a simple thing to run a kosher kitchen. But *Purim* shows that, ideally, we are all one team, so committed to our common destiny and way of life that we can rely one hundred percent on each other's *kashrus*. Indeed, we are taught that we have no need even to desire the tables of kings, for ours is better in every aspect.[173] A closeness like this is indicative of true brotherhood and companionship. His table is my table. My table is his. We are indeed one loving family, one intimately bound people.

The last *mitzvah* of *Purim* is the festive meal, a magnificent banquet celebrating the saving of our lives from Haman's extermination plan.[174] Moreover, included in this sumptuous feast

---

172. Even though everyone had done something wrong (*TB Megillah* 12a), the chain reaction began when some failed to follow the guidance of our Torah leaders. See *Michtav*, Vol. 1, p. 75.

173. *Pirkei Avos* 6:5.

174. *Purim* is often contrasted to *Chanukah*, where the Hellenist Seleucids had just the opposite intention: the Jews could stay alive, but their Torah way of life and culture had to be eliminated. This finite world constantly poses challenges for the Jew, either to his body or his soul.

134 / *Self Beyond Self*

is the unusual requirement to become intoxicated, and an obvious question arises: What happened to our all-important Jewish self-restraint and control? Amid the abundance of wine, whiskey, vodka, gin and *hamantashen*, we hardly appear to be mastering our physical desires! Such letting loose on *Purim* seems very much out of character. What is happening here?

What is happening is one of the secrets of being Jewish.

The lion sits ever so placidly in his lair, his regal calmness creating the impression of total disinterest in any foul play or molestation. But of course, with relative ease, he could be aroused to deadly ferocity. Even though we know all too well how wine and alcohol can arouse the worst behavior in men, we are not worried on *Purim* because we are dealing with a Jew and not with a hidden beast.

The Jew who has been working on controlling his lusts and cravings for 364 days of the year — and consistently every year — about such a Jew we are not concerned that, on this one day of reduced inhibitions, he will overturn all this effort. On the contrary, and this is the whole point, we dramatically demonstrate the validity of the entire Torah method by "letting the inside come out" on *Purim*. For what comes out now after the system has developed the Jew is no longer a lion, but a lamb.

Indeed, we are taught that *Yom Kippur* (referred to as *Yom Kipurim* in the Torah) — ostensibly the holiest day of the year — only resembles (*ki* in Hebrew means "like") *Purim*. In other words, *Yom Kipurim* is being described as something only *like Purim*, implying that *Purim* itself is actually on a higher level.[175]

On *Yom Kipurim* when a Jew is fasting and praying, seriously thinking about life and his mortality, he is exercising

---

175. In the name of the Arizal, explaining the *Tikunei Zohar* 21.

maximum control over his instincts and bodily desires. But on *Purim*, we now see how much these controls have actually become *integrated* into his personality, even subconsciously. If on this day of unbridled indulgence he *still* shows his inner purity and refinement by exercising control over his actions, *then* we know that he is truly righteous, through and through. The Torah has actually helped produce a stellar success.

Particularly in our times, with the greatest economic prosperity the world has ever known, uninterrupted physical pleasure is an alluring and all-pervading theme. Money can buy us enjoyments once reserved only for monarchs. Three-hundred-horsepower engines and jumbo jets accelerate our euphoric illusions that life is one long joy ride. True, one occasionally notices that there seems to be a lot of movement with very little direction, but no matter. Just keep plopping down that credit card in time to the advertiser's jingle and fasten your seat belt. We're off to a good time! No?

Purim tells us, "No!" The real "good time" is when a person is able to control his desire to just have a good time. For pleasure for its own sake eats away and ultimately destroys the individual's moral fiber. He will naturally desire more and more physical satisfaction, ignoring the spiritual purpose of existence and failing to raise himself much above the level of a craving animal. There is no elevating purpose to a life whose dominant ideology is to make enough money so that more enjoyments can be purchased — tennis rackets, golf clubs, computer games, video tapes, professional cameras, exotic vacations, fancy restaurant meals, expensive clothes, luxury cars, summer homes . . . ad infinitum.

Building a world where the Ultimate is manifest, the Jew has very little time or need for self-indulgence, except on *Purim*

— the day when he proves that his drive to satisfy his appetites is joyously under control.

Part Five:
Keys to Eternity

   XVI An All-Pervading Theme
  XVII Very Rewarding Meals
 XVIII Only in Heaven's Hands
   XIX Effort-filled Presents
    XX The Final Resolution

XVI
An All-Pervading Theme

The picture should be clear by now that the key to being Jewish is a threefold attack on the human being's basic failings: arrogance, lust and jealousy. In actuality, these three are the causes of all life's travails and difficulties.[176] For example, why do people speak evil of each other, destroying reputations and promoting enmity? Because, generally, they are either jealous of those more successful or are arrogantly seeking to dominate and control. Why are people unhappy in marriage or having trouble getting married? Because they have not learned the art of giving, or lack control over their physical desires. Why do people feel alienated and alone? Because their feelings of superiority or inferiority isolate them from their fellow human beings. Why do people sense little real meaning in their lives, continually attempting to distract themselves with work, entertainment, sports? Because they are imagining life as self-created or randomly constructed, with no possibility, much less necessity, of relating to the Cause of their existence.

---

176. *Pirkei Avos* 4:21, Tiferes Yisroel, note 108.

An All-Pervading Theme / 139

Examining various other Torah sources, we find support for the centrality and relevance of our basic thesis.

For example, *Chazal* so clearly perceived these three fundamental life challenges that they synthesized our whole discussion with an ingenious mnemonic, alliterative epigram: "In three ways a person is known: *b'koso, b'keeso* and *b'ka'aso*" — through his drinking cup, his pocket and his anger.[177]

His *kose* — how he indulges himself in physical pleasures.

His *keese* — how he opens his pocket to give to others.[178]

His *ka'as* — how angry he becomes when people do not conform to his opinion.[179]

Further, to emphasize the difference between the path that corrects our weaknesses and the path that allows them to intensify, *Chazal* exhort us to follow the example of Avraham and not of Bilam, who was a great prophet among the world's nations.[180] They trenchantly describe the critical differences

---

177. *TB Eruvin* 65b. A fourth category — his levity — is additionally mentioned by the *Gemora*, indicating the level of seriousness with which a person approaches the whole purpose of his life.

   The same idea can be discerned in the third sentence of the *Shema*: "And these words which I command you today shall be upon your heart." *Devorim* 6:7. Unification and the Threefold Key of achieving it should be our constant concern, and we should realize how vitally important our Jewish mission is (see Chap. VIII).

178. Rashi defines this term as referring to honest business practices. Still, the subject is our monetary dealings with others.

179. See Rambam, *Hilchos Deos* 2:3: "One who becomes angry is as if he worshipped idols." Anger is often a factor of arrogance, and arrogance is connected to false idols because the person thinks that he is totally in charge as if he were a god. See Chap. VII, pp. 66-7. See also Rabbi Aharon Feldman, *The River, the Kettle and the Bird*, CSB Publications, Jerusalem, 1987, pp. 119-21: 'Fundamentally, anger is an expression of glory-seeking" (p. 121).

180. *Pirkei Avos* 5:19.

between the two men:

Avraham had

- **a goodly eye**: he looked upon others benevolently, without envy or self-interest.
- **a humble spirit**: he never was domineering, even though he was one of the most powerful and important men of his day.
- **an abstaining nature**: he lived the most simple life style with no self-indulgences, even though he was very wealthy.

Whereas the antithesis was epitomized in Bilam, who

- **had an evil eye**: he was jealous of other people's success and status.
- **was arrogant and overbearing**: even in his relationship with the Creator he behaved as if he were an equal.
- **was self-indulgent**: separating the spiritual from the physical, he freed moral restraints and encouraged the unlicensed pursuit of bodily passions and desires.

In another example, we find our Threefold Key in the dramatic encounter of Yaakov with his twin brother, Esav. In order to overcome Esav, who represented the *sitra achra*, Yaakov prepared three defenses:[181]

1. He equipped for war.
2. He prayed to Hashem.
3. He sent presents.

Learning Torah is compared to war because it is the battle of the mind to understand reality and truth.[182] Prayer is a way

---

181. *Bereishis* 32:9, Rashi.
182. See *Shir Hashirim* 3:8; *TB Chagigah* 14a; *TB Kiddushin* 30b, Rashi, "Es

to keep a spiritual perspective on the physical world and its tests. Presents to others promote love and peaceful interaction.

Also, many are familiar with the famous expression, "The threefold cord is not quickly broken."[183] One explanation is that it is referring to the threefold protection from error which the Jew secures when he is wearing *tefillin* on his head and arm, has *tzitzis* on his clothes and has a *mezuzah* on the entrance [of his home].[184] We have previously explained how *tefillin* represent Torah learning and protect against arrogance.[185] *Tzitzis* help prevent immorality and even improper thoughts.[186] The *mezuzah* on the entrance symbolizes a Godly home which is open to bestowing lovingkindness on everyone, as *Chazal* teach us, "Let your home be open wide [to receive guests]."[187]

Our Key is also described in the prophetic literature. The prophet Micah succinctly asked and answered what the goal of life is:[188] "He has told you, O man, what is good and what Hashem seeks from you:

- that you do judgement": follow the exact rules that help us control our physical drives
- "and love acts of kindness": constantly being involved with others, giving our time, concern and money
- "and walk humbly with your God": learn true humility

Vahaiv B'sufa."

183. *Koheles* 4:12. One of the explanations of this verse by *Tanna d'Bei Eliyahu* (Chap. 3) is that it is referring to the *Avos*.
184. *TB Menachos* 43b.
185. See Chap. V, pp. 42-52.
186. *Bemidbar* 15:39, Rashi; *TB Menachos* 44a.
187. *Pirkei Avos* 1:5, Harav m'Bertinoro.
188. *Micah* 6:8.

by being close to Hashem, a closeness that comes through the intimacy of learning His thoughts — Torah.[189]

In fact, these three qualities are actually what keep the world going, as we are taught in the *Mishnah*:[190] "Through the fulfillment of three principles, the world continues:

- Judgement": correct adherence to the system of control
- "Truth": recognition of the Creator, His sovereignty and our concomitant humble obedience
- "Peace": unifying humankind, using the art of giving to bring each person closer to his fellow.

These three principles are the same as our basic formula of Jewish existence: *Avodah* — to control desire and lust; Torah — to constrain arrogance; acts of lovingkindness — to prevent jealousy. For when we fully activate this Threefold Key, we will necessarily create and establish a world of judgement, truth and peace.

But lest we think, "Very nice; certainly the world could do with more peace, etc., but I'm just a bit busy with my business, my career, my familial, civic and social responsibilities, my exercise program . . . ," in that case, we must realize the absolute importance of this threefold system. For if we fail to use it, we could find ourselves vulnerable to *Chazal's* pithy warning:[191]

---

189. See Ibn Ezra and Metzudas Dovid on *Micah* 6:8.
190. *Pirkei Avos* 1:18.
191. *Pirkei Avos* 4:21. Elsewhere in *Pirkei Avos* 2:11, we are taught that the "evil eye," the *yetzer hara* and hating others take a person out of the world. Putting these two statements together, the Eitz Yosef (2:16/4:28) explains that the evil eye is connected to jealousy, the *yetzer hara* to lust, and hating others to arrogance, for a prideful person considers that others do not honor him sufficiently and, therefore, grows to dislike them. Compare Chart B: Integrated Dynamic, p. 232.

"Jealousy, lust and arrogance take a person out of the world."

Very significantly, the three negative traits which our emotions, instincts and intellect produce **when used for self** are the exact three traits that take us out of this world. Now we see why these three were particularly selected, for they correspond to the three basic parts of the human. Further, we are taught that these three take us out of not only this world but also the World to Come,[192] and the reason for both is clear:

Hashem created this world so that the finite human could earn his own infinite existence, which in practical terms means that he goes from self to beyond-self. When the person behaves in a self fashion (jealousy, lust, arrogance), he takes himself **out of** the purpose for which **the world** was created. For really he should be behaving in a beyond-self fashion (infinitely), but instead he is behaving for self (finitely). Consequently, he is depriving himself of the World to Come because this dimension is the infinity which he would have been achieving had he been going beyond self. He simply failed to use his talents, energies and resources to build his own World to Come.

Amazing as it may sound, when *Chazal* in *Pirkei Avos* explain that the world stands on three pillars and then a few chapters later define the three prime negative traits, they are summarizing in three continua the basic challenge and test of life. Quite profoundly, even while life is extremely complex, it is at the same time very straightforward and to the point.

Concluding this chapter, we bring two further exemplifications of our theme.

The Jewish People are very much family oriented. Origi-

---

192. See *Pirkei Avos* 4:21, Tiferes Yisroel, note 108.

nally, there were Twelve Tribes organized under four banners, three tribes per banner.[193] This body of people was called *B'nei Yisroel*, the Children of Yisroel, the name given Yaakov when he showed his dedication to truth.[194] However, there were also two other parts of the Jewish People, considered separately in the census of *B'nei Yisroel*.[195] They were the *Kohanim* and the Tribe of Levi, the *Levi'im*. As we will now explain, these three basic national subdivisions also fit into our Threefold Key to being Jewish.[196]

The *Kohanim* were designated to perform the service in the *Beis Hamikdosh*, where the physical was raised to the highest spiritual purpose. Their intentions and all their activities — dress, washing, eating — were guided by a very precise, disciplined system, culminating in the most controlled example when the *Kohain Gadol* did the complicated and detailed service of *Yom Kippur*.[197] In other physical areas as well, such as whom they could marry,[198] the *Kohanim* were given additional rules that particularly sanctified them.[199] Sanctification is the process whereby the physical is elevated to the spiritual,[200] and the

---

193. *Bemidbar* 2:1-31.
194. *Bereishis* 32:28.
195. *Bemidbar* 1:49; 3:14-39.
196. We remind the reader: Each category may very well include the lessons of the other categories, but, in its group, it best represents a particular aspect of the Threefold Key. Compare, for example, another component of the *Kohanim* and *Kehunah* discussed on pp. 147-8.
197. See, for example, *Shemos* 28:1-43; *Vayikra* 15:1-34; *Mishnayos* in *Yoma, Zevachim, Minachos, M'elah, Tamid*.
198. *Vayikra* 21:7, 13-14.
199. *Vayikra* 21:6, Ramban.
200. *Vayikra* 19:2, Rashi: "Wherever one finds a control of sexual activity, one finds sanctification."

Kohanim are the classic paradigm of this Jewish potential. Clearly, then, this section of the Jewish People represents the control of appetites and instincts through rule and discipline.

The *Levi'im* were completely dedicated to following Hashem and His Torah. As mentioned, unlike the rest of the nation, they were never subjected to the Egyptian bondage because they maintained their single-minded commitment to Torah learning.[201] In the desert, as a result of their full subjugation to Torah, only they were able to withstand the test of the Golden Calf. At that time, only they stood obediently together with Moshe and stalwartly fought to quell the rebellion.[202] They transported the *Mishkan* and were camped directly around it,[203] showing their intimate involvement in the process that brings Hashem into His world.[204]

Both in the desert and in the Land of Israel, they were the prime teachers of Torah to the Jewish People, as we are specifically taught: "They shall teach Yaakov Your judgements, and Yisroel, Your Torah."[205] The forty-eight Levite cities set up in *Eretz Yisroel*, including the six Cities of Refuge, were spread throughout the country, providing Torah education centers for everyone,[206] and they were supported in their studies through special tithes.[207] Without question, the *Levi'im* represent the

---

201. See p. 123.
202. *Shemos* 32:26-9. It should be very indelibly noted that all the women stayed faithful to Hashem and refused to worship the Golden Calf.
203. *Bemidbar*, Chaps. 3-4.
204. The *Levi'im* were also specifically designated to carry the *Aron* with the Two Tablets of the Covenant. *Devorim* 10:8; 31:25.
205. *Devorim* 33:10.
206. *Bemidbar* 35:1-8.
207. *Bemidbar* 18:24; Rambam, *Hilchos Shemitah V'Yovel* 13:12; *Sefer Hachinuch, Mitzvah* 395.

146 / *Self Beyond Self*

Torah/intellect aspect of our Threefold Key.

B'nei Yisroel symbolized the sum total of humankind:

- The Twelve Tribes corresponded to the twelve signs of the Zodiac — representing all the extraterrestrial forces influencing human behavior.[208]
- The encampment in the desert was specifically arranged to cover the four directions of the compass — east, south, west, and north.[209]
- They made up a census population of six hundred thousand — *six* representing the six days of creation and the six cubic planes encompassing the totality of our physical world.[210]

Further, as the descendants of one father, Yaakov, they really were all brothers, direct blood relations, one big family responsible each for the other, as it says, "All Yisroel are guarantors, one for the other."[211] Molded and unified as one people and one nation, they experienced together the great Exodus, the receiving of the Torah at *Har Sinai*, the conquest of the Land of Israel, the settlement of the Land, and the flourishing of great kings and kingdoms. Even in this scattered and afflicted Diaspora, the indestructible link of one Jew to his brother has insured a ready home and all necessary financial support to every wayfarer, immigrant and refugee. Without question, the valiant history of the Jewish People expresses the central core of the Torah's humanitarian teaching, "And you shall love your neighbor as yourself."[212]

---

208. See Rabbi M. Glazerson, *Above the Zodiac*, Jerusalem, 1985.
209. *Bemidbar* 35:2:1-31.
210. *Shemos* 12:37; *Bemidbar* 2:32; Maharal, *Netzach Yisroel*, B'nei Brak, 1980, p. 39.
211. *TB Shavuos* 39a on *Vayikra* 26:27.
212. *Vayikra* 19:18; *TY Nedarim* 9:4 (30b).

Lovingkindness — the selfless concern for others — could never be more eloquently manifest than in the living drama of the Children of Yisroel.

In summary, there is no question that every Jew must work to perfect all three of his basic components. However, it underscores the importance of the Threefold Key when we see how it helps to explain the three principal subdivisions of the Jewish People, *Kohanim* (instincts), *Levi'im* (intellect) and *B'nei Yisroel* (emotions).

Finally, we would be remiss if we did not mention the famous Three Crowns, which are derived from the three gold, crown-like rims that were part of three holy objects in the *Beis Hamikdosh*:[213]

    the Ark   =   the Crown of Torah
(which contained the Two Tablets of stone)
    the Golden Altar   =   the Crown of *Kehunah*
(on which incense was burnt)
    the Golden Table   =   the Crown of *Malchus*
(on which rested the twelve shewbreads)

The very word "crown" suggests that we are discussing the very top of the Jewish leadership, those most prominent in representing the mission and goals of the Jewish People. Indeed, one commentator specifically assigns each crown to a particular category of leader:[214]

    The Crown of Torah: a judge or Head of the Sanhedrin
    The Crown of *Kehunah*: the High Priest or his assistant
    The Crown of *Malchus*: the King or those of the greatest wealth.

---

213. *TB Yoma* 72b; *Pirkei Avos* 4:13(17), Rabbeinu Yona.
214. *Pirkei Avos* 4:13, Tiferes Yisroel, note 72; *cf. op. cit.*, Harav m'Bertinoro.

Correlating these people with the utensils in the Temple, we can now understand not only what each crown symbolically represents, but also how our Threefold Key applies even at these highest levels of activity:

Torah: Concerning our Torah leaders, the higher the people are, the *more* they have to obey Hashem's will. The ability to decide the law in specific cases means that the judge must totally submit himself to Hashem and completely adhere to His rules.[215] With humility, he will arrive at the proper decision, proving that he merits the Crown of Torah.

Kehunah: As the one personally responsible for serving Hashem in His Sanctuary, the High Priest represented all of the Jewish People. Therefore, he was required to have an intimate concern for every single Jew, as represented in the *ketores*,[216] the incense made up of many spices, one of which was unsavory.[217] For the job of the top Jewish holy men is to bring *everyone* — even the unsavory ones — into the fold, using love to heal and bond an entire people into one unit.[218]

Malchus: The shewbread on the Golden Table represented

---

215. Underscoring this total identification with Hashem, the Torah actually gives judges one of the same names attributed to God. See, for example, *Shemos* 22:7, 8.
216. See Chap. X, fn. 108. The *ketores* was burnt on the Golden Altar. *Shemos* 30:1-10.
217. *Shemos* 30:24; TB *Kerisus* 6b.
218. Compare *Pirkei Avos* 1:12 and *Avos d'Rebbi Nossan* 12:4, describing Aharon Hakohain's peace-pursuing qualities. Also see *Bemidbar* 35:25, *Targum Yonason*, where on *Yom Kippur* the *Kohain Gadol* was required to pray that no Jew commit any of the three major transgressions: idol worship, immorality or murder. His responsibility for his people was very great, and, for this reason, if any person was even negligently killed, the manslayer stayed confined in a City of Refuge until the *Kohain Gadol*'s death. See also TB *Macos* 11a.

the dedication of our physical resources to the service of Hashem.[219] Yet, with ease, those who have great material success could be the worst examples of misusing wealth for self-indulgence and instinctual pleasure. However, those who are at the top of the financial ladder in the Torah world understand the shewbread's profound lesson that materiality is only a means to a spiritual end. As a result, they work to control their instincts by avoiding indulgences and luxuries, gaining thereby the Crown of *Malchus*. Indeed, we can further learn from the shewbread that all the plenty in the world derives *only* through the merit of those who properly use material means for spiritual purposes.[220]

Concluding this far-ranging chapter, we see quite clearly that our Threefold Key is a pervasive theme throughout Judaism, not only at the individual level but also at the level of the entire nation and its leadership.

---

219. Compare Chap. XXIII, p. 218 and fn. 324.

220. See *TB Berachos* 17b and *TB Taanis* 24b, which describe how through the righteousness of Rebbi Chaninah ben Dosa, the world was provided with its sustenance.

We note that after the *Mishnah* [*Pirkei Avos* 4:13(17)] says that there are three crowns and lists them, it then goes on to state: "and the Crown of a Good Name surpasses them all." This fourth category is interpreted as a necessary ingredient in each of the other three. See Commentaries on *Pirkei Avos* by Rabbeinu Yona and Harav m'Bertinoro. See further App. C: The Fourth Component, p. 247.

XVII

Very Rewarding Meals

To describe even more graphically the stakes that are involved in appreciating, internalizing and utilizing the Threefold Key, we have several other examples in this and the next two chapters that illustrate the significance and importance of our basic theme.

We are taught that everyone who fulfills the three meals of *Shabbos* will be saved from three hardships:[221]

1. The travail at the time when the *Mashiach* comes
2. The rule of *Gehenom*
3. The war of *Gog* and *Magog* (cataclysmic war)

Without question, we are given quite an incentive to wash and break bread for these three meals!

But looking deeper, *Chazal* explain that each repast actually represents one of our *Avos*:[222]

    – the first meal, in the evening: Avraham

---

221. *TB Shabbos* 118a.
222. *Shemos* 16:25; *Zohar, Parashas Yisro*, 88a,b. We have followed in our discussion the first statement of Rabbi Shimon towards the end of page 88a.

– the second meal, generally in the late morning: Yitzchak

– the third meal, in the late afternoon: Yaakov

Considering what we have already learned about how the *Avos* represent our Threefold Key to realizing our potential as Jews, we can begin to understand how these meals afford protection from adversity. For *Shabbos* symbolizes the purpose of creation, the day upon which the Jew experiences the most spirituality possible in the physical world. In order for this dimension to be truly felt, however, the other half of the coin — our human character traits and behavior — must also have been raised to a high level. On this special day, we come closest to correcting the three basic errors that block us from bringing Hashem into the world and as a result, more than on any other day of the week, we feel closest to the Infinite.

As mentioned previously, *Shabbos* strongly represents the concept of giving to others, particularly strangers and guests.[223] So, certainly, its entrance through the first meal symbolizes Avraham, whose foremost quality was lovingkindness.

With this perspective, we can determine how the *Shabbos* evening meal protects us against the first hardship listed above. Examining what *Chazal* say concerning the travails which will accompany the *Mashiach*'s coming, we see that the dominant theme is alienation of man from his fellow, with lack of communication, indifference to others, disrespect and selfishness in ascendancy.[224] *Chutzpah* — unabashed audacity — reigns supreme, for each person has become an island of self-concern, unaffected by what others may have to say, even those wiser in

---

223. See pp. 37-8.
224. *Mishnah Sotah* 9:14.

knowledge and experience. This isolation causes estrangement and separateness, which many would agree is a fairly accurate synopsis of what in our time most obstructs the *Mashiach*'s arrival: the disunity and factionalism of the Jewish People.[225]

When we promote our interconnection and concomitant obligation to reach out and actively help others, insularity is ameliorated. We see how much we really need our fellow human beings, for how can we become true givers if we stay wrapped up in our own little worlds? Once we realize that other people are a necessary part of our world, we can no longer deal with them flippantly or derogatorily, for such behavior would clearly contradict our goal of caring and giving to them. *Chutzpah* builds barriers between people; lovingkindness, bridges.

The first meal of *Shabbos* heralds the dimension of closeness: the Creator with His People, husband with wife, parent with child, sibling with sibling, friend with neighbor, host with guest, resident with stranger. Such interaction promotes selflessness and builds communication and respect for each other. Insularity is dissipated in an atmosphere of unification.

As previously described,[226] the radiant glow of *Shabbos* candles, the vibrant warmth of the festive table and food, the joyous intonation of the *Kiddush* melody, subsequently followed with song after song from the family and guests gathered

---

225. See *Yalkut Shimoni, Netzavim* (first section): "Yisroel will not be redeemed until they are one united group."

   It would be appropriate to add here that, often, jealousy and arrogance are like two sides of one coin, for they both effectively distance a person from his neighbor. Indeed, when we bless our sons each *Shabbos* night to be righteous brothers like Ephraim and Menashe, we are praying that they behave like these two brothers, specifically because Ephraim and Menashe succeeded in overcoming haughtiness and envy.

226. See pp. 38-9.

together — all contribute to a magical transcendence where nothing exists but a loving oneness. Achieving this union, we shed our selfish concerns and save ourselves from the travail of isolation. The first meal thus inoculates us from such trouble, using lovingkindness to overcome alienation and separateness. And then, as an ultimate consequence, having worked hard and sincerely to unite ourselves, we will have formed a unified whole that will naturally follow a leader — the *Mashiach*.[227]

In the morning, moving to the second *Shabbos* meal, we sense quite a different central motif: strict adherence to rule. How so? Instead of running around involved in our own business or pleasure, we subject ourselves to a totally complete system of special laws. For "day" symbolizes human activity and creativity, but on *Shabbos* we Jews strive to exemplify that Hashem is the Creator and Controller of the world. So, quite obviously, our stores, offices and factories are closed, and all the machines and contrivances that demonstrate our power are put away from our immediate control. In this way, we are proving that, in actuality, Hashem is the *only* power. True, all these rules began at sunset the night before. But the clearest, most open demonstration of Hashem's dominion occurs on Saturday morning when everyone else in the world is occupied with his own interests, and we Jews ignore all our own affairs and concern ourselves just with Hashem and His special laws of *Shabbos*.

So, this second meal — which is in honor of Yitzchak — demonstrates the quality of discipline and rule observance. A person who keeps this meal (i.e., lives its full implications)

---

227. See further pp. 190-1.

shows his capacity to follow a standard above his own desires and inclinations. Although he might have preferred on this day to make his biggest profits of the week, or to drive to the beach for sun and fun, or to use the new barbecue on his back-yard patio, instead he has learned to control his preoccupation with the physical, disciplining himself to use it when and how Hashem has directed.

As a result, he is saved from the rule of *Gehenom*, which Judaism defines as the place most distant from Hashem. For what, most practically, prevents a person from being close to Hashem? His physical nature, his craving for earthly pleasure, with no thought or feeling for the spiritual essence within the physical.[228] Pursuing our personal desires blanks out all other considerations — even the Creator. So in the end, even now in this world, we suffer *Gehenom* — distance or absence from Hashem. And this separation is really quite upsetting. To think how easily we could have learned control mechanisms but, instead, overindulged our appetites and sensual drives. How frustrating to know that a golden opportunity to reach a higher plane of behavior was missed! How, with some discipline and rules of self-regulation, we could have overcome our natures and come closer to the Ultimate! Instead, we now suffer the very rule which we lived by — the physical, which can have no real meaning in and of itself, and no lasting satisfaction. However, truly living the second meal of *Shabbos* corrects this whole mentality, for we are proving our control over the physical and our total commitment to the spiritual — an approach to life which necessarily will save us from the rule of *Gehenom*, now and forever.

---

228. See *Mishnah Chagiga* 2:1, Harav m'Bertinoro.

By the time *Shabbos* is reaching its conclusion, something very interesting has happened to us. Besides a whole day of giving to others and following Hashem's rules, we have had the time to read and learn about Hashem's thoughts in His Torah. Life's many daily obligations and distractions often prevent just plain thinking about the purpose of it all. Too busy, no time. But on *Shabbos*, we have the time to settle down, to gain our perspective and sense our true place in creation. True, all week we were very important, even very powerful, people, but on *Shabbos* we stop just long enough to realize how fragile and ephemeral we really are. And gaining this deeper awareness, we feel an overwhelming sense of truth and peace. No games, no illusions, just clear reality.

For this day of rest provides the opportunity to put away our legal briefs, research papers, professional periodicals, newspapers, magazines, popular reading, and to instead pick up the volumes and volumes of our holy literature which give us a tiny window into the Ultimate Mind. Using as much of the day as possible to try to learn the ideas and thoughts of Hashem, we find our whole being expanded and humbled. Expanded — because the thought process involved increases our clarity and truth-perceptivity; humbled — both because our limitations are so blatant vis-à-vis the wealth of wisdom involved and because the understanding which we attain is itself such an open gift.[229]

All this effort counteracts the askew picture which man has of himself. His centrality on the local, regional, national and international scenes has him blown out of proportion to the truth. And all the human wisdom which he applies to comprehending his situation only intensifies his perception of his own

---

229. See also pp. 171-2.

self-importance. Why? Because a person is biased against threats to his ego, against accepting criticism, against really changing himself for the better. Insecurity, fear, guilt, diffidence, embarrassment, inertia, laziness — all prevent facing the truth. And even if critics and criticism are not lacking, they are fended off as fallible, biased, uninformed . . . . Besides, it is a given that no one is perfect, so why try? Who can really criticize with rectitude, anyway? Isn't everything just relative and a matter of personal opinion?

But the Torah helps us see the truth about ourselves, for its source is beyond man and can, therefore, be a check against egocentricity, biases and avoidance of responsibility. While learning Torah we come face to face, as it were, with the Infinite. From that perspective, we begin to realize that we are just a few milliseconds in the span of eternity. With such little significance, where is there room for pride or arrogance, for haughtily pushing our weight around, for self-importance?

And if we take this issue a step further, we can understand why, without Torah, discord exists between people. Each person builds his ego in order to dominate as far as the particular ambit of his power can reach, using all means available — his mind, his personality, his dynamism, his finesse, his pen, his money, his temper, his rage. And since everyone else is doing approximately the same thing, it is not hard to imagine how conflict can arise.

Now, what happens when we project this problem from the level of individuals to the level of nations? Nations, after all, are just collections of individuals, and each nation is only an aggregate extension of individual temperaments. With almost everyone striving to succeed and dominate, it is no wonder that nations do the same on an international level. In fact, we could say that "nationalism" is just another word for egocentricity at a national level.

Again, looking further, we can ask: What happens to power that has no check on itself? Answer: it reaches self-destructive proportions.

On the individual level, the person becomes a bastion of impregnability, avoiding both serious self-examination and constructive criticism from others. Once he denies the necessity for changing himself, he has essentially — from a Jewish standpoint — destroyed his life goal: to reach higher and higher levels of self-perfection. He has undermined the very justification for his continued existence. Since he is imperfect and continues to avoid correcting his imperfections, they eventually will undo him. For example, a person fails to control his anger. Other people will not desire to be with him, and he will be left basically alone, dissatisfied and unhappy.

And on a national and international level, power and superiority drives involve countries in competition and self-destructive warfare. The Olympic games are supposed to sublimate the problem, but instead, they merely epitomize it. (Consider where the Olympics just prior to World War II were held.) Today, with nuclear, chemical and biological weapons, the danger is so great that, for lack of capacity to absorb it, we simply block it out of our minds.

But the source of the problem is the same: the desire for ego-ascendancy and dominance — man's omnipotence! Counting up its GNP, its nuclear warhead stock piles, its jet fighter planes, is just a nation doing what the individual does when he calculates his net worth by counting up his savings, real estate, or stocks and bonds — even the number of children he has. In the end, both the individual and the nation have sealed their fate, for this ego-inflation is self-destructive, inevitably causing latent or overt hostility and conflict.

Having arrived at the end of *Shabbos* for the third meal (in honor of Yaakov) and having used the day to learn Torah, the Jew is also told that he well merit begin saved from the war of *Gog* and *Magog*. This cataclysmic battle epitomizes the ego conflicts on an international level. Having striven to overcome his own arrogance through learning Torah, the individual has saved himself from the destructive effects of egocentricity and has earned the promise of being saved at the international level. For we are taught that if he succeeded in changing what was in his capacity to change, then what was beyond his ability to alter he is not held responsible for.[230] Once he is diligently working to change his own egocentricity and that of others whom he can influence, he is exempt from any further responsibility.

The stories of total catastrophes where, despite all odds, some remnant survived, are known to every reader.[231] Miraculous events — clear interventions from a Higher Source — indicate that Hashem can save however and whomever he wants. The question is only: How to improve ourselves in order to merit in some small, infinitesimal way, this thin chance of survival? By correcting arrogance, we can extricate ourselves from that classic and universal downfall, as we are taught: "Pride goes before the destruction, and haughtiness of spirit before a fall."[232] Thus, may we use our next *Shabbos* — and the

---

230. *Pirkei Avos* 2:21; *TB Shabbos* 65b; Rambam, *Hilchos Deos* 6:7.
231. See, for example, the story of how the rabbis and students of the Mir Yeshivah were saved during the Holocaust. Yecheskel Leitner, *Operation Torah Rescue*, Feldheim Publishers, Jerusalem/New York, 1987. See also *Bereishis Rabba*, Sec. 96, Nechmad L'mar'eh.
232. *Mishlei* 16:18.

concept behind its third meal — to learn Torah wholeheartedly and hopefully, with Hashem's compassion, remain humbly unscathed.

The three meals of *Shabbos* provide very exceptional protection, for they symbolize our efforts to move our emotions, instincts and intellect from self to beyond-self. This achievement avoids the negative results that come from self: selfishness/jealousy (birth-pangs of the *Mashiach*), lust (the rule of *Gehenom*) and arrogance (the war of *Gog* and *Magog*). No wonder that *Shabbos* is called "Day of Eternity,"[233] for anyone who properly observes it actually experiences a dimension beyond the finite, closer to the Infinite.

---

233. See Rabbi Aryeh Kaplan, *Sabbath, Day of Eternity*, NCSY Publication, New York, 1991.

XVIII
Only in Heaven's Hands

Another fascinating example demonstrating the Threefold Key and its importance is this famous dictum of *Chazal*:[234] "In the hand of Hashem are three keys which He does not give over to any messenger:

- the key to the rains,
- the key to birth,
- the key to the revival of the dead."

How can our basic thesis help elucidate this amazing statement of *Chazal*?

Perhaps many of us — particularly city-dwellers — are unaware of how essential rain is for the survival of humankind. The farmer plants a seed and then the "heavens" bring rain. Irrigation is helpful, but the wheat and rice baskets of the world are full only to the extent that the rains fall. Hashem does or does not literally shower His kindness on His creatures by sending or not sending the food-producing, life-giving rain.

What prompts this blessing?

---

234. *TB Ta'anis* 2a.

It is a basic Judaic concept that Hashem often deals with us in relation to how we are behaving: *mida k'negid mida* — measure for measure.[235] Applying this principle to Heaven's blessings, we find that to the degree that we are full of lovingkindness, Hashem can deal with us in the same fashion. To the degree that we are selfish, ungenerous, greedily keeping our wealth for ourselves, He also can hold back His bountiful giving.

Indeed, realizing how much we owe Hashem for every drop of rain, which combines with others to bring us every morsel of our food, we should be practically jumping for joy and genuinely eager to reciprocate in every way possible. For this reason, the term "charity" is actually a misnomer: we are really doing ourselves the biggest favor.[236] For how could we better prove our gratitude, and what better investment for our own financial future? Although, without question, Hashem compassionately bestows His blessing as He sees fit, even when we might be undeserving, we can still see the correlation between this key which He holds onto and the lovingkindness category of our threefold model.

Moving to the next key solely in Hashem's hand, we normally assume that having children is a fairly natural event, almost to the point of taking it for granted. Sadly, miscarriages, stillbirths, births of children whom we consider deficient or abnormal occur from time to time. Moreover, many of us know of childless families or families who would like to have more children but cannot. Indeed, it is

---

235. *TB Sanhedrin* 90a; *TB Megillah* 12b. See Chap. IV, fn. 32.
236. The Hebrew term for charity is *tzedoka*, which actually means "rightful due." In the context of our discussion, we can add that money given to those in need is actually no more than the right way to show our appreciation.

only when we so much want to have a child and cannot that we realize how much the power is beyond our control.

Without doubt, Hashem desires that life procreate. Indeed, it is the first commandment in His Torah, for He desires that His creation continue and that humans have a role in creating.[237]

In order to motivate this participation, the sexual drive was implanted, for without it there would be no world.[238] But what happens when this drive is misused and converted into a personal pleasure trip, with no thought of the purpose for which it was given? Very simple. Instead of being a joy and a blessing, it can corrupt and destroy.

For example, in another issue, food is essential for life, but overindulging in it actually destroys life. Being overweight shortens one's life, making it harder for the body's organs to function. Eating too much meat increases cholesterol and contributes to heart disease. Sweets and pastries corrode the teeth and adversely effect one's whole body. Alcoholic beverages, if overused, are very harmful. Food just for the sake of eating food is often our undoing.

The Jew is commanded to sanctify — i.e., elevate to a spiritual plane — all the physical world. If he controls his lusts and physical desires, directing them to the goal for which they were given, then he receives the blessing which relates to that particular desire.

We are advised by the Torah to eat what we need in order to live, and not to overindulge.[239] Looking for that third helping or the next tasty treat or exotic restaurant belies the seriousness of our destiny. For our purpose is to transcend the physical, to

---

237. *Bereishis* 1:28; *Sefer Hachinuch, Mitzvah* 1; *Shulchan Aruch, Even Ha'ezer* 1:1.
238. *TB Yoma* 69b.
239. *TB Berachos* 32a; *TB Chulin* 84a; Rambam, *Hilchos Deos* 4:15; 5:10.

use it as a means to a greater end. If we remember that food is to preserve a healthily-functioning body, then it will not destroy us but will, instead, aid us in fulfilling our true goal.

The same principle exists regarding the sexual drive. If it is controlled and directed toward the purpose for which it was given, it brings life and health and productive results. If it is misused as an end in itself, we can expect all sorts of negative consequences: overindulgence, promiscuity, broken homes, dissatisfaction, medical and psychological malfunctioning.

So Hashem holds on to the key of birth, watching how we behave with our sexual desires. If we show Him that we can control them as the Torah directs,[240] His compassionate power may bring birth and all that birth implies: healthy, whole progeny, who will continue generation after generation sanctifying the physical world.[241]

---

240. See Rambam, *Hilchos Isurei Be'ah* (22 chapters of laws). See, also, our discussions pp. 39-42, 85-7. We hasten to add that sexual desires can also be expressed in a Torah fashion whenever the intention of their use is for the benefit of the other. In other words, the person is going beyond self. He is not seeking his own finite pleasure, but rather, he is concerned to give to the other person love, commitment, companionship and happiness. Such control over self and focusing on beyond-self is precisely the behavior which the Torah is asking us to achieve *all* the time and in *every* situation.

241. *Koheles* 11:2; *Vayikra Rabba* 14:7. **Clearly, as finite beings, by definition, we can never fully comprehend the reasons for Hashem's actions**, as many unknown factors can easily be involved. Every situation is unique and calls for the sage counsel of Torah authorities in order to glean the most understanding possible. For example, when we see righteous people denied children, we can understand that their love of Hashem is so strong that they love Him even when He withholds a blessing normally due them, a principle graphically represented by the first Jew, Avraham, who had to reach 100 years of age before his son and spiritual heir, Yitzchak, was born. On all issues involving children, the greatest degree of sensitivity must be exercised, for the subject touches the deepest recesses of the Jewish heart.

The third key which Hashem specifically retains is revival of the dead.

Resurrection is probably the hardest concept in Jewish belief for us to comprehend. Indeed, most unknowing Jews believe that it is a Christian idea and immediately dismiss it. But, in fact, it is Jewish and is an essential pillar in the whole infrastructure of the Torah's ontology.[242]

"Sure," you say, "it would be nice to live forever. Such a beautiful dream where death, pain, sorrow just disappear. But you really have pushed me beyond my ability to accept what I can't verify. Even if I admit that Hashem controls the rains and birth, I don't see, realistically, what it means when you say that He revives the dead. Furthermore, you're asking me to change my whole outlook on life. The implications of another dimension would force me to behave quite a bit differently!"

Fair enough. Please be patient as we endeavor to explain.

This third key is another example of the third category of the Jewish improvement system. Pride and egotism are corrected by constantly learning Torah, which tells us what Hashem wants and humbles our seeming omnipotence and independence.

As the mind gets closer to understanding something about the absolute greatness of Hashem, we start to gain a truer perspective on ourselves. We begin to see that, in essence, we are really next-to-nothing. No matter how great we may be, we are nothing compared to Hashem's greatness. Further, we see clearly our mortality and our meaninglessness compared to Hashem's unendingness: a drop in the ocean, a grain of sand on the beach, a lit match opposite the sun.

---

242. *TB Sanhedrin* 90a,b; Rambam, Thirteen Principles, Number 13.

So why, then, despite our insignificance, do we still strive with all our effort to achieve anything in life, anyway?

Because we realize one basic fact: Since we *can* understand *something* of Hashem, then, in fact, there is a part of us that has something in common with Hashem. And that part which we have in common *is* eternal like Hashem Himself.

Thus, every bit of effort which we can put into maximizing this eternal dimension in our lives is certainly worth our time. Then, no longer do our lives have an end, but rather, they can tie into the eternity of Hashem's existence. And revival of the dead is then the natural consequence of our mind and body having transcended the physical and having totally identified with Hashem.[243] We have tried our very best to become as much like the Eternal as possible. Indeed, as explained in this book's beginning, Hashem's purpose in creating the finite world was precisely to give humankind the opportunity of earning its own infinity. And by going **beyond self**, the person has actually gone **beyond the finite** (self=finite), which — within the limitations of finite human existence — is the most he can do to achieve the infinite.

Another way to understand this capacity is to realize that our physical beings are the only blockages between us and Ultimate Spirit. If we use our minds to direct all of our being towards this Ultimate, then this potential physical blockage is

---

243. Clearly, if only the mind connects to the Infinite but the body does not follow suit, then no one can expect a revival that would include the body. Therefore, whatever the mind learns must be converted into action, as we learn in the *Mishnah*: "Action and not study is the main thing" (*Pirkei Avos* 1:17). This idea is also expressed through the two parts of *tefillin*: one *bayis* on the head with four separate compartments and one on the arm with all the inscriptions on a single parchment — the plurality of ideas must lead ultimately into one, unified action.

eliminated.[244] What remains is only the spiritual — and this part does not die. Having passed the test where the mind (spirit) has successfully controlled the body, we can be granted a new form of body (revival of the dead) which has within it no contradiction to spirit and can, therefore, last forever.

Those who know Jewish ontology also understand that, originally, humankind was not created to die. Only because man denied the Source of his creation did he cause death to enter the world.

How did this disaster come about?

When Adom held his mind to be equal or even superior to Hashem's mind, he took the next logical step: he challenged what Hashem said to do and, instead, did what he thought was more correct. A very straightforward approach, but truly a very great error and, even more to the point, a very great exercise in human arrogance. How could he have thought that he knew better than the Creator of the world?! Yet, strange as it may sound, since man was given free will, with this power he can actually think and act contrary to the Creator.

Applying our self—beyond-self continuum,[245] we can readily see that such a decision reflected the person using his intellect as he — self — viewed appropriate. By acting in such a fashion, he stayed on the self side of the continuum, which necessarily included remaining finite and mortal. (See Part Seven, Chart C.) Had he gone beyond self by using his mind completely consistent with the Ultimate Mind, then he would have maintained his link to the Infinite and Eternal. Death would have never entered the picture, for the **total** bond be-

---

244. See p.5-11, where we described the choice between self and beyond-self.
245. See Chart A: The Self—Beyond-Self Continuum, p. 231.

tween the created being and his Creator would never have been broken.

Today when we learn Torah and thereby humble our minds to work consonant with the will of the Creator, we are reversing the process that caused death to exist and are, in effect, creating eternal existence.

But what about the absolutely righteous person who has succeeded in this challenge? Why does he die?

Hashem's purpose in creating man was to give him the opportunity to achieve his own eternity. From the time that the first man (Adom) failed in this test, no single human being could achieve the perfect, total resolution of the physical into the spiritual. The first man had this great potential, but his failure almost resulted in total disaster.[246] From then on, to prevent such further huge mistakes, Hashem divided the responsibility among a group of people working together to perform this herculean task of achieving perfection. The Jewish People, striving and sacrificing for over three thousand years, have gradually moved the problem closer to its final resolution. No one individual can realize this purpose of humankind, for he is tied into a whole People, who must attain this goal together. He is just part of the picture, and his role depends upon the whole picture being filled in before his own final realization can be achieved.[247]

We must be aware that, even though we have this opportunity of tapping into the infinite, this gift of eternal existence

---

246. Adom's sin brought death into the world, although Hashem commuted his sentence and granted him many years of life in the meantime. See *Bereishis* 2:17, Ramban; *Tehillim* 25:6, Rashi; *TB Shabbos* 55b.
247. Rabbi Yehudah HaLevi, *Kuzari* 3:19; Arizal, *Likutey Torah, Ta'amey Hamitzvos, Vayikra* 19:18, cited in Rabbi Aryeh Kaplan, *Reaching Out*, NCSY Publication, New York, 1991 (3rd ed.), p. 25.

— like the one that began our physical lives — is still a gift, completely within Hashem's discretion. He bestows it how, where, when, and on whom He so chooses. True, He has promised this reward.[248] But we, in order to earn it, must try our absolute best to maximize our minds' complete identification with the Ultimate. Learning Torah gains us this union, as we are taught succinctly: "The Torah of the wise is the source of life, removing from the snares of death."[249]

Clearly, Hashem is holding onto a very special key — the key to eternity. He is willing, however, to turn this key if we use the third part of *our* Threefold Key to being Jewish, taking our intellect and moving it from self to beyond-self through learning and fulfilling the Torah to our utmost capacity.

---

248. The essential paradox of a promised reward dependent upon effort is beautifully captured in the *Mishnah*: "Everything is foreseen, yet freedom of choice is given. **The world is judged for the good, yet everything depends on the preponderance of good deeds**" (*Pirkei Avos* 3:10).

249. *Mishlei* 13:14. Compare *TB Baba Basra* 16a, where the *soton*, *yetzer hara* and *Malach Hamoves* are equated. In other words, learning Torah gives us the capacity to overcome the *yetzer hara* (*TB Kiddushin* 30b), which necessarily means also overcoming the *Malach Hamoves*.

XIX
Effort-Filled Presents

Finally, we want to answer an as-yet-unstated question from one last threefold formula.

Why has there been such a long, tortuous history in the effort to achieve these three goals of Jewish development with still, apparently, no clear resolution? Or more simply stated: Why has it been so hard to do what has been described rather simply?

Chazal say that the Creator has given three goodly presents to the Jewish People, but all of them have been granted only through great difficulty and travail:[250]

- Torah
- The Land of Israel
- The World to Come

From the beginning, the promise has been accompanied by the blunt qualification that life is going to be hard work. If it would have been easy or simple, then the entire undertaking would not have been worth creating in the first place. The

---

250. *TB Berachos* 5a.

Master of creation was a master craftsman in devising a challenging creation.

Why?

Few people like consistent hand-outs or overt charity. Dignity and self-respect are practically destroyed when the person is a passive recipient. Better a modest income earned from honest labor than a gold mine bestowed gratuitously. Sure, we fancy the life of easy luxury. But if we would look deeply into ourselves, we would realize that the only sense of life-satisfaction which we can ever experience is when we have worked hard ourselves to achieve our goals. And if we succeeded primarily because of some manipulation or some indulgent benefactor, then the sense of accomplishment which we honestly feel inside is considerably diminished. The very self-identity which we each so intensely perceive is the same self-identity that yearns to know its exclusively-own achievement.[251]

Thus, the simple answer is that, considering the rewards that Hashem has in store for His creatures, the greatest kindness is to allow us a part — however small — in meriting them.

So, now we may appear to have countered the statement which we first brought that Hashem has three presents to give us. After all, presents which have to be earned — and only through great difficulty — are hardly presents! Somehow we seem to be misusing our terms.

An answer to this apparent contradiction is that as much

---

251. See *TB Baba Metzia* 38a, concerning a person's strong preference for his own effort. Hashem created man in order that he should endeavor and accomplish. *Bereishis* 2:3,16. This principle contravenes some Far Eastern religions and philosophies that advocate passivity and disengagement from life.

as we work to earn them, in the end their achievement is really a present. They are so challenging to attain that ultimately there is no way to receive them except through an act of benevolent bestowal. Still, we must strive as diligently as possible even to be within range of receiving them, for the goal is always to *earn* our own infinity, putting in as much of our own effort as possible.

What is the meaning of these three presents and why are they obtainable only through arduous effort?

"Torah" means to know the Mind of the Creator, as far as the human mind can know it. To know Hashem's Mind, as it were, the Jew must become completely humble, extracting every ounce of pride and self-importance from within himself. For as soon as his ego and conflicting personal opinions intervene, he can no longer be a vessel to receive Hashem's wisdom, nor can he be a conduit of Hashem's ideas to others. His own self blocks this Higher Force from coming into and through him.

Clearly, then, to learn Torah properly requires a huge effort. First, the amount of information involved is endless, and second, the ego has to be constantly effaced. Both tasks can be quite beyond the individual, and therefore, Hashem has to give him a present of the knowledge. Yet this present is still a factor of how much the individual truly desired and exerted himself to know the wisdom of the Ultimate: how many hours he labored, how much sleep and comfort he sacrificed, how much he humbled himself to seek out help from others when necessary, how much he prayed for understanding, how much he honestly opened up to what is far beyond him.[252] The key in this

---

252. Compare *Pirkei Avos* 6:4,6: "Such is the path of Torah ... ; Torah is acquired in forty-eight ways ...." See also p. 199 concerning Moshe Rabbeinu's humility.

process is breaking his ego and humbly learning with all his capacity.

The Land of Israel (the second present) — as the term itself implies — is a physical gift, namely, a place, a home, an area of land in which the Jew can perform his task in the world. Just as the body is a repository for the soul, *Eretz Yisroel* is the physical venue for the spiritual mission of the Jewish People.

Here too, however, we are not speaking of a free gift, but of one which must be merited with great effort.

Why?

Because, for us Jews, the rule is that to earn the physical, we must show that we are in control of the physical. In other words, we must be working to elevate our sensual drives, for they are merely a test to see if we will use them in a pure and sanctified fashion. Any form of moral laxity will deprive us of the physical gifts which Hashem wants to give us. Indeed, the Torah says openly that the Land will spew out its inhabitants if they behave inconsistently with the highest level of morality.[253]

For the Land of Israel is not just any place in the world. It is the Palace of the King, the headquarters of the world. In order to reside in such a special home, one must act accordingly. If the King of Kings is in residence, then certainly His attendants must behave with absolute impeccability — everywhere in the world, but certainly, especially, in this Inner Sanctum. To deserve such close physical proximity to the Holy One, Blessed Be He, we are required to live with the most physical purity

---

253. *Vayikra* 18:24-7;20:22. See *TB Berachos* 48b, where *bris* and Torah must be mentioned in the blessing on the Land in *Birkas Hamazone*. To preserve our right to the Land of Israel, we must maintain the many laws of physical purity given to us in the Torah.

possible. Otherwise, we would be directly contradicting our closeness with the more immediate presence of Hashem in *Eretz Yisroel*, a presence easily affronted by any decadence.

Earnestly striving to control our lusts and instincts is the only way to merit, in some small degree, residence in this Kingly Abode. Matters of sexual morality and modesty are obviously included in the purity required.[254] But other areas of our physicality are also thoroughly legislated. When the *Beis Hamikdosh* stood, countless rules for the preparation, offering and eating of the sacrifices guided the spiritual elevation of the *kohanim* and the entire Jewish People. The regulations concerning agriculture (eg., *kilayim, Shemitah*) and all food grown in the Land (eg., *terumos, ma'aseros*) — applicable to this very day — graphically illustrate the high control of materiality essential for continued living in such a holy land.[255] Other laws include removal of all idol worship, open fields around the cities, pilgrimages to Yerushalayim, the Cities of Refuge where a person could flee if he committed a negligent homicide, etc . . . . These rules are complex and all-encompassing, but striving diligently to fulfill them, we can earn some merit to remain in the King's Palace.

Again, no matter how much we do, we can still claim the Land of Israel only as a present, for Royal real estate is obviously beyond our means.

At this point, the reader may ask, "But we Jews now have the State of Israel, and no more than 20% of its residents even

---

254. The warning that the Land will spew us out is preceded by a long list of illicit sexual practices which the Canaanites indulged in and which we were explicitly prohibited from doing. *Vayikra* 18:3-30.

255. In the future, when we fully merit being in *Eretz Yisroel*, delicious cakes will naturally come forth from the Land. *TB Shabbos* 30b.

claim to be following Hashem's rules!"[256] But he has only to look around at all the other countries of the world and ask if any of them are under such perennial threat of attack and extinction. Even after many years of statehood, the hold on the Land is still constantly being contested.

Indeed, with so many of its citizens having moved away[257] and the incessant tension wearing on its current residents, one wonders how long a Jewish state which denies its Jewish rules and heritage will survive — particularly if we recall that we have no claim to the Land even as a present if we ignore the system of physical control, which is a prerequisite for tenure.

Unfortunately, most people discuss only political solutions for the Middle East. Were it that we understood the real nature of this Holy Land, the true solution would be far faster in coming. May Hashem soon enlighten our searching minds.

As for the third present — the World to Come, everyone will agree that tremendous effort is definitely being expended to receive it. In fact, so much travail has already been suffered that the World to Come should be arriving within the hour, if not sooner!

The Torah teaches us that the goal of this world is to achieve the Oneness of Hashem, as it says in the *Shema*: "Hear, O Yisroel . . . the Lord is One." In other words, all the billions

---

256. The percentage of Torah-observant Jews appears to be increasing, with higher birthrate, larger percentage immigration to Israel and lower percentage emigration from Israel as visible factors. How the huge influx of Russian Jews will influence this trend remains to be seen.

257. The Israeli Government officially estimates that since the establishment of the state, 10-12% of the population has left the country. *Yated*, 29 Sivan 5753 (June 18, 1993), p. 24. This figure would mean that close to half a million Israelis have abandoned their homeland.

of parts are destined to come back and be again whole with Hashem and His Totality. All the rules have been given to aid us in this extremely difficult endeavor. For it is upon us, in the first instance, to create this unity. Indeed, just as the natural world works in harmony and absolute wholeness as it follows the rules ordained by the Creator, so too, humankind can gain the same harmony if it follows the rules provided.[258]

But what single issue blocks this unity more than any other?

The division between man and his brother.

Instead of feeling our solidarity, we isolate ourselves and build walls between each other. Instead of joining together, we each go our own way. Instead of sharing, we keep our possessions for ourselves. Instead of lovingly reaching out our hand to help, we put our hands in the air, proclaiming helpless inability. Instead of smiling and speaking with concern, we mouth our hellos and hide from closeness.

And these are the least of the divisive factors, for we also act overtly to destroy our unity.

We label our brother under a certain category and, henceforth, have nothing further to do with him. We speak ill of him needlessly, spreading idle remarks and partial untruths as if he were our enemy, alien and foreign to us. We find ways to climb over and even supplant him, and it's all legal because that's competition. We laboriously build our personal bastions of financial security, obviating the need to join forces with others. The system is everyone for himself, with no goal or intention of creating unity.

---

258. As we say in the *Birkas Hamazone* and at the end of the *Amidah* and the *Kaddish*, "He who makes harmony (*shalom*) in His upper realms, may He make harmony upon us and upon all Yisroel."

In truth, though, *Olam Habah* (the World to Come) means the world where Hashem's Oneness is manifest, where everything is synchronized to function exactly according to His Being, His will.

Imagine a factory where production is coordinated and organized along a smooth assembly line, with each person doing his assigned task, cooperating with his fellow. No one is trying to overcome the other. Rather, each realizes that he must work in a manner which complements everyone else's part, thereby contributing to and maximizing the total combined effort. Yet even this superb, well-synchronized system of factory production is only a dim shadow of what the Creator planned for His human creation. Instead of monotonous, mechanical activity, the production line that Hashem envisions fulfills the complete, total dynamic of every human's potential. But the exciting part is that, in the first instance, it was the plan of creation for us to make this happen. It is our opportunity and obligation to create a coordinated and harmonious system of human interdependence. Unfortunately, the distance between this achievement and the way we now live is the difference between the world we see today and the World to Come.[259]

The vital element is to understand that there is no room for jealousy and envy in this "factory." Instead, we must constantly remind ourselves that each person is our partner in building a

---

259. See Chap. XVII, fn. 225. See, also, *TB Berachos* 17a: "Rav was accustomed to saying: The World to Come is not like this world. In the World to Come there is no eating, drinking, marital relations, commerce, **jealousy, enmity, competition.** Only *tzaddikim* sitting with their crowns on their heads, enjoying the splendor of the *Shechinah*." As explained before (Chap. III, fn. 11), any one category can often include the other parts of the Threefold Key. But in juxtaposition to others in its group, one category is being used to highlight a particular aspect of the Key. Our emphasis here is the end to jealousy, etc.

common enterprise, where both his job and ours are similarly important. He must complete himself in his own way just as each of us must complete ourselves in our own ways, and only when everyone has accomplished his mission is the story finished. Therefore, ultimately there is no way for anyone of us to be fulfilled without all the rest of us also being fulfilled. And it should be quite obvious that it is really in our own best interest when we help the other person to succeed. His success is also our success.

There is a parable told that portrays this point:[260]

What is the difference between *Gan Aden* and *Gehenom*, metaphorically?

In both, there is a long table with endless delicacies being served. Everyone is seated alongside the table, but each person's hands are tied so that he is unable to feed himself. In *Gehenom*, the people are only able to look at all that is being offered without being able to taste it. But in *Gan Aden*, the ropes are just loose enough so that each person can feed his neighbor.

A tasty thought, helping our fellow human — more so, perhaps, than we ever realized.

Of course, this challenge is a huge, unending task, and for this reason, again, Hashem will have to make a present of *Olam Habah*. But, for our part, we must always be diligently striving to do all we can to love and give to each other, for in this way we will hasten the day when Hashem will compassionately bestow upon all of us the World to Come.

---

260. This parable can probably be traced through different cultures and people, for its truth is universal.

XX
The Final Resolution

Having attempted to show the all-pervasive importance of the Threefold Key to being Jewish, we would like to clarify a question which may have already occurred to those who are knowledgeable of Torah sources. Many statements in the *Gemora* describe the Final Redemption of humankind — i.e., the coming of the *Mashiach* — but do not appear to be dealing with the principles which we have outlined. On closer analysis, however, we hope to explain that our Key is actually *the* means of unlocking the door to the final resolution.

Initially, it should be made clear that the many differing viewpoints in the *Gemora* are not contradictory, but are rather different facets of a total picture.[261] Also, there are various stages in the process, and no one stage stands alone, but each fits in with the others.[262] With these two points clear, let us begin our inquiry into some of *Chazal's* statements concerning the redemption.

---

261. *TB Eruvin* 13b; *Michtav*, Vol. 3, p. 353, citing *Tikunei Zohar*.
262. See, for example, *TB Nidah* 13b, Tosefos "*Ahd.*"

We are taught that the son of Dovid (the *Mashiach*) will come only

- when those of haughty spirit will have ceased among the Jewish People.[263]
- when all the souls that are to be in bodies will have come through this world.[264]
- in a generation which is wholly worthy or wholly culpable.[265]

The first statement clearly refers to the vital correction of pride and arrogance. The second hints to the necessity of sanctifying our physical desires for their true spiritual purpose, i.e., that our intention should be to bring holy souls into the world.[266] The third suggests how crucial unity among brothers is — even when they are misbehaving — as was demonstrated during the Generation of the Dispersal, where Hashem dealt leniently because fellowship existed.[267]

Another series of references describes very negative circumstances which will arouse the Jews to *teshuvah*, and then the *Mashiach* will come:[268]

- all the governments will deny Hashem's existence: Secular power politics often expresses man's egocentric denial of anything beyond himself.

---

263. TB *Sanhedrin* 98a.
264. TB *Yevamos* 62a; TB *Nidah* 13b.
265. TB *Sanhedrin* 98a.
266. See the Ramban's special prayer, which is said before conjugal relations and which states this idea very emphatically.
267. *Bereishis* 11:9, Rashi: "and they behaved with love and comradeship amongst each other . . . ."
268. TB *Sanhedrin* 97a, Maharsha.

- informers who report others to the authorities will increase: The less that love for others is prevalent, the greater each person will try to harm the other.
- students of Torah will decrease: Truth is a very high standard to follow, and both its students and their supporting communities can easily lack the requisite level of humble dedication to maintaining this high commitment.
- every last penny will be emptied from the pocket: The insatiable desires for consumer consumption can easily exhaust one's bank account.
- people will despair of the redemption ever coming: The ego often concludes that if it can't do something, it can't be done.

We are also taught that "If Yisroel would keep two *Shabbosos* according to the law, they would immediately be redeemed."[269] As explained by one commentator, the two *Shabbosos* refer to the *Shabbos* of creation (i.e., the Seventh Day) and the *Shabbos* of *Eretz Yisroel* (*Shemitah* — the Sabbatical Year).[270] The laws of both *Shabbos* and *Shemitah* are very complex and all-encompassing. They show how both time (*Shabbos*) and space (*Shemitah*) can be used exclusively for Hashem. Were we to completely follow such total systems of control and discipline, we would in effect be transcending the physical world.

Additionally, as we saw in Chapter XVII, fully actualizing the three meals of *Shabbos* corrects the three prime deficiencies. And *Shemitah* also has three main concepts that improve the

---

269. *TB Shabbos* 118b.
270. *Yeshayahu* 56:4, Radak.

three parts of the human being:

1. Training control over our physical food needs by restraining the normal reliance on agriculture and by emphasizing the holiness of all grown food. (Instincts)

2. Opening the gates of private, food-producing property and cancelling all debts, demonstrating the close interconnection and brotherhood of the Jewish People. (Emotions)

3. Free time from regular work in order to concentrate on Torah learning. (Intellect)

We may suggest that fully observing *Shabbos* and *Shemitah* is particularly meritorious since they openly reveal Hashem's presence in His world, showing the Jew's full acceptance of His care and control.[271]

On another issue, *Chazal* explain that rebuilding the *Beis Hamikdosh* depends on understanding why it was twice destroyed. The first time, idol worship, promiscuity and murder caused the destruction.[272] If we refer back to Chapter VII, we will recall that these three reasons fit precisely into our Threefold Key to being Jewish. And here we see how the failure to fulfill this system of human perfection can sometimes cause disastrous consequences.

---

271. We can also explain the importance of these two *mitzvos* if we recall that doing them "according to the law" means that the person must be a *talmid chachom*, and a true *talmid chachom* is metaphorically called "*Shabbos*" because of his increased perfection and closeness to Hashem. These three "*Shabbosos*" thereby represent the three basic dimensions of life: time (*Shabbos*), space (*Shemitah*) and person (a *talmid chachom*). They become analogous to the *Kohain Gadol* (person) on *Yom Kippur* (time) in the *Kodesh Hakodoshim* (space), which altogether attained the yearly atonement for the Jewish People. We can, therefore, understand why *Chazal* tell us that as soon as we Jews perfect these dimensions, the Final Redemption will automatically occur.

272. *TB Yoma* 9b.

The destruction of the second *Beis Hamikdosh* was brought on by causeless hatred.[273] The Exile that followed this calamity has lasted until this day, and the question here is: why so long? An answer given is that when the First Temple was destroyed the three transgressions were more external. Therefore, since outward behavior is more easily correctable, that exile lasted only seventy years. However, on the second occasion, the error was an internal one and, therefore, has taken considerably more time to be rectified.[274]

Causeless, unjustified hatred can be instigated by a variety of factors: arrogance, envy, frustration caused by insufficient physical satisfaction. The main point is that the source of the problem is deep inside the individual. Few people commit obvious idol worship, but it is easy to deny the absolute sovereignty of the Creator: all it takes is one petulant complaint, one burst of anger, one sigh of frustration or sadness. Few are overtly promiscuous, but impure thoughts can enter the mind in a minute. Few commit murder, but the tongue can become such a quick weapon for stabbing others. The underlying cause for all of them is an unthinking self-centeredness that blindly blocks out everyone else. However, the Torah system trains us to go from self to beyond-self, which will automatically help us gain the proper perspective on ourselves. Through diligently learning humility before the Almighty, controlling our instincts and giving to others, we have, with Hashem's help, the best opportunity of converting selfish and unfounded enmity into selfless and positively-directed love.

There is another interpretation for the greater duration of this

---

273. *Ibid.* See further App. C: The Fourth Component, p. 247.
274. *Ibid.*

The Final Resolution / 183

Exile: Causeless hatred is specifically connected to arrogance, for a haughty person will dislike and eventually hate people for failing to honor him sufficiently.[275] The preclusion of everyone else's importance will ultimately lead to precluding even Hashem's importance, directly causing the removal of His presence in the world and the destruction of the *Beis Hamikdosh*, the place where His presence was most manifest. Causeless hatred can, therefore, be a very effective catalyst for dire catastrophe.[276]

With this approach, we can understand the many reasons given for the destruction of Yerushalayim. We shall briefly list them, suggesting the possible connection to our Key-system:[277]

1. Profaning *Shabbos*: failure to activate all or any one of the three aspects of our Key that are included in *Shabbos*, as discussed in Chapters V and XVII.

2. Neglecting to say *Shema* morning and evening: again, a subject which reflects all the main issues, as discussed in Chapter VIII.

3. Neglecting to educate the young children: the purity of their learning epitomizes the goal of converting physicality into spirituality.[278]

---

275. *Pirkei Avos* 2:16, 4:28, Rashi, Eitz Yosef. See also Chap. XVI, fn. 191.

276. Causeless hatred is connected to *loshon hara*, which is also blamed for the destruction of the *Beis Hamikdosh*. See TB *Gittin* 55b, 57b (Rashi: "*v'heinu*"); *Chofetz Chaim*, Introduction, p. 1. See also TB *Arachin* 15b, which equates *loshon hara* to the three major transgressions, just as was done here with causeless hatred (TB *Yoma* 9b). But, again, if we analyze the reasons for *loshon hara*, they compare quite similarly to those of causeless hatred: arrogance, envy, etc. See App. C: The Fourth Component, p. 247.

277. The first eight reasons are taken from TB *Shabbos* 119b; the last from TB *Baba Metzia* 30b. The Maharsha's explanation in TB *Shabbos* has been drawn upon for our discussion.

278. As we are taught, "One cannot compare the breath (i.e., utterances) that

4. A lack of shamefacedness between each other: the very quality of conscience that typifies a Jew, as dealt with in Chapter IV (pages 29-32).

5. Equating "lesser level" people with "greater level" people: arrogance causes disrespect for our Torah leaders.

6. A failure of those in upper positions to reprove one another: haughtiness corrupts truth-seeking such that each affords the other immunity from criticism in order to gain it for himself.

7. Scorning *talmidei chachomim*: the height of arrogance.

8. Dishonest business practices: the competitive urge, when based on selfish envy, will eventually lead to ignoring legalities.[279]

---

has sin with the breath that has no sin." *TB Shabbos* 119b.

279. After completing his commentary on this section, the Maharsha added this revealing contemporary insight:

"In reality, most, if not all, of these listed transgressions are present in our current generation. Only a very few are careful with the prohibitions of *Shabbos*, with many ignorant of the things which they are doing wrong. Indeed, every community should be organizing classes to teach about the prohibitions which are being violated. And on *motza'ei Shabbos*, many feel that it is required for them to go out and become intoxicated, and as a consequence, they miss the time for *k'rias Shema* in the morning. The neglecting of our young children's Torah education is prevalent in every community, and the *yeshivah* students waste most of their semester breaks with idleness and touring. Equating the lesser with the greater is a societal breakdown in our own generation, for each one wants to be the chief rabbi and chief judge, though lacking the commensurate Torah credentials, expressing the concept that 'many profane....' And each one wants to display his wealth, whether through clothes or homes or whatever, and this trait leads to stealing from one another. Reproof of the community leaders is impossible, since each one worries about the other's so-called honor. The disgracing of *talmidei chachomim* and the ignoring of their admonitions are daily occurrences. People transact business dishonestly, with so many varieties of deception, usury and thievery that it even appears

The Final Resolution / 185

9. An insistence on civil court litigation: when people are unable to compromise, they demonstrate a false self-righteousness and a lack of compassion and concern for others.

Finally, there is the famous statement that "The only difference between our present world and the time of the *Mashiach* is subjection to foreign governments."[280]

As we will learn a bit later when we bring in the Rambam's discussion, one of the three primary goals of the *Mashiach*'s kingship is to turn the Jewish People and the nations of the world towards Hashem through the power of Torah learning. The main global indicator of the Exile is that instead of Torah (i.e., Hashem) governing humankind, man — his governments, his legislatures, his laws, his armies — rule the world. This is what the expression "foreign governments" is teaching us. The reason for this state of affairs is man's egoism, and the correction is humbly accepting the Torah's sovereignty. This crucial change of authority will be established under the *Mashiach*'s leadership.

In actuality, the process of the Final Redemption was already hinted at from the very beginning of the Jewish People. We are taught that for three reasons Avraham's descendants were subjected to the Egyptian slavery, the prototype of all the exiles:[281]

---

permissible to take deposit of someone's money and then deny ever having received it.

"Every God-fearing and pious Jew should be personally aware of these things that are happening, and where it is within his power, he must protest, even each reproving the other. It would be appropriate to say more, but I realize that perhaps my words will be ignored, and *Chazal* already cautioned in such circumstances, 'Better that they be unwitting than witting offenders.' "

These words were written by the Maharsha approximately 400 years ago.

280. *TB Berachos* 34b; *TB Sanhedrin* 93b; Rambam, *Hilchos Melachim* 12:2.

1. When Avraham drafted Torah scholars for military service to help save his nephew Lot, he was caught in an inherent dilemma: the immeasurable value to society of *talmidei chachomim* completely dedicated to their learning, *versus* the necessity of using these righteous and committed Torah scholars to benefit society in other ways. (Intellect)

2. When Avraham questioned how his offspring would merit the Land of Israel, he foresaw the issue of whether his progeny would maintain the physical purity commensurate with possession of the Holy Land. (Instincts)

3. When he returned rescued captives to their idol-worshipping masters, he indicated the difficulty of giving absolutely perfect love to our fellow humans, who all deserve being brought under Hashem's benevolence.[282] (Emotions)

Continuing this pattern, when Yaakov and Yosef later conveyed to their descendants the formula for knowing who would be the redeemer from the Egyptian slavery and exile, they each made a one-sentence declaration, which can be divided into three parts:

Yaakov (*Bereishis* 48:21)	Yosef (*Bereishis* 50:24)
1. I die	1. I die
2. Hashem will be with you	2. Hashem will surely visit you
3. and will bring you back to the land of your fathers	3. and will bring you up out of this land to the land ....

---

281. *TB Nedarim* 32a.

282. We know that the *Avos* were on such a high level that it is practially impossible for us to understand the tests that they were given. Our explanation here simply shows that Avraham's situation revealed the classic three issues which are the constant challenges of the Jewish People.

Quite significantly, the *Midrash*[283] deduces from these statements that the redeemer would be coming with three signs. He would

1. speak in the style of *anochi*.
2. use the expression *pakode*.
3. appoint the Elders, i.e., judges.

We can explain these indicators and how they fit with what Yaakov and Yosef said as follows:

1. *Anochi* ("I" in English) connotes that the human redeemer is acting only as a messenger of Hashem, Who is the real and only *Anochi*.[284] In other words, the "I" of the human ego is totally effaced, as expressed in the statements of Yaakov and Yosef, "I die." So humble is such a person that he is only a conduit of Hashem's will in this world, his mind and intellect being totally subservient to this will. This quality was true of the redeemer from Egypt — Moshe Rabbeinu, who was called the most humble of all men[285] and was, therefore, the most suitable conveyor of Hashem's Torah to all humankind.

2. The expression *pakode* (visit, remember) first appears when Hashem promised Avraham offspring and then later granted him and Sarah a son.[286] Because Avraham "remembered" Hashem constantly through his total commitment to making Him manifest in the world, Hashem "remembered" Avraham by granting him continued existence, first through

---

283. *Bereishis Rabba* 97:6. The Chidushie Haradal explains that Yaakov and Yosef's statements are really the same. We have slightly rearranged the order of the signs as listed in the *Midrash* to match the order of the statements in the *Chumash*.
284. Compare *Shemos* 20:2: "*Anochi* (I am) the Lord your God."
285. *Bemidbar* 12:3. See our discussion pp. 171-2.
286. *Bereishis* 15:5; 17:19; 21:1, Rashi.

having a child and second through ensuring that Avraham's progeny would always continue. In other words, because of Avraham's lovingkindness totally reaching beyond self, Hashem chose him to father the people who would complete the very task which Avraham started and which was the intended destiny of all humankind — striving to achieve the infinite.[287]

This choice meant that Hashem had committed Himself not only to never abandoning the Jewish People, but also, ultimately, to definitely redeeming them, i.e., to bring them to fulfill their goal and purpose — eternity. As a clear precedent and model to prove Hashem's commitment, He redeemed us from Egypt to show that He intends to keep his promise of releasing mortal man from the bonds of the physical, from the bonds of the finite. Indeed, the Hebrew word for Egypt — *Mitzrayim* — comes from a root that means "narrow, constrained." When the Torah says that Hashem took us out of *Mitzrayim*, it is also saying that He took us out of the narrow constraints of the physical and the finite.

Thus, when Moshe, Hashem's agent, came and used the expression *pakode*, he was actually signalling the initiation of the process to which Hashem had committed Himself through His promise to Avraham. For all times, Avraham's lovingkindness generates Hashem's lovingkindness, which guarantees the transformation of slavery to exodus, of exile to redemption, of finite to infinite. And when we follow in Avraham's footsteps by reaching emotionally beyond self, loving Hashem and others, we ensure our own participation in the realization of this great and wonderful promise — *pakode*!

---

287. See Chap. II, pp. 11-4.

3. The successful administration of an entire people depended on a system of courts and judges, with the Great Sanhedrin of Seventy Elders at the top. This judicial network was to enforce the high level of purity that would maintain continued possession of the Promised Land, a place that cannot tolerate any form of decadence. Leaving the immorality of Egypt, the Jewish People could possess *Eretz Yisroel* as their rightful inheritance only if they unfailingly sanctified the physical and controlled their instincts. Moshe immediately gathered the Elders and, later, instituted the court system.[288] The goal was clear: to preserve the holiness of the People from its beginning, and onward, into its ultimate destination, the Holy Land.[289] Therefore, when Yaakov and Yosef promised that the redeemer would return the Jews to the land of their forefathers, the *Midrash* relates this promise to the appointment of judges, for they would be the ones responsible for ensuring the continued possession of the Land by enforcing the highest level of morality and sanctity.

With this explanation of the *Midrash*, we can now understand how the three factors which caused the bondage of Avraham's descendants were conceptually the same as the signs brought by the redeemer.[290] Understanding and working on the issues that have to be corrected is *the* way to bring the redemption.

---

288. *Shemos* 4:29, 18:13-26; *Bemidbar* 11:16, where judges were appointed to help quell the people's complaints that their physical pleasures were being limited. See Maharzu, *Bereishis Rabba* 97:6, connecting judges with *v'hayshiv* (and He will bring [you] back [to the land]). See also *Devorim* 16:20, Rashi: "*L'ma'an.*"

289. As we discussed before, *Eretz Yisroel* cannot tolerate any moral degeneracy. See pp. 172-4 and fns. 253, 254.

290. The Jews who left Egypt also merited being saved because they stayed strong in these three categories. See Chap. IX.

190 / *Self Beyond Self*

Indeed, in the same vein, the Rambam gives three main qualifications for the person who will be the *Mashiach*:[291]

1. He will return the kingship of Dovid (really, the Kingship of Hashem) through the greatness of his Torah learning and wisdom. He will activate the performance of all the laws of the Torah by the entire Jewish People and the Seven Noahide Commandments by all the non-Jews. His absolute commitment to Hashem and His Torah will thwart any and all counterforces or ideologies, leaving them totally eliminated while he and the Kingdom of Hashem will remain forever triumphant.[292]

2. He will rebuild the *Beis Hamikdosh* on its location and reinstate the sacrifices. These offerings are termed in Hebrew *karbonos*, a word derived from the verb "to come near." Physicality can mistakenly become an end in itself, but the *karbonos* teach us that the physical is clearly only a means to a higher end — spiritual ascension, coming near to Hashem.[293] Not by coincidence, the chamber of the Great Sanhedrin was within the area of the *Beis Hamikdosh*, indicating the judicial role in enforcing physical purity.

3. He will gather together all the dispersed elements of the Jewish People. All the main soul-energy implanted in this world lives in the bodies of humans, primarily in the Chosen People. Bringing all this potential together is a main objective of the *Mashiach*, for then he is unifying Hashem, so to speak, in

---

291. Rambam, *Hilchos Melachim* 11:1,4.
292. From here we see clearly that the *Mashiach* cannot die. Rambam, *Hilchos Melachim* 11:3.
293. See our discussions elsewhere, for example, Chap. III, pp. 19-21 and fn. 16. See *Mishnah Megillah* 3:6 and *Pirkei Avos* 1:2, where Harav m'Bertinoro explains that because of the *karbonos*, heaven and earth continue. We can understand that the purpose of the whole world is to bring the physical to a spiritual plane.

the earthly world as He is unified in the spiritual world. Such fusion, obviously, includes every Jew, no matter how far removed he is from his People, from his Torah Judaism, from his Source. Moreover, it embraces every human being on the globe, for to the degree to which any living soul can conceive of Hashem and act accordingly, it should be guided and assisted to achieve this potential. This unification of humankind under Hashem is the end goal and completion of world history, for creation will have reached union with the Eternal. As a result, the basic dilemma of life will have been resolved:[294] When we are completely like our Source, then Hashem will be everywhere, as it says, "and the Lord will be King over all the world; on that day, the Lord will be One and His Name One."[295]

Having seen clearly what the *Mashiach* represents, we now understand our own role in the Final Redemption. For what he will accomplish in the macrocosm is precisely what each of us is supposed to be working on in the microcosm. By learning Torah, following the rules of physical control, and extending lovingkindness to each other, we are doing the same thing as the *Mashiach*, only within our more limited range of activity. As our combined efforts grow and intensify, the whole world can ultimately modulate into one frequency: 100% dedication to making manifest the presence of Hashem. With the symphonic orchestra in as perfect tune as possible, the conductor — the *Mashiach* — can then enter to lead the grand finale.

One could argue that the sooner we succeed in fulfilling our goal through the Threefold Key to being Jewish, the sooner

---

294. See Chap. II, pp. 11-4.
295. *Zechariah* 14:9.

the *Mashiach* will be able to assume his leadership position.

Indeed, the *Mashiach* is walking around somewhere right now. The only question is and has always been: When will the generation be ready? When will we accomplish what we need to do in order to prepare for his appearance? Now we know clearly what our task is. May we pray that we soon achieve it, hastening the *Mashiach*'s arrival and the final triumphant resolution of history for all humankind.

Part Six:
From Theory to Actualization

    XXI Practical Applications for Torah-aware Jews

   XXII Practical Applications for Jews Unfamiliar with Torah

  XXIII Conclusion for Torah-aware Jews

  XXIV Conclusion for Jews Unfamiliar with Torah

           Epilogue: Success!

           Postscript

XXI
Practical Applications for Torah-aware Jews

As promised in the beginning, we would like to offer some practical applications of this book's basic thesis. In truth, we have mentioned throughout our discussion various suggestions, but the following is a more systematic presentation.

Acts of Lovingkindness

We start with an important piece of advice:[296]

A chasid came to R. Avremele of Stretin and begged, "Rebbe, please help me acquire *yiras shamayim* (fear of Heaven)."

"I have no advice on how to acquire that," answered R. Avremele, "but I can tell you how to acquire love of Heaven."

"That's even better, Rebbe," the man said, "because love

---

296. Shmuel Himelstein, *A Touch of Wisdom, A Touch of Wit*, Mesorah Publications, Brooklyn, New York, 1991, pp. 110-11.

Heaven is even greater than fear of Heaven."[297]

"The way to acquire love of Heaven," R. Avremele counseled him, "is by loving your fellow Jew."

It would appear from this story that even for Torah-aware Jews, the popular epigram, "Love is the answer," has considerable relevance. Indeed, Rabbi Eliyahu E. Dessler succinctly divided the world between givers and takers, with the goal to make oneself into a true giver.[298] If we recall that giving is really, in Hebrew, the definition of love,[299] then it follows that to become a giver is to learn how to love others. In fact, it is the major principle of the Torah — love your neighbor as yourself[300] — and the subject of very much Torah literature. Rabbi Zelig Pliskin, in his book, *Love Your Neighbor*, wrote 437 pages of suggestions concerning how to put this principle into practice, summarizing his effort with the following from the *Orchos Tzaddikim*:

> You should help others in every way possible according to your ability. You should trouble yourself for the rich and poor alike. You should lend money to anyone who needs a loan. Give presents to the poor according to your ability, and from time to time send presents to the wealthy also. If you have business dealings with others, be entirely honest. Do not be strict with others in small matters. Always wish to give pleasure to others, and not vice versa. Speak pleasantly to everyone. If someone deceived you, do not deceive him. Bear the yoke of others, but do not cause others trouble. Do not quarrel. Greet every person with joy and a pleasant facial expres-

---

297. See *TB Yoma* 86a.
298. *Michtav*, Vol. 1, pp. 32-51, *Strive for Truth!*, Vol. 1, pp. 119-58.
299. See p. 37, fn. 38.
300. *Vayikra* 19:18, Rashi citing *Toras Kohanim*.

> sion, for this will strengthen love. Deal with others for their good. When others are sad or worried, comfort them. If someone confided his secret to you, do not reveal it to others even if he angers you. Do not speak evil of others and do not listen when others speak evil. Always try to find merit in others. You should honor every person with deeds and with words. You should not act condescendingly toward anyone.[301]

For the Jew aware of Torah values, this advice is both intense and to the point. In the terminology used by this book, we should go beyond our concern for self and be concerned for the other person as much as possible. For this reason, the list of possible good deeds is endless, as it says: "These are the things that have no measure (i.e., limit): ... acts of lovingkindness ...."[302] It is a lot of work, but then, did anyone imagine that achieving beyond-self — i.e., infinity — would be an easy task? And, furthermore, as is implied in the story which we initially quoted, no one should fool himself into thinking that he loves Hashem when, in fact, he only minimally loves others.

When we consistently give to other people, we learn to go beyond our self-interest and eliminate our competitive attitude towards our fellow human beings. We extend to them our emotions — our commitment, attachment, closeness. We want what is good for them and are not concerned for what we receive in return. Our feelings are trained to go beyond self until we reach the point at which we are completely happy and eager that good be bestowed upon others. As a result, when they succeed, we actually feel joy and are never jealous about their

---

301. *Orchos Tzaddkim, Sha'ar Ha'ahava* (The Gate of Love), Feldheim Publishers (Hebrew edition), 1991, pp. 52-3.
302. *Mishnah Pe'ah* 1:1. See, further, App. B: Love Your Neighbor, p. 243.

success.

Moreover, when we hear that someone whom we know has been blessed with good news, we should check for any pang of envy or insecurity that might be aroused. Likewise, when talking with others, we should avoid pointed questions that allow us to evaluate their levels of achievement so that we can then compare how well we are competing. For example, "How many children do you have now?", "What yeshiva has your son been accepted to?", "What is the name (i.e., family lineage) of your prospective son-in-law?" Although all of these inquiries may well come from a genuine interest in the other's well-being, all too often, they really stem from an insecure and selfish attitude that stems from our fear of the advancement of others.

This problem can have even more disastrous consequences when latent feelings of jealousy subconsciously cause people to talk about others. *Loshon hara* can often be a way of attacking and trying to diminish someone else's success. Similarly, *ayin hara* can be a real phenomenon when we realize how strongly people desire their own success, even if it should come indirectly, through others failing.

Lovingkindness is such a strong antidote to all these destructive forces that we are specifically taught, *olam chesed y'baneh*[303] — "the world is built through lovingkindness." Such a world is a positive and wonderful place to live in, for all jealousy and selfishness have been eliminated. Moreover, this achievement is not only for now but also forever, for the world *olam* implies this world *and* the World to Come.[304] In other words, as we have been explaining all along, we can earn our

---

303. *Tehillim* 89:3. See *Pirkei Avos* 1:2, Harav m'Bertinoro.
304. The word *olam* is also very close to the word *l'olam*, which means "forever."

own infinity. We just have to go beyond self.

Avodah

Actually going beyond self at the level of our instincts is quite a complicated process. Our bodies seem to work almost automatically due to the necessity of fulfilling their natural functions. Our physical nerve endings register responses which are undeniably satisfying, for without them, vital life functions would, of course, simply stop. Furthermore, it is also very hard to extract any beyond-self dimension from these pleasures which are, by their very nature, so personal. So what practical advice is there to help us move our instincts into the realm of beyond-self?

The concept of *Avodah* teaches us that our instincts must and can be raised to a higher level of service.[305] Control and discipline are essential components in preventing our bodies from endlessly craving more and more satisfaction. In Torah Judaism, every one of our instincts has many well-defined guidelines as to when and how they may be used. What we can eat, what we are permitted to see, to hear, to touch, etc. — all have many specifically tailored regulations which help us contain and productively control those strong forces within us that sometimes seem almost independent entities.

In our contemporary life-style, when physical abundance has reached a zenith unknown in world history, the temptations to indulge in this cornucopia are almost overwhelming. Indeed, today very many of these delights even come with kosher labels: connoisseur wines and kosher shrimp, Passover *l'mehadrin* in Aruba and a bar mitzvah party at the Hilton grand

---

305. See Chap. III, pp. 19-21.

ballroom with kosher caterer, not to mention *parve* ice cream as creamy as the original, the perfect dessert for the best meat meal!

Abstaining from such endless pleasures is not a Jewish requirement. However, seeking after them is definitely not maximizing the opportunity to go beyond the instinctual aspect of self. What we need to keep ourselves functioning healthfully should be our prime intention. Otherwise, in numerous ways we have to train ourselves to limit or even avoid many physical stimulations. Luxurious hotels, costly gala celebrations, exotic vacations, all pander to our weaker inclinations. Instead, we should try to emulate the *kohanim* in the *Beis Hamikdosh* who sought, even with their eating, to go beyond self and bodily desires and, instead, serve only Hashem. The intention is all-important. And as an added incentive, the *Gemora* specifically teaches us that the more we fill our stomachs, the more harm we cause ourselves.[306] Indeed, the Rambam states that eating more than we need is the main source of all illnesses and recommends that we leave the table with our stomachs one-quarter empty.[307]

Even those of us who control their appetites and consume modestly can also continually raise their level by infusing physicality with greater and greater spirituality. This task can mean that our instincts will increasingly avoid private gratification and operate, instead, only for a higher purpose. This potential can be so developed that even in our thoughts we would not be aroused by a bodily pleasure merely for the sake of that pleasure.

If this *avodah* sounds difficult and even superhuman, that

---

306. *TB Berachos* 32a.
307. Rambam, *Hilchos Deos* 4:2,15.

200 / *Self Beyond Self*

is precisely why we have the inspirational stories of our great *tzaddikim*. They were humans like ourselves who consistently lived the most temperate and modest life-styles.[308] No frills, no icing, never anything more than required.[309] Their achievements can spur us to strive harder in the beyond-self use of our instincts, while, of course, at the same time we pray that Hashem will constantly help us in this very challenging endeavor.[310]

Torah

Although we have all heard the expression "lording it over others," most of us would never imagine that such an undesirable character trait is part of our own personalities. Yet human nature is such that, almost invariably, when someone else is less endowed with intelligence, knowledge, wealth or status, we immediately start feeling superior. It seems to strengthen us to know that we are better than others, ahead of others, more successful than others — and how much more so when honestly and objectively this happens to be the case. Even if overtly we do nothing to flaunt our superiority, just the private, inner

---

308. For two of the countless examples, see *A Tzaddik in Our Time* (Rabbi Aryeh Levin), Feldheim Publishers, Jerusalem/New York, 1977, p. 79; *Guardian of Jerusalem* (Rabbi Yosef Chaim Sonnenfeld), Mesorah Publications, Ltd., Brooklyn, New York, 1983, p. 210.

309. The Chofetz Chaim succinctly described the issue here: " . . . The main point is that each individual should sincerely analyze what are his true requirements, without which he could not survive." *Mishnah Berurah*, 156:1, note 2. In the *Sha'ar HaTzion* (note 3), he proposed an objective standard to determine one's needs: what he would give to support another person of his same economic level.

310. In *Birchos Hashachar* (the Morning Blessings), we openly request that Hashem "will force our evil inclination to be subservient" to Him.

knowledge boosts our egos and nourishes the satisfying sense that we are on top.

As a result, it turns out that we *have* actually set ourselves up as lords over others. And even though most contemporary cultures have dismantled baronages and dukedoms, we have created new ones, called the Affluent Circle, the Important Families Association, the Best Yeshivahs Club, the Exclusive Orthodox Clique. Quality and achievement are certainly realities of life, but if we are not careful, we can also, unfortunately, tack on that extra little layer of pride, just what it takes to inflate our self-image of importance and status.

Moreover, prideful feelings are just a step away from outright arrogant behavior. Speaking condescendingly of others, ignoring or slighting them, talking derogatorily of them, failing to listen to their criticism — can all derive from an ego that holds itself above others, sure of its ascendancy and eager to maintain its supremacy.

Indeed, the ego's continual drive for success distances us from other human beings and even allows us to push them aside, whether because they block our progress or because we are so preoccupied with ourselves that we do not even notice that they are there. In brief, pride's successes just precede its downfall, simply because by falsely lording over others, we isolate ourselves from our fellow Jews, inevitably falling into a lonely pit.

Realizing the ease with which the superiority trip can move in the wrong direction, we must labor persistently to save ourselves from such disaster. How? There is one prime way: learning Torah. The learning of Torah constantly shows us that Hashem is actually the *only* Being who possesses any superiority. The greatness and expanse of Torah humbles every human being. Relative to this huge body of knowledge, it becomes obvious that we have no real power, no supremacy, no rulership.

At the same time, by our regular study of Hashem's thoughts in His Torah, we overcome our personal biases and attain a truth-perspective. Eternal concepts of *absolute* right, *perfect* justice, *total* morality blaze their way through our ephemeral, compromising, vacillating, convenience-oriented existence. Our minds are cleared of the endless falsities that cloud our true perception of reality. Again, we patently see that it is totally foolish to play ego games, for the only superiority is in the Ultimate Mind, a glimpse of which we can gain through assiduously learning Torah.

Of course, this effort also entails our humbly going to the Torah Sages of then and now, our constant mentors, for without them we would be lost in the Torah's immensity. Only they have any significant grasp of this wisdom. This gives them true authority, for Hashem specifically invested them with sufficient ability in order to teach and guide the rest of us. And they, with all their greatness, continue to remain humble because the more they know, the more they know how much more they *still* have to learn. Also, they profoundly understand that their abilities and achievements are given them solely for the benefit of the Jewish People and not to inflate their egos. Indeed, should they ever become arrogant, they would, perforce, break their intimate tie to the Master of creation, simultaneously disillusioning and alienating their followers.

We point out that the *Gemora* is compared to an ocean — its depth and breadth are beyond the capacity of a human being to traverse, and the serious and honest student automatically feels humility in its presence. Indeed, every tractate begins on the second page; there is no first page. Even the accomplished learner is reminded that, as much as he knows, he still has yet to complete the first page. Humility must be the essence of the true Talmud scholar.[311]

As an important example of how to inculcate humility, when we study with others and an idea is granted us, we should understand that we are only trustees with the responsibility of conveying the idea to our learning partner so that he will benefit from it as well. In giving us our intellect and ingenuity, Hashem intended that we should use them for the benefit of others and not as tools for domination and personal gain. Whatever understanding and talent we possess are solely largess from Above. Any element of superiority would immediately poison the waters that were meant to give clarity, cleansing and healing to ourselves, our fellow Jews, and even the whole world.

In brief, the practical approach to achieving humility and avoiding arrogance is through occupying ourselves with learning Torah as much as we possibly can, realizing that every page we understand and every idea we think of are constant reminders of how humble we should feel and behave.

---

311. We are taught that, Jewishly, true greatness is always accompanied by humility. *TB Megillah* 31a.

We would like to recommend an excellent book that expands on many of the themes presented in this book: *Beyond Your Ego*, Dr. Judith Mishell/Dr. Shalom Srebrenik, CIS Publishers, New York/London/Jerusalem, 1992.

XXII
Practical Applications for Jews Unfamiliar with Torah

As promised in the first chapter, we would like to bring together some practical applications of this book's basic thesis. But before we do, a quick review of what we have learned so far would be useful.

If we were to sit down and analyze all the problems of the world — international, national, local, individual — in addition to having a long list and a bad headache, we would also be able to clearly see that most of the problems evolve because of man himself. For example, wars and violence reflect the strong ego drive; corruption exhibits the insatiable drive for money and power; pollution manifests selfish desires with no concern for others; loneliness and depression stem from the inability to reach out of one's own little world; escapism is a response to the seemingly meaningless existence of a creature born to die.

Then, if we were to break down the human into his component parts, we would see that he is made up of three basic ingredients:

– Emotions

- Instincts
- Intellect

In truth, these elements are neutral and can each be used in one of two ways (plus all the degrees in between): either for the individual himself or for beyond-self.

When they are used for self, they result in some fairly severe problems:

1. Jealousy, envy, selfishness
2. Lust, promiscuity, self-indulgence
3. Arrogance, egocentricity, glory-seeking

When they are used for beyond-self, they bring about some very positive results:

1. Acts of lovingkindness to others
2. Self-restraint, discipline, transcendence of the physical
3. Humility, self-effacement

In other words, we humans are both the problem and the solution, depending which way we direct our component parts — to self or to beyond-self. Everyone is already functioning in life somewhere on the continuum between these poles, and it is very rare to find either extreme. We note in passing that going beyond self does **not** mean that the special abilities and qualities of each person are being ignored or abandoned. On the contrary, every single aspect of each human personality and individuality is being utilized. Rather, the whole question is: For what purpose is our uniqueness being used? What is the goal of all this life effort — for self or for beyond-self?

Torah Judaism attempts to carefully guide the Jew through a highly sophisticated and totally integrated system to reach beyond-self — a more elevating, salutary, productive and dynamic dimension. Every person has the free will to decide for himself or herself, and we hope that the reader has been sufficiently impressed with the simplicity and elegance of the basic Torah system that he or she will want to investigate it further.

Summary complete, let's consider a few examples of how our Threefold Key actually works in practice, giving us at the same time practical solutions to many of life's problems.

Emotions

The subject of emotions is, obviously, quite complicated. We find people often feeling that they are not receiving enough love or attention. Their emotional needs require further reinforcement, and, lacking this support system, they can suffer sadness, diffidence, a sense of inadequacy, even depression. It can happen that the individual's needs become stronger and even more difficult to satisfy since, in general, others are also looking out for themselves and are not much concerned for his requirements. The spiral of dissatisfaction will intensify the person's dependency, arousing both his feelings of isolation and his jealousy at others' success. In other words, life can end up lacking essential emotional fulfillment.

We have explained that the solution to this psychological down-spin depends on going beyond one's self. This idea means that we cease to be concerned for ourselves — except for our basic requirements — and instead, concentrate the great majority of our thoughts and energies on the needs of others. By constantly being involved in this way, we gradually switch our focus from self to beyond-self. We no longer want to receive; we just want to give.

Giving to others is a central theme in Torah Judaism. In the secular world, however, there is very little incentive or structure which assists, much less encourages, this process as a central goal. As a result, the true fruition of going beyond self rarely occurs. Inertia, financial responsibilities, a minimal amount of spare time, all obstruct development, making any real changes in these deep-set personality weaknesses quite unlikely.

On the other hand, after spending some time and effort to learn the Torah system of lovingkindness, the reader will quickly see how much more productively his emotions will develop, how a whole new world of beyond-self potential can be created and realized.[312]

In conclusion, to give a beautiful example of how just the communal aspects of what we are describing *are* realized, we would like to bring the following newspaper article, which quotes from another article which appeared in *Ma'ariv*, a prominent secular Israeli newspaper. *Ma'ariv* was commenting on the unique behavior of the residents of B'nei Brak, a predominantly Torah-observant city near Tel Aviv:

MA'ARIV ON THE *CHESED* OF B'NEI BRAK

> The Israel daily *Ma'ariv* recently ran a long, appreciative article, entitled "Unbelievable *Chesed*," on the *chesed* (lovingkindness) organizations of B'nei Brak. The article contrasted the way the doing of *chesed* is interwoven into the very fabric of *chareidi* (religious) life to the situation in the secular world where doing something for others without recompense is considered aberrational behavior.
>
> According to the *Ma'ariv* article, "*Gemilut chassadim* (bestowing kindness) is not only a *mitzvah*, it is a pleasure for the residents of B'nei Brak. It is amazing how much people there wish to help others and to what degree they will put themselves out to do so."
>
> Of particular interest to the writer for *Ma'ariv* was

---

312. For just a small sampling of this system, see App. B: Love Your Neighbor, p. 243.

the manner in which the doing of *chesed* has been institutionalized in the form of more than 300 *gemachim* (lovingkindness organizations) in B'nei Brak. In addition to the large number of traditional free loan societies [that lend money without interest], there are *gemachim* available to answer every imaginable need — from the apparently trivial to the potentially life saving, from *arbes* (chickpeas) for a last minute *shalom zachar*, matching outfits for twins and triplets, or candles for escorting the bride and groom, to blood and eyeglasses. Cribs, carriages, baby bottles, baby scales, hair trimmers, vitamins, tablecloths, electric drills, and heaters are just some of the items available through the various *gemachim*.

The article concludes, "In contrast to the secular society in which a strong desire to help others without the expectation of reward is considered unusual — *gemilut chassadim* is a *mitzvah* which is particularly sought after in B'nei Brak, even for matters which are neither urgent or necessary.... In the *chareidi* society in general, and in B'nei Brak in particular, when someone needs something in the middle of the night, he always has somewhere to turn where he will get what he needs — no questions asked. Whether his need is great or small it will be answered for no other reason than that it is a *mitzvah* to do so."[313]

Caring for others is the Torah solution for growing emotionally. By going beyond our own emotional needs and focusing on the other fellow, we are creating a whole environment of love. For if we desire merely to receive love passively, we create nothing. But if we actively reach out to build relationships and help others, we set in motion a vitality and spirit that

---

313. *Yated*, 28 Tishrei 5750 (October 27, 1989), p. 3.

lifts everyone up — including ourselves.

Instincts

Since World War II, a clear trend in the morality of Western society can be discerned. Affluence and modern technology have made physical pleasure-seeking a way of life. Every day, new ways are devised so that people will spend more money to satisfy their bodily instincts. Competitive capitalism, together with a legal system protecting individual rights of expression and enjoyment, has successfully created a "liberated," permissive society. Particularly on issues of sexuality, Western culture has effectively deleted the word "promiscuity" from the collective vocabulary. As one best-selling American writer and philosopher put it:

> Sexual liberation presented itself as a bold affirmation of the senses and of undeniable natural impulse against our puritanical heritage, society's conventions and repressions, bolstered by Biblical myths about original sin. From the early sixties on there was a gradual testing of the limits on sexual expression, and they melted away or had already disappeared without anybody's having noticed it. The disapproval of parents and teachers of youngsters' sleeping or living together was easily overcome. The moral inhibitions, the fear of disease, the risk of pregnancy, the family and social consequences of premarital intercourse and the difficulty of finding places in which to have it — everything that stood in its way suddenly was no longer there. Students, particularly the girls, were no longer ashamed to give public evidence of sexual attraction or of its fulfillment. The kinds of cohabitation that were dangerous in the twenties, and risqu' or bohemian in the thirties and forties

> became as normal as membership in the Girl Scouts. I say "particularly" girls because young men were always supposed to be eager for immediate gratification, whereas young women, inspired by modesty were supposed to resist it. It was a modification or phasing out of female modesty that made the new arrangements possible. Since, however, modesty was supposed to be mere convention or habit, no effort was required to overcome it....[314]

This synopsis is obviously quite a different picture from the self-control and restraint which Torah Judaism trains and encourages. "Puritanical," "Biblical myths," "original sin" are all labels which are completely inapplicable to Judaism. For these terms reflect an arbitrary clamping down with no other goal than to inhibit and suppress. However, the various Torah guidelines actually have the profoundly edifying purpose of raising man above the level of simple animal behavior, of moving his instincts from self to beyond-self. In other words, even within our most physical and instinctual aspects, we can achieve an infinite dimension. We can truly sense that we are attaining ultimate meaning and purpose when we are properly using our sensuality.

Without question, each person has the free will to decide that he prefers to live without any external restraints or system of right and wrong. However, if he would look around at the modern world and give the subject more thought, he could very likely conclude that structure and order would, in fact, not only make him a happier and more satisfied individual but also produce a healthier and more productive society. For when we

---

314. Professor Allan Bloom, *The Closing of the American Mind*, Simon and Shuster, New York, 1987, p. 98.

compare Torah society and non-observant society, we find a stark statistical contrast. A ruleless culture necessarily produces a whole list of "unstructured" behavior: divorce, juvenile delinquency, drug abuse, alcoholism, homosexuality, violence, alienation. Indeed, the same author quoted above was forced to admit that modern, "liberated" culture can have negative byproducts:

> A university teacher of liberal arts cannot help confronting special handicaps, a slight deformity of the spirit, in the students, ever more numerous, whose parents are divorced. I do not have the slightest doubt that they do as well as others in all kinds of specialized subjects, but I find they are not as open to the serious study of philosophy and literature as some other students are. I would guess this is because they are less eager to look into the meaning of their lives, or to risk shaking their received opinions. In order to live with the chaos of their experience, they tend to have rigid frameworks about which is right and wrong and how they ought to live. They are full of desperate platitudes about self determination, respect for other people's rights and decisions, the need to work out one's individual values and commitments, etc. All this is a thin veneer over boundless seas of rage, doubt and fear.[315]

In comparison, the Torah world suffers negligibly from the ills of contemporary society. Indeed, the greater the adherence

---

315. *Ibid.*, p. 210. The author heavily criticizes America's educational system and proposes the return to the serious study of the classical philosophers, like Socrates and Plato. How ironic it is that a Jewish thinker could arrive at exactly the right answer — proper education — except that, given his ignorance of his own heritage, his best suggestion is to use non-Jewish sources! Had he studied Torah, he would have known of an infinitely superior solution, right in his own back yard.

212 / *Self Beyond Self*

to the Torah system, the greater the wholesomeness and purity of each person and the entire community. And sometimes this qualitative difference is readily observable, as the following excerpt from the book *The Eternal Jewish Home* dramatically shows:

> The famed Israeli humorist, Ephraim Kishon, in an unusual public confession, expressed his admiration for the behavior of religiously-educated young people. A loyal Jew and Zionist, Mr. Kishon had long been noted for his anti-religious position. However, in an article entitled "The Knitted *Kipa* (head covering)," he wrote:[316]
>
>> In any case, this humorist is happy to admit his mistake.... [H]e willingly acknowledges that these old-fashioned — in his eyes — concepts have produced better Israelis; that the [heretofore] mocked rigidity of religious parents has made better youth; that the kosher kitchen has proved to be a stronger spiritual institution than the fortresses of intelligence and progress. It is difficult for us to imagine the State of Israel without this religious faith, even though we personally may not hold by it. Nevertheless, if as a precondition for the nurturing of such youth ... we, the intellectual irreligious, are required not to ride buses on *Shabbat* or not to go to the movies on Friday nights, the writer of these lines is willing to stay home! ...
>>
>> In a society which is losing face, the young faces of today's youth have remained unchanged under the *kipa* — good, clean faces. There is still a

---

316. Taken from the Israeli newspaper *Hamodia*, 17 Adar 5735 (February 28, 1975), from the original article appearing in the newspaper *Ma'ariv*, the week before.

Practical Applications for Jews Unfamiliar with Torah / 213

> place in the world for politeness and seriousness, a place for love of one's homeland, a place where even silence exists. Any lecturer speaking before high school or university students will quickly sense the difference in the level of the questions when religious youth are before him. They act differently and question differently. Never was heard from them an unwarranted remark concerning the State.... They don't amuse themselves with the idea of leaving the country; they don't have short memories and long tresses....
>
> To tell the truth, when seeing a good face around, we automatically turn to see if there is a *kipa* just behind it....[317]

One man's opinion, however convincing, is certainly not enough to prove the case. Nor is the reader expected to accept merely on faith or logic the contention that rules governing our instincts make for a better way of life. One has only to study the Torah system and see how it is lived in practice, by visiting the homes, schools and communities, and then further convincing will be unnecessary.

Intellect

The mind is such a rich resource that it deserves to be listed as one of a person's assets, without any connection to any income it actually produces. Ideas, concepts, clarity of thought, understanding life — all *are* pleasures, though they have no price tag. Indeed, one could argue that they are even more valuable than gold and jewels. For if, deep down, a person is confused or perplexed in his thinking, then what good will all

---

317. Rabbi Yoel Schwartz, *The Eternal Jewish Home*, Jerusalem, 1982, pp. 16-18.

his wealth bring him? Instead, he walks around subliminally quite unhappy, for life is an unsolved riddle which he has no real clue of how to figure out.

Or, if he has somehow avoided the issues and remained blissfully ignorant, we objectively could consider such a fellow as missing a major aspect of being alive. After all, little children are also occupied all day long with little or no awareness of their life's purpose, and no one would imagine that an adult should live in such a fashion.

And if he claims that there is nothing so vital to unravel or understand, then maybe he should read this list:

1. Why were you born a Jew rather than a non-Jew?

2. Why are the Jewish People still here when all other ancient peoples have disappeared?

3. Why have the Jews suffered so terribly throughout the ages: persecutions, expulsions, inquisitions, pogroms, holocausts?

4. Why have the Jews returned to their Biblical homeland after 2000 years of exile?

5. Why are the Jews in Israel still under threat of attack after all these years of statehood?

6. Why is it so important to have a Jewish spouse? Isn't everybody the same?

7. Are you sure that your work is the main reason you were put on this earth?

8. Why are life's pleasures so fleeting, with no lasting satisfaction?

9. If you are just a speck in time and space, what does it matter that you were created in the first place?

10. Why do people die?

A Jew who is unaware of his Jewish heritage and its wealth

of wisdom can use his wonderful mind for many things. But if he does not know the answers to some very basic questions about life, which his own ethnic background can help answer, then how can he pretend that he is an educated, aware and knowledgeable person?

Perhaps our minds have been so much into self (i.e., information primarily for one's personal advancement) that no beyond-self alternatives have even had the possibility of entering. Or if they did manage to get in, there was not enough serious opportunity or effort to pursue the implications.

If so, would it not be wise to find out before it is too late? Would it not be wise to admit that perhaps we do not know all the answers, and then to seek out those answers. What do we stand to lose? We might even be surprised to wake up to some very important issues that we have simply overlooked until now.

In this one-shot gamble for meaning which we call our lives, wouldn't it be wise to use our minds to their maximum capacity, confident at least that we wasted none of our resources? Wouldn't it be worthwhile to seek wisdom and understanding, investigating the greatest source of knowledge in humankind's hands — the Torah, with its immense library of law, philosophy, history, literature, ethics, science and psychology?

It would appear that we could use our intellect for something more. We just have to make an effort, with nothing to lose and everything to gain.

XXIII
Conclusion for Torah-aware Jews

The Torah-aware Jew knows that he is living his life with a Torah of truth but often does not consciously realize how this truth actually changes and improves his life. Although no one would dispute that the *mitzvos* do result in making a better person and a better community, there is so much Torah to learn and so many *mitzvos* to do that the complexity and immensity of the entire system can seem both overwhelming and inexplicable.[318]

In the beginning of this book, we stated that there is a

---

318. We sometimes wonder whether observant Jews are reticent to approach non-observant Jews simply because they feel unable to explain to an outsider how Judaism works. Getting a handle on the subject would not only give each *frum* Jew greater confidence in dealing with other Jews, but it would also strengthen his own deeper appreciation and actualization of Judaism. We would like to recommend a new book which will help observant Jews explain issues in Judaism to less observant Jews: *The Eye of A Needle*, Aish HaTorah's Kiruv Primer, Feldheim Publishers, Jerusalem/New York, 1993. Also a very useful book which organizes and explains all the *mitzvos* in a lucid, contemporary style is *Masterplan, Judaism: its program, meanings, goals*, by Rabbi Aryeh Carmell, Feldheim Publishers, Jerusalem, 1991.

simple approach which allows one to organize and clarify the goal of life according to Judaism, as well as how this goal can be achieved. Succinctly stated, the goal is to bring the presence of the Creator into the world or — from the other side of the coin — to transform finite existence into an infinite reality. Practically speaking, however, we take what we have called the Threefold Key to being Jewish and use it to go from self to beyond-self.

This Key enables every observant Jew to measure his *mitzvos* — and, indeed, all his activities — on a very precise continuum: How much was I acting for self compared to beyond-self? The more one has achieved in the beyond-self direction, the more of the infinite he has brought into the world. Why? Because even one step beyond one's self and one's finiteness is, at the same time, a step towards the infinite. The person is expanding his entire world by breaking through the boundaries of his small, self-enclosed existence. And, in effect, he is dynamically creating a more infinite-like environment:

- The Infinite is a giver — and so is he, when he gives his money, effort or concern to others.
- The Infinite is truth — and so is he, when he learns Torah and lives its truth.
- The Infinite is spiritual — and so is he, when he uses his physicality for spiritual goals.

The *mitzvos* constantly point us in the direction of such infinite actions, gradually changing us from self and finite to beyond-self and infinite-like.[319] There should be no doubt in

---

319. Of course, there are many levels here, depending on how far the person actually went beyond self in the quality and self-sacrifice of his actions, as we are taught, "According to the difficulty is the reward." *Pirkei Avos* 5:26. *Cf.*, for example, Rambam, *Hilchos Matanos Anei'im* 10:7-14 (The

anyone's mind that a person's life can gain no greater or more fulfilling achievement.

Torah Judaism has traditionally understood that life is purposely built with fundamental problems, tests, challenges. The effort here has also been to define these clearly and sharply: In three major ways, *we* are the problem and *we* are the solution. If, in any split second of our lives, we even *feel* arrogance, lust or envy, we have momentarily failed in our Jewish mission.[320] If ever we are lax in learning Torah, following the rules of self-control, or extending lovingkindness, we are like soldiers unarmed in battle. How can we expect to survive, much less win?

True, *a mensch iz nur a mensch un nisht a malach*,[321] and the *Gemora* explains that the *yetzer hara* has to have some play in order for this world to exist at all.[322] But we know that if the *Beis Hamikdosh* is not built in our time, it is as if we destroyed it with our own hands.[323] And many of us may already know that the components of the *Beis Hamikdosh* symbolically corresponded to the human form: the *Aron* — the heart, the *Menorah* — the mind, the *Shulchan* — the stomach ... all to teach what Hashem also wants us to build,[324] namely, ourselves, as it says, "And they will make for Me a *Mikdosh*, and I will dwell in *them* [and not just in the *Mikdosh*]."[325]

Eight Levels of Charity).

320. See *Shemos* 4:14, discussed in Chap. VIII, fn. 88.
321. A Yiddish expression which means: "A human being is only a human being and not an angel."
322. TB *Yoma* 69b.
323. TY *Yoma* 1:1(5a).
324. TB *Menachos* 29a, *Ein Yaakov, Chidushei Gaonim* in the name of the Rambam. It is noteworthy that these three main parts of the *Beis Hamikdosh* correspond to the emotions, intellect and instincts.

As we move closer to the end of world history, we simply must try harder, even if it is very difficult, so that the final resolution will come through the more pleasant means: through our efforts, rather than perforce. Let us not lull ourselves into a false sense of security or business-as-usual attitude. If, *chas v'shalom*, we do not take the initiative and strive to go beyond self, we have only ourselves to blame.

May Hashem grant that this small book help us all understand better how to fulfill our unique and absolutely vital Jewish destiny.

The Key is in our hands. Please, may we use it.

---

325. *Shemos* 25:8.

XXIV
Conclusion for Jews Unfamiliar with Torah

Almost everyone is fascinated by elaborately or intricately constructed machines, be they giant space ships, jumbo jets or luxury motor cars, fully equipped with all the accessories. Modern life excites us with the wonders of technological progress.

But if we turn our attention away from all the machines for just a moment and look deeply into ourselves, we will realize that issues of personal happiness and fulfillment are still unanswered by all that swirls around us. Even with push-button this and automated that, easy comfort here and whirlwind travel there, we still peer out from behind our two eyes wondering where all this is leading us. Somewhere or nowhere? What does life mean? What is the purpose of it all?

What has perhaps struck us secularly-educated Jews after reading this small book is that there is a system more intricate than all the machines put together; one which allows us to make sense out of existence. With this system, we can unequivocally understand that there is a purpose, that there is a goal, that there *is* a greater dimension to life. And — most importantly — there are precise, practical means of achieving this ultimate destiny.

Already, for over three thousand five hundred years, our ancestors have tenaciously held on to this system, sacrificing their lives, fortunes and comfort, rather than abandon what they knew to be true. Up until today, we may have been unaware of what it was that kept them so stubbornly committed. But now, through seeing many of Judaism's major concepts integrated into a clear, unified theme, perhaps we have felt a surge of justifiable pride in the deeper reality of being Jewish. Perhaps we have even been a bit amazed by the wisdom and profundity of our great Torah heritage. And perhaps we have come to the conclusion that it's time we seriously learned more about Judaism.

If so, then an important next step can be taken. We should seek out Torah Jews who are putting this system into action, and they can help us learn how the power and dynamic of Torah Judaism can be integrated into our lives. For growing beyond self is both a challenging and exhilarating experience, tapping into the maximum potential that life has to offer. We all want to get the very most that we can out of life. Torah Judaism enthusiastically supports this approach, extending it to its most logical, joyful and meaningful fruition — the Infinite.

Epilogue: Success!

What is the Jewish definition of success?

Before reading this book, we probably would have answered, depending on our backgrounds:

- Finishing the *Shas*[326]
- Earning great wealth
- Leading a citizen's campaign that stops government corruption
- Having healthy, wonderful children
- Being able to travel the whole world
- Having the top reputation in town
- Forcing the big corporations to improve their anti-pollution standards
- Giving great sums of money to *tzedoka*[327]

---

326. There is no question that this is an extremely admirable achievement. But we are taught, in the name of Rabbi Yisroel Salanter, that it is easier to finish the *Shas* than to change one bad character trait.

327. We are referring to a situation in which the person is very wealthy, in which case he has a far greater potential of lovingkindness to fulfill.

- Being elected to any important governmental, professional, civic or Jewish communal position
- Discovering a new medical cure, mathematical formula, invention . . .
- Buying that "dream" home, with a tennis court and a swimming pool
- "My son, the doctor"
- Renovating an entire inner-city slum into a model community
- Being promoted to partner, executive vice-president, etc.

After reading this book, we now know that none of these fulfill the real Jewish definition of success, even if we Jews *are* successful in doing them.

Jewish success means one thing and one thing only:

Making Hashem more manifest in the world, as it says, "*Shema Yisroel* . . . ,"[328] i.e., bringing the Infinite into the finite. Or, seen from the other side of the coin: making the finite like the Infinite, moving self to beyond-self.

Why is this our true success? Because the world was created only in order for us to earn the infinite. When we are making Hashem more manifest, we are, in effect, achieving truth, good, purity, wholeness, the infinite.[329]

And this success is a discernible reality, for Judaism is not a religion or a set of traditions. Nor is it a philosophy or a system of ethics. Judaism is a way of life. And in order for it to be a way of life, it actually has to happen. In other words, Hashem

---

328. See Chap. VIII.
329. See Chart C: Basic Dichotomies, p. 236.

224 / *Self Beyond Self*

actually has to be more in this world because of our behavior — our thoughts, our words, our actions.

This book has endeavored to take the more abstract terminology and give it a clear, precise definition: moving from self to beyond-self is the practical expression of moving the finite toward the Infinite. By applying **Torah, acts of lovingkindness** and *Avodah* to our *mind, emotions* and *instincts*, we counter **arrogance, jealousy** and **lust** and create *humility, selfless giving* and *transcendence of physicality*. As best as we could,[330] we have transformed our finite selves into infinite-like beings. Succinctly stated, this dynamic process of going from self to beyond-self gains for us our only true and real success.

Hashem has fixed both the challenge/problem of life and its solution[331] — all for our benefit and advantage. As is well known, "If you're not part of the solution, you're part of the problem!" But *now* we clearly see both. With this realization, we

---

330. Several points are important to mention here:
   1) Ultimate success is never in our own hands. All we can do is try our best to go beyond self; the rest is in Hashem's hands. See further Chap. XIX.
   2) So long as the person is maximizing his own potential, he never has to be concerned whether others are doing more. See further pp. 176-7.
   3) Since we are generally subjective about ourselves, we can err in judging whether we are making our best effort. Therefore, it is essential that we include sage, Torah-rabbinic advice in our self-assessment. *Cf. Pirkei Avos* 1:16.

331. See our discussion, Chap. II, pp. 7-11. Just in case it is not already 100% clear, we want to add a simple note:
   Let no one imagine that now that he clearly knows the main problems of life, he can go and work out his own solutions. Hashem so intricately constructed the problems that there is no other way to solve them other than by using His solutions. Just as the manufacturer knows best how his product works, Hashem — the Chief Manufacturer — obviously knows what operating instructions (Torah) are best for His product (the creation).

can drink another *l'chaim* and this time be joyously grateful to Hashem for the opportunity to turn all the problems of life into solutions, all the ephemerality of life into an unending reality.

Postscript

We began this book with the chapter, "What's in It for Me?", for it is a given that people naturally act in their own self-interest. The major thrust of the book, however, seems to fly in the face of this given, for we are advocating that people go beyond self and, therefore, apparently deny their self-interest.

Nevertheless, it should really be quite clear, through all we have presented, that it is in the self's most ultimate self-interest to go beyond self, for this is its greatest achievement and fruition. In other words, since the self's goal is to gain infinity and since going beyond self is the way we can achieve this goal, then it follows that it is in the self's best interest to go beyond self.

Now "What's in it for me" means that I can gain the most if I cease to be concerned about finite *me* and focus, instead, on the *me* that can go beyond, the *me* that can reach toward the infinite. For this *me* is the greatest accomplishment that I can ever achieve, and for this purpose I was created.

Remember: this is not a denial of *me* or self. On the contrary, self *must* be maintained and properly cared for so that it can then be dynamically and wholeheartedly directed beyond self. Torah Jews enjoy good food, dress nicely, get married, have a family and make a living like everyone else. The difference is the ultimate *goal* of all this effort: Is it for the finite or for the infinite? The Torah and every *mitzvah* direct us to the infinite, ensuring that every moment of time and every particle of matter will reach their highest reality. *Me* is the crucial component, crucial precisely because of its potential and opportunity to become part of something infinitely greater.

Part Seven:
Internalizing Mechanisms

Included in this section are various means to help internalize the ideas presented in this book.

Chart A: **The Self—Beyond-Self Continuum**

Chart B: **The Integrated Dynamic of the Self—Beyond-Self Continuum**

Chart C: **Basic Dichotomies of Life**

Chart D: **Summary Review of *Self Beyond Self*: The Threefold Key to Being Jewish**

Appendix A: **Special Prayer**

Appendix B: **Love Your Neighbor**

Appendix C: **The Fourth Component**

Chart A
The Self—Beyond-Self Continuum
(This Chart is explained in Chapter II, pages 5-11.)

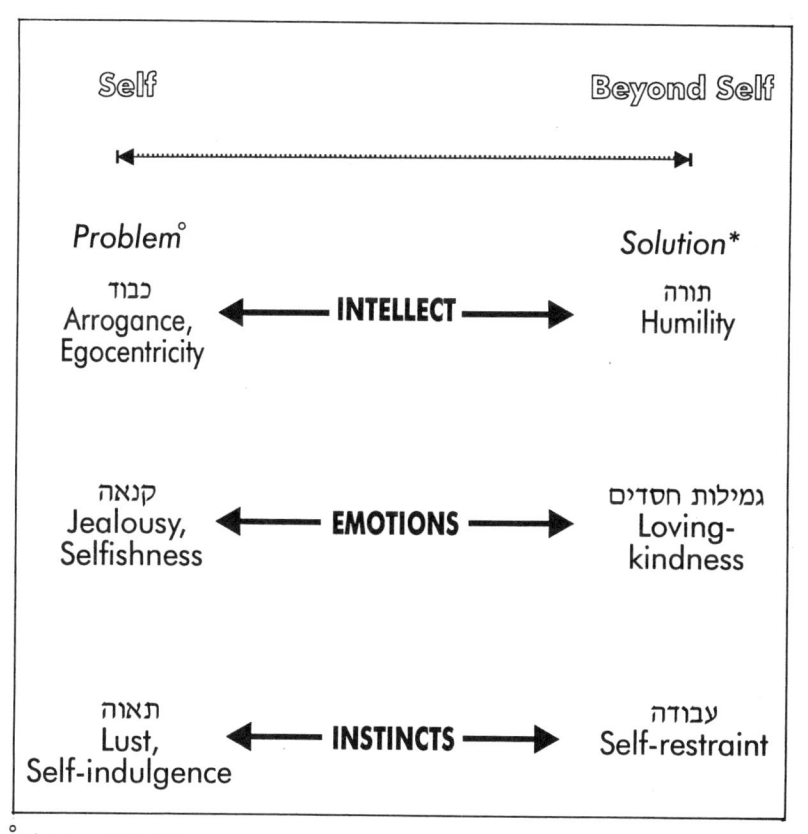

Self   Beyond Self

Problem°   *Solution**

כבוד
Arrogance, Egocentricity ⟵ **INTELLECT** ⟶ תורה
Humility

קנאה
Jealousy, Selfishness ⟵ **EMOTIONS** ⟶ גמילות חסדים
Loving-kindness

תאוה
Lust, Self-indulgence ⟵ **INSTINCTS** ⟶ עבודה
Self-restraint

°*Pirkei Avos 4:21 (28)*   **Pirkei Avos 1:2*

232 / *Self Beyond Self*

Chart B
The Integrated Dynamic of the Self—Beyond-Self Continuum

The continuum discussed in this book and diagramed in Chart A is not merely linear. In reality, all three parts of the human being work together. Obviously, the brain is the command center for everything, with its three major parts controlling the intellect, emotions and instincts.[332]

Chart B on pages 234-5 represents this interaction. For example, on the "self" side, intellect moves into the instincts realm when the person thinks impure thoughts. For example, on the "beyond-self" side, instincts move into the emotions realm when the person acts faithfully.

This chart also highlights the overall qualities and failings produced by each polarity. The beyond-self person radiates wisdom, benevolence and bodily purity, whereas the self person manifests three great evils: the evil tongue, the evil eye and the evil inclination. We note that "evil" has been defined as

---

332. The three parts of the brain — cerebrum, limbic system and central core — very roughly compare to the intellect, emotions and instincts, with of course a great deal of overlap among the three.

meaning "substandard," i.e., the person is behaving in a way that is below what he is capable of and what is expected of him.[333] In the terminology which we are using, he has chosen self over beyond-self, a decision which an aware Jew will realize is considerably substandard.

Again, we emphasize that everyone is somewhere on the continuum between self and beyond-self.[334] It is very rare to find either extreme: the perfectly self-only person or the perfectly beyond-self person. We all are between these two, and the sole question is: Will we use the system which Hashem gave us — Torah and *mitzvos* — to reach towards the ultimate dimension of beyond-self rather than live our lives predominantly focused on self?

This challenge is the purpose of the human's creation, for in this way we can earn eternity/infinity through our own persistent effort. **Remember this basic analogy: finite is to infinite as self is to beyond-self.** As self — which is finite — moves to beyond-self, it is doing, practically speaking, the most that it can to move towards the infinite.

---

333. Rabbi Dr. Eli Munk, *The Seven Days of the Beginning*, Feldheim Publishers, Jerusalem/New York, 1974, p. 167.
334. See Chap. II, pp. 6-7.

234 / Self Beyond Self

The Integrated
The Self—Beyond-
Self ←——————————————————

Problem

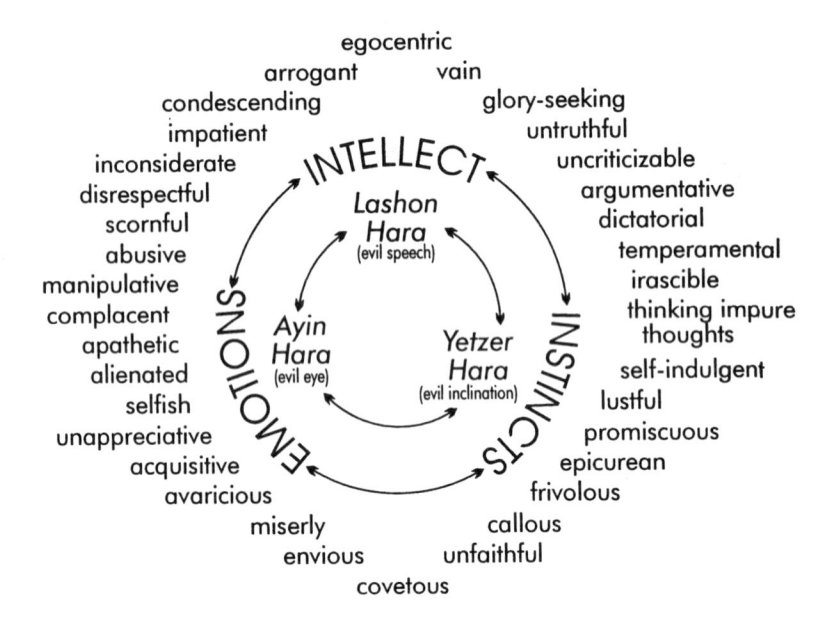

```
                    egocentric
            arrogant         vain
        condescending    glory-seeking
           impatient        untruthful
        inconsiderate  INTELLECT  uncriticizable
         disrespectful              argumentative
            scornful    Lashon     dictatorial
             abusive     Hara      temperamental
          manipulative (evil speech) irascible
           complacent                thinking impure
            apathetic  Ayin    Yetzer  thoughts
            alienated  Hara    Hara    self-indulgent
             selfish (evil eye)(evil inclination) lustful
         unappreciative                promiscuous
            acquisitive              epicurean
              avaricious           frivolous
                  miserly        callous
                   envious    unfaithful
                       covetous
```

(EMOTIONS / INSTINCTS labels around the circle)

Dynamic of Self Continuum

┈┈┈┈┈┈┈┈► **Beyond Self**

Solution

```
                    self-effacing
              humble      respectful
           patient            truthful
       considerate               forgiving
    compassionate  INTELLECT   unpretentious
       thoughtful                conscientious
        empathetic   Wisdom       studious
          amenable                  prudent
           amicable                  diligent
         cooperative                  responsible
           altruistic  Benevolence   thinking pure
            generous                  thoughts
          kindhearted       Purity
           hospitable               disciplined
             EMOTIONS              law-abiding
              genuine    INSTINCTS  self-controlled
               grateful            modest
                spirited        abstemious
                  selfless   unostentatious
                      faithful
```

Chart C
Basic Dichotomies of Life

This chart shows some of the very many dichotomies of life according to Judaism, adding the self—beyond-self dichotomy. Extensive explanation would be necessary to adequately cover each entry on this chart. In brief, we can say simply that, Jewishly, free will is the basis of life, for a person must be able to act independently in order to be judged on whether he earned his own eternity. And, obviously, for choice to exist, there must be at least two alternatives.

In actuality, at the top of the list (which we did not include) is Hashem (right side) and the counterforce (left side), which He purposefully put into the world to give us our test. This counterforce is sometimes called the *sitra achra*, the "other side," and its job is to pull us away from Hashem, again to give us choice.

Although each dichotomy is obviously different from the other, it should be clear that by listing them under each other, we can see that, in essence, they are really very similar. For by achieving truth, we are also achieving the infinite, wholeness, positivism, happiness, and so on.

Basic Dichotomies of Life

Challenge/
Problem *Solution*

Challenge/Problem		Solution
Falsehood	←-----→	Truth
Evil	←-----→	Good
Impure	←-----→	Pure
Profane	←-----→	Holy
*Physical	←-----→	Spiritual
*Body	←-----→	Soul
Finite	←-----→	Infinite
Limitedness	←-----→	Unlimitedness
Parts	←-----→	Whole
Disunity	←-----→	Unity
Sadness	←-----→	Happiness
Death	←-----→	Life
Darkness	←-----→	Light
Negativism	←-----→	Positivism
Yetzer Harah (evil inclination)	←-----→	Yetzer Hatov (good inclination)
Not for the sake of Heaven	←-----→	For the sake of Heaven
*Self	←-----→	Beyond Self

*When used solely for itself

Chart D
Summary Review of *Self Beyond Self* in Chart Form

The charts below summarize all the material covered by this book, placing each part of each threesome into its appropriate category: 1 = emotions; 2 = instincts; 3 = intellect.

As explained on several occasions, a particular part can also have within it all three categories. But once it is in a specific triad, it will be focusing on one of the three categories. For example, in the subject of "Signs" in Part Two, *tefillin* are under the intellect category. However, they also also have within them the other two categories: emotions, in that the *shel yad* is opposite the heart, and instincts, in that the right head strap is required, according to one opinion, to go down to the *bris*.[335]

> **Note:**
> Page numbers in regular type: 123
> Footnote numbers in bold type: **123**

---

335. *Kitzur Shulchan Aruch* 10:13. See *Shulchan Aruch, Orach Chaim,* 27:11, *Mishnah Berurah* 41.

	Subject	1	2	3	pp/**fn.**
Part One:	Solution	Lovingkindness	Self-restraint	Humility	10
In The Beginning	Challenge/Problem	Jealousy	Lust	Arrogance	8
	Spiritual Forces	*Ruach*	*Nefesh*	*Neshamah*	1
	Human Components	Emotions	Instincts	Intellect	6

	Genealogy	Avraham	Yitzchak	Yaakov	16
Part Two:		Tent	Altar	Ladder	16
The Fundamentals of Jewish Identity	History	Kayin and Hevel	Adom & Chava	Earth & Moon	24
		Kayin and Hevel	The Flood	The Dispersion	24
	Qualities	Doing lovingkindness	Shamefaced	Compassionate	26
	Signs	*Shabbos*	*Bris milah*	*Tefillin*	34
	Woman's Power	Separating *challah*	Family purity	*Shabbos* lights	53

	Major Crimes	Murder	Adultery	Idolatry	66
	Unification	Heart	Being	Substance	68
	Identity Savers	Names	Dress	Language	82
Part Three:	Three Pillars	Acts of lovingkindness	*Avodah*	Torah	90
A System Vital for Life	Blessing a new baby	Good deeds	Bridal canopy	Torah	**116**
	Within Lovingkindness	With money and body	To both poor and rich	To both living and dead	93
	Within *Avodah*	*Shacharis*	*Minchah*	*Ma'ariv*	95
	Within Torah	*Nezikim*	*Pirkei Avos*	*Berachos*	96
	Mitzvos	*Eidos*	*Chukim*	*Mishpatim*	**123**

	Rosh Hashanah	*Malchuyos*	*Zichronos*	*Shofaros*	106
Part Four:	*Unesane-tokef*	*Tzedoka*	Prayer	*Teshuvah*	108
Exemplary Celebrations	Holidays	*Pesach*	*Shavous*	*Succos*	114
	The *Seder*	*Pesach*	*Matzah*	*Maror*	119
	Purim	Gifts to the poor and a friend	Festive meal	*Megillah*	127

240 / Self Beyond Self

	Subject	1	2	3	pp/**fn**.
Part Five: Keys to Eternity	Behavior Indicators	*Keese*	*Kose*	*Ka'as*	139
	Avraham	Goodly eye	Abstaining nature	Humble spirit	140
	Bilam	Evil eye	Licentious	Arrogant	140
	Yaakov / Esav	Presents	Prayer	War preparation	140
	Three-twined cord	*Mezuzah*	*Tzitzis*	*Tefillin*	141
	Micah	Acts of lovingkindness	Judgement	Walk humbly	141
	World Continues	Peace	Judgement	Truth	142
	Negative behavior	Evil eye	*Yetzer hara*	Hating others	**191**
		Jealousy	Lust	Arrogance	143
	Jewish People	*B'nei Yisroel*	*Kohanim*	*Levi'im*	143
	Three Crowns	*Keser Kehunah*	*Keser Malchus*	*Keser* Torah	147
	Shabbos Meals	Travail before *Mashiach's* coming	Rule of *Gehenom*	War of *Gog* and *Magog*	150
	Three Keys	Rain	Birth	Resurrection	160
	Three Presents	World to Come	*Eretz Yisroel*	Torah	169
	Sabbatical Year	Land open to all and debts cancelled	Refraining from food production	Time to learn Torah	181
	Destruction of the First Temple	Murder	Adultery	Idol Worship	181
	Avraham and the Egyptian Bondage	Returned captives	Questioned about the Land	Used Torah scholars in war	185
	Redemption	"*Pakode*"	Appoint judges	"*Anochi*"	186
	Mashiach	Ingathering of the exiles	Rebuilding *Beis Hamikdosh*	Kingship of *Beis Dovid*	189

Appendix A
Special Prayer

The following prayer is printed in many Hebrew *siddurim* after the weekday *Shemonah Esreh*, in the middle of the concluding paragraph, "My God, guard my tongue from evil . . . ." It turns out that this prayer focuses on the three major problem areas discussed throughout this book, beseeching Divine assistance to avoid:

1. Jealousy
2. Anger (which derives from arrogance)
3. The evil inclination (most often referring to lust[336])

יְהִי רָצוֹן מִלְּפָנֶיךָ ה' אֱלֹקַי וֵאלֹקֵי אֲבוֹתַי, שֶׁלֹּא תַעֲלֶה קִנְאַת אָדָם עָלַי וְלֹא קִנְאָתִי עַל אֲחֵרִים, וְשֶׁלֹּא אֶכְעוֹס הַיּוֹם וְשֶׁלֹּא אַכְעִיסְךָ, וְתַצִּילֵנִי מִיֵּצֶר הָרָע, וְתֵן בְּלִבִּי הַכְנָעָה וַעֲנָוָה. מַלְכֵּנוּ וֵאלֹקֵינוּ, יַחֵד שִׁמְךָ בְּעוֹלָמֶךָ, בְּנֵה עִירְךָ, יַסֵּד בֵּיתְךָ וְשַׁכְלֵל הֵיכָלֶךָ, וְקַבֵּץ קִבּוּץ גָּלֻיּוֹת וּפְדֵה צֹאנֶךָ וְשַׂמַּח עֲדָתֶךָ:

---

336. *Cf.* Chap. XVI fn. 191, Chap. XXIII, fn. 322.

Translation:

May it be Your will, O Lord, my God and God of my fathers, that no one should be jealous of me nor I, of others, and that I should not become angry today nor make You angry. And save me from the evil inclination and make my inner being submissive and humble.

Our King and our God, unify Your Name in Your world, build Your city [Yerushalayim], establish Your House and perfect Your Temple, and bring about the ingathering of the exiles. Redeem Your flock and cause Your congregation to rejoice.

Appendix B
Love Your Neighbor

Going beyond self in giving to others has endless opportunities. To give the reader a small sampling, we quote from the book Love Your Neighbor *(with the kind permission of the author, Rabbi Zelig Pliskin) forty examples under just the one* mitzvah *of loving your neighbor as yourself* (Vayikra 19:18). *As mentioned previously, the book has over four hundred pages which cover innumerable other acts of lovingkindness which can help us grow constantly beyond self.*[337]

To love one's fellow man as oneself is not merely a lofty ideal devoid of practical significance. Rather, it is a Torah commandment with specific obligations and restrictions. In every encounter with other people you have an opportunity either to fulfill or violate this commandment. **It is impossible to enumerate every single aspect of this commandment since it encompasses so many details.** [Emphasis added.] Listed below are some of the fundamental details:

The general rule for this commandment is that anything

---

337. See *Love Your Neighbor*, pp. 302-12, for the sources of each example and illustrative stories.

you would want others to do for you, you should do for others.

You fulfill this commandment when you

1) visit someone who is ill.
2) comfort someone who is mourning.
3) offer someone assistance in enabling him to get married.
4) help a bride and groom rejoice.
5) are hospitable to guests.
6) attend someone's funeral and help in any aspect of the burial.
7) lend money or any other article to someone.
8) pray for someone's well-being.
9) forgive others for wronging you.
10) teach others Torah.
11) greet others with a friendly countenance.
12) give someone change for a larger coin.
13) run to tell someone good news.
14) correct someone who does something that others will consider odd, for this will prevent others from looking down at him.

All the more so this commandment obligates you to correct someone if you see him transgressing. If someone is drowning and you fail to try to save him, it would be a gross understatement to say that you do not love him. Your obligation to save someone from drowning spiritually is even greater. As the *Midrash* states: "All love that does not include mutual correction is not true love."

15) A craftsman fulfills this commandment if he has in mind that he is making his product for the benefit of the person who will use it, and not merely as a source of income.
16) A doctor fulfills this commandment when he heals someone.

This commandment obligates you to

17) supply others with *kosher* food if they are unable to obtain it themselves.
18) protect others from injury.
19) share the feelings of sorrow and suffering of others.
20) feel happiness for the good fortune of others.
21) warn others about possible loss or damage.
22) pick up someone's garment if you see it lying on the floor.
23) give others helpful advice whenever possible.
24) cheer someone up when you see that he is sad or lonely.

25) write letters to your relatives in other cities so that they should not worry about you.
26) return books to their proper place in a library, synagogue, or yeshiva so that others will be able to find them without delay.

27) This commandment forbids you to rejoice at the misfortunes of others.
28) This commandment forbids you to unnecessarily make noise that would disturb the sleep of others.
29) This commandment forbids you to curse others.
30) This commandment forbids you to cause someone pain or unpleasantness through your actions or words. Some examples are: spitting in someone's presence; banging a hammer within the hearing range of someone with a headache; smoking when it annoys someone; scraping a chair along the floor, causing it to make a screeching noise; cracking knuckles; slamming doors; talking in an excessively loud voice.
31) If you see someone suffering, this commandment obligates you to save him from further suffering. Moreover, even before a person suffers, if you are able to save him from future suffering, you are obligated to do so.

A person who is sensitive to the feelings of others will relinquish his seat to a latecomer to a meeting at which all the seats are already taken. Someone who arrives late might feel uncomfortable to look for a chair himself, while a person who came earlier feels more at home.

32) A person who fulfills this commandment will not be jealous of the good fortunes of others.

The idea has been expressed that the meaning of "as yourself" in this verse refers to the type of fellow man. It is not difficult to befriend and love a person who far exceeds you in wealth or prestige. In the same way, if a person is of a far lower status, you would show warmth to him out of pity. However, the Torah requires you to befriend a fellow man who is "as yourself," of the same social and financial status. You must overcome any feelings of competition or jealousy and show sincere friendship even in this case.

33) A person who fulfills this commandment will not speak *loshon hara* about others, for no one wants others to speak *loshon hara* about him.
34) A person who fulfills this commandment will always judge others favorably, for if

he himself would do something improper, he would want others to judge him favorably and find merit in his actions.

35) A person who fulfills this commandment will not keep people waiting because of him.

36) A person who fulfills this commandment will try to save others needless exertion.

37) A person who fulfills this commandment will do all he can to give others pleasure. As the Vilna Gaon wrote: "A great part of the Torah is concerned with a person's bringing happiness to others."

38) A person should be very careful not to grow angry at others, for when a person is angry at others he not only feels no love for them, buy may even hate them and wish them harm.

39) Our parents are included in our obligation to love others as ourselves. The same applies to one's spouse, children, and brothers and sisters. Although this might seem self-evident, it is still necessary to mention since some people are careful to do *chesed* for strangers but forget that they have a similar, and even greater, obligation toward their relatives.

40) Many people are willing to spend much money and effort to fulfill other *mitzvos*, but when it comes to helping others, the smallest amount of effort or expense will deter them. Therefore, whenever a person has a question about his obligation to help others, he should not rely on his own judgment. Rather, he should consult a halachic authority.

Appendix C
The Fourth Component

Anyone familiar with Torah Judaism knows that numbers play a significant role in its methodology. This book has shown how important the number three is in explaining Judaism's goals and structure. While a detailed examination is beyond the scope of this present work, we would like to mention briefly how the number four fits into our basic thesis. Our purpose is to further demonstrate the centrality of our Threefold Key and its usefulness in elucidating Judaism.

It occurs often in Torah numerology that a number is used to join together the series that preceded it. Thus, for example, three can be used to join together one and two, very much on the model of thesis, antithesis and synthesis. The last in a series combines with that which went before it to synthesize the entire series.

The Hebrew terminology for what we are describing is called *kollel*, which here means "all-inclusive," "all-embracing." The number is serving to collect together — *kollel* — whatever came before it.

Applying this concept to our Threefold Key and the number four, we maintain that the fourth component is the composite of all the prior three. For example and without elaboration, we can say that after Avraham, Yitzchak and Yaakov, the fourth component is Dovid Hamelech, for Dovid as representative of the *Mashiach* embodies all the qualities of the *Avos* in one dynamic entity.[338] This idea is further reflected in the fourth head on the letter *shin* of the *tefillin* and the fourth element of the "Celestial Chariot."

We are taught that the first *Beis Hamikdosh* was destroyed because of murder, sexual offenses and idolatry, and the second, because of causeless hatred.[339] This last reason can be interpreted as a fourth, all-encompassing component, for underlying the three major transgressions can be a thoughtless self-centeredness that ignores everyone and everything, all propriety and all restraint. In effect, the person can end up worshipping himself, wantonly indulging his instincts and even eliminating all others who get in his way. This deeper level of human fallibility is what can cause an exile which has lasted 2000 years.

Indeed, we can say that this fourth exile which we are now in — Edom — is the culmination of the three that preceded it. As the Maharal explains, the current exile contains all the elements that were subverted by the prior three exiles: Babylonia — body/instincts; Media/Persia — emotions; Greece — intellect.[340]

As a final example, mentioned also in our Conclusion for

---

338. *Cf. Shmuel* II 23:8; *TB Moed Katan* 16b.
339. See Chap. XX, pp. 181-3.
340. See *Gevuros Hashem*, B'nei Brak, 1980, p. 51. The Maharal uses the term *nefesh* for emotions, i.e., inner essence.

Torah-aware Jews, the three main articles of the Temple represented the human's three main elements: the *Aron* — emotions; the *Menorah* — intellect; the *Shulchan* — instincts. Together with these inside the Temple was a fourth object: the Golden Altar, upon which the *ketores* was burnt. This incense came to atone for *loshon hara*, which can derive from the misuse of any one or all of the human's three parts. The Golden Altar and the *ketores* symbolized the correction and proper use of our intellect, emotions and instincts, creating an exhilarating, harmonious and transcendental world.

This concept of *kollel*, therefore, shows how a fourth component actually represents the coalescence of our Threefold Key into one entity. As such, this explanation underscores the importance of our Key as an effective tool in understanding Judaism.

GLOSSARY

A

Abarbanel: Rabbi Yitzchak (1437-1508), great Torah scholar and statesman; wrote *Zevach Pesach* on the *Hagadah*

Aderes Eliyahu: commentary on the *Chumash* by the Gra.

Adom: Adam, the first man

Aharon: Aaron, the older brother of Moses and the first High Priest of the Jewish People

Akeidah: the binding of Yitzchak (see *Bereishis* 22:1-19)

Aleinu: lit., "On us"; prayer which ends the three daily services

Aley Shor: book on Jewish thought and ethics by Rabbi Shlomo Volbe

Amidah: formal prayers, said in a barely audible voice, while standing

Anochi: Hebrew word for "I"

Aron: the Ark in which was contained the two stone Tablets of the Ten Commandments

Arbes: cooked chickpeas, traditionally served at a *shalom zachor*

Arizal: acronym for Rabbi Yitzchak Luria (1534-1572), who explained many of the concepts and ideas in the *Kabbalah*

Avinu: lit., our forefather; see *Avos*

Avodah: lit., "service," referring to the offerings of the *karbonos* by the *kohanim* in the *Beis Hamikdosh*

Avos: the Forefathers, referring to Avraham, Yitzchak and Yaakov

Avos d'Rebbi Nossan: a greatly expanded version of *Pirkei Avos*

Avraham: Abraham

Ayin Hara: lit., "evil eye"; the negative force resulting from viewing others enviously

B

Ba'al HaTurim: see Tur

Bertinoro: see Harav m'Bertinoro

Batei Kenesses: houses of worship

Batei Midrash: houses of study

Bayis: "house," herein referring to the hardened leather compartment of the *tefillin* in which Torah inscriptions are placed and strapped down on the head and arm

Beis Dovid: lit., "the House of David," referring to the direct lineage from King David to the *Mashiach*

Beis Hamikdosh: the Holy Temple, located in Jerusalem and twice destroyed by invading armies

Bemidbar: lit., "in the desert," the fourth Book of the *Chumash*, referred to as *Numbers* in English

Bemidbar Rabba: a *Midrash* on the Book of *Bemidbar*

Ben Ish Chai: Rabbi Yosef Chaim from Bagdad (1834-1908), important Torah scholar, author and community leader

Beracha(chos): blessing(s)

Bereishis: lit., "in the beginning," the first Book of the *Chumash*, referred to as *Genesis* in English

Bereishis Rabba: a *Midrash* on the Book of *Bereishis*

Birchos Hashachar: sixteen morning blessings which give detailed praise for the awakening process each day

Birkas Hamazone: the grace after meals when bread is eaten

B'nei Yissachar: book on *Shabbos* and the holidays by Rabbi Tzvi Elimelech of Dinov (d. 1841)

B'nei Brak: a city of Torah-observant Jews near Tel Aviv, Israel

Bris Milah: Jewish circumcision

C

Chaim: life

Challah: a portion of the dough which the Torah requires to be given to the *kohain* but which today, in the absence of the Temple, is burned

Chametz: leavened product; a Jew is prohibited from owning or eating *chametz* during the seven (or eight) days of *Pesach*

Chareidi: strongly Torah-observant

Chasid: a kindly, pious and devoted Jew; since the middle 18th c. also refers to a Jew who follows a particular Chasidic sect

Chas v'shalom: lit., pity and peace!; may Heaven spare us!

Chava: Eve

Chazal: acronym for "our Wise Men, may their memory be for a blessing," referring to the Sages

Chesed: lovingkindness

Chet: sin, with the connotation of "missing the mark"

Chidushei Haradal: commentary on *Midrash Rabba* by Rabbi David Luria (1795-1855)

Chofetz Chaim: Rabbi Yisroel Meir Kagan (1839-1933), very righteous and scholarly leader of the Jewish People; called the Chofetz Chaim ("seek life") after the title of his first book, which deals with the laws of *loshon hara*

Chukim: "statutes," Torah laws whose reasons are obscure

Chumash: the Five Books of Moses, the Pentateuch

Chutzpah(-dik): audacity (audacious), effrontery, impudence

D

Davening: praying

Dayeinu: "It is sufficient for us," refrain used in the *Hagadah*

Derech Hashem: *The Way of God*, classic logical explication of Judaism by Rabbi Moshe Chaim Luzzatto (1707-1747)

Devorim: lit., "words" or "things," the fifth Book of the *Chumash*, referred to as *Deuteronomy* in English

Dovid Hamelech: King David

E

Edom: the Hebrew term for the Roman exile, which began at the destruction of the Second Temple in 70 c.e. and has continued until today

Eidos: lit., "testimonies," *mitzvos* relating to the historical experiences of the Jewish People

Eitz Yosef: commentary on *Midrash Rabba* and *Pirkei Avos* by Rabbi Chanoch Zundel ben Yosef (d.1867)

Erev: evening; also the day before *Shabbos/Yom Tov*

Eretz Yisroel: the Land of Israel

Esrog: citron, fruit used as part of the Four Species on *Succos*

Even Ha'ezer: lit., "the help-stone," the section of the *Shulchan Aruch* dealing with the laws of marriage and divorce

Even Sh'leimah: book collecting various ideas and explanations on Torah topics by the Gra

F

Frum: Yiddish for "religious," "Torah-observant"

G

Gan Aden: the Garden of Eden

Gehenom: Hell, i.e., the place furthest from Hashem

Gemachim: organizations/individuals that publicly do *gemilut chassadim*

Gematria: the use of the numerical values of Hebrew letters (and, consequently, words) to compare words of equivalent values

Gemora: the Talmud

Gemilut chassadim: the bestowal of acts of lovingkindness

Gog and Magog, The war of: cataclysmic war preceding the *Mashiach*'s arrival

Guf: body

Gra: acronym for the Gaon Rabbi Eliyahu ben Shlomo Zalman of Vilna (1720-1797); called "Gaon" (genius) because of his extraordinary intellect and vast knowledge of Torah

H

Hagadah: book used at the *Pesach Seder*, which includes the various *mitzvos* of the evening — the recital of the Exodus from Egypt, *matzah*, the four cups of wine, the bitter herbs, etc.

Halachic: of or pertaining to Torah law

Hamantashen: the triangle-shaped pastry eaten on *Purim*, symbolic of Haman's three-cornered hat

Har Hamoriah: Mount Moriah, the place from which the teaching ("morah") originates; the Temple Mount in Jerusalem

Har Sinai: Mount Sinai

Harav m'Bertinoro: Rabbi Ovadiah from Bertinoro, Italy (c. 1450-1510), famous commentator on the *Mishnah*

Hashem: lit., "the Name," referring to God and used in place of the ineffable Holy Four-letter Name of God

Havdalah: lit., "Distinction," referring to the ceremony on Saturday evening, marking the distinction between the ending of the holy *Shabbos* and the entrance of the regular work-week

Hester panim: lit., "the hidden face" of Hashem, when He, so to speak, hides from us His direct involvement in our lives

Hevel: Abel

Hilchos: the laws of . . . (referring to different sections of the Rambam's *Mishnah Torah*)

I

Ibn Ezra: Rabbi Avraham (1089-1164) from Spain, author of an important commentary on the *Chumash*

Infinite: when capitalized, refers to Hashem; when lower case, refers to a dimension which is indefinitely great, unbounded, unlimited

K

Ka'as: anger

Kabbalah: the deeper, esoteric explanations of the Torah

Kaddish: lit., "sanctification," the proclamation of Hashem's power and greatness, said in a *minyon* (10 men) at various stages during the *davening* and after Torah study

Kara Soton: lit., "tear (i.e., remove) the hinderer," i.e., the force that tries to stop us from observing Hashem's *mitzvos*

Karbonos: the animal offerings on the outside Altar of the *Beis Hamikdosh*

Kashrus: the laws of kosher (proper) food

Kayin: Cain

Keese: pocket

Kehunah: the priesthood

Keser: crown

Ketores: the incense used in the *Beis Hamikdosh*

Kiddush: the blessings said, usually over wine, to sanctify *Shabbos*

Kilayim: prohibited mixture of diverse seeds, e.g., grains and legumes, when planting

Kinyon: halachic process of transferring possession or ownership

Kipa: head covering (often referred to as *yarmulka*)

Kodesh Hakodoshim: lit., "the Holy of Holies," the most sanctified area of the Temple which contained the *Aron* and the Ten Commandments and which no one was allowed to enter except the *Kohain Gadol* on *Yom Kippur*

Kohain: priest

Kohain Gadol: High Priest

Kohanim: priests

Kose: cup

Kosel: lit., "wall," referring to the Western Wall of the Temple Mount, located in Jerusalem and built originally by King Solomon, with subsequent generations adding further tiers of stone

K'rias Shema: the recitation of the *Shema* at its required times

L

L'chaim: lit., "To life!", a toast, usually accompanied by a drink of some alcoholic beverage

Levi'im: levites, assistants to the *kohanim*

L'mehadrin: doing a *mitzvah* in the most precise, careful and quality fashion

Loshon Hara: lit., "evil tongue," derogatory speech (forbidden even if true)

M

Ma'ariv: the evening prayer; (also the name of a contemporary Israeli evening newspaper)

Ma'aseros: tithes on produce grown in *Eretz Yisroel*

Machzor: the special prayer book used on *Rosh Hashanah* and *Yom Kippur*

Magen Dovid: lit., "the shield of David," the six-pointed star of David, formed by two opposite overlapping equilateral triangles

Maharal: acronym for Rabbi Yehudah Loew ben Bezalel (1512-1609), who lived in Prague and wrote profoundly and extensively on Jewish thought and philosophy

Maharsha: acronym for Rabbi Shmuel Eliezer Edels (1555-1631) of Cracow, Poland, who wrote an erudite and comprehensive commentary on the *Gemora*

Maharzu: acronym for Rabbi Zeev Wolf Einhorn (end of 19th c.) who wrote a commentary on *Midrash Rabba*

Malach Hamoves: the Angel of Death

Mal'achim: angels, messengers

Malchuyos: Kingship, referring to the absolute dominion of Hashem, and the name given to one of the sections of the *Rosh Hashanah* prayers

Malchus: kingdom, government, official authority

Mashiach: lit., "the anointed one," Messiah

Matanos Kehunah: commentary on *Midrash Rabba* by Rabbi Yissachar Ber Katz Berman Ashkenazi (late 16th c.)

Me'am Lo'ez: unique anthology of *Midrash* and *halacha* covering the entire *Tenach*, written by Rabbi Yaakov Kuli (1598-1641)

Megillah: lit., "scroll," often referring to the Scroll of *Esther*

Meleches Shlomo: commentary on the *Mishnah* by Rabbi Shlomo Adeni (1567-1625)

Menorah: the 1.8 meter, seven-branched gold candelabra which stood in the main sanctuary of the *Beis Hamikdosh*

Mesillas Yesharim: *Path of the Just*, classic *mussar* (character-improving) work by Rabbi Moshe Chaim Luzzatto (1707-1747)

Metzudas Dovid: commentary on the Prophets and the Writings by Rabbi Dovid Altschuler (18th c.)

Mezuzah(-zos): parchment(s) with Torah inscriptions (the first two paragraphs of the *Shema*) which is (are) placed on the doorposts of every room

Mida k'neged mida: measure for measure

Midrash: the handed-down oral interpretations which elaborate and explain the stories and concepts of the Torah

Midrash Rabba: lit., "the Great *Midrash*," a very large collection of Midrashic explanations assembled during the early Gaonic period

Midrash Shochar Tov: an ancient *Midrash* on *Tehillim* (Psalms)

Mikdosh: see *Beis Hamikdosh*

Mishkan: Tabernacle, the portable Temple used by the Israelites in the desert for 39 years and for the first 440 years that they lived in *Eretz Yisroel*

Mishnah: the codification of the Oral Law by Rabbi Yehuda HaNasi in the second century of the common era

Mishnah Berurah: the Chofetz Chaim's commentary on the *Shulchan Aruch, Orach Chaim*

Mishnah Torah: See Rambam

Mishnayos: plural form of the word *Mishnah*

Mishpatim: judgements, laws

Mitzrayim: Egypt

Mitzvah(-vos): commandment(s) from Hashem in the Torah and also from the Sages, as authorized in the Torah (*Devorim* 17: 10)

Mizmor: song, psalm

Moshe Rabbeinu: Moses, our teacher

Motza'ei Shabbos: the going out of *Shabbos*, Saturday night

N

Nefesh: soul; the lowest of the five levels of the soul, often termed the "animal" soul in that it is the life force that humans share in common with animals

Neshamah: soul; one of the five levels of the soul, referring to the "intellectual" soul, present exclusively in human beings

Nezikim: the laws of damages; tort law

O

Olam Habah: the World to Come

Orach Chaim: lit., "the way of life," the section of the *Shulchan Aruch* dealing with daily Jewish practices

Oral Law: the oral explanation of the written Torah, told to Moshe by Hashem and orally transmitted for 1500 years until codified in the *Mishnah* and explained in the *Gemora*

Orchos Tzaddikim: *The Ways of the Righteous*, a book which outlines ways to improve behavior and motivations; written anonymously by a 15th century rabbi

P

Parve: "neutral," food that is neither meat nor milk, e.g., fish, vegetables

Pakode: remember, visit

Pesach: Passover

Pirkei Avos: lit., "Chapters of the Fathers," section of the *Mishnah* which contains the ethical sayings and maxims of the Sages

Purim: the Feast of Lots, rabbinic holiday celebrating the miraculous overthrow and defeat of those in the Persian Empire who sought to destroy the entire Jewish People in the fourth century before the common era

R

Radak: acronym for Rabbi Dovid Kimchi (1160-1235), Torah scholar from France who wrote an important commentary on the *Tenach*

Rambam: acronym for Rabbi Moshe ben Maimon (Maimonides) (1135-1204), extraordinary halachic scholar and philosopher who codified all of the Torah law in his 14-volume *Mishnah Torah*

Ramban: acronym for Rabbi Moshe ben Nachman (Nachmonides) (1094-1270), great commentator on the Torah and *Gemora*

Rashi: acronym for Rabbi Shlomo ben Yitzchak (1045-1105), unparalleled commentator on *Tenach* and *Gemora*

Rabbeinu Yona: rabbi from Gerona, Spain (1200-1263), who wrote commentaries and authored several important books on moral and ethical improvement

Rebbe: close, personal teacher, often referring to Chasidic rabbis

Rebbi: rabbi

Rosh Hashanah: lit., "head of the year," the Jewish New Year

Rosh Yeshivah: the head or dean of a *yeshivah*

Ruach: spirit, one of the five levels of the soul, corresponding to the vitality, enthusiasm, personality, inner essence of a human being

S

Sages: the rabbis of the Talmudic period

Sanhedrin: Jewish court of 23 judges; the Great Sanhedrin in Jerusalem was composed of 71 judges/sages

Seder: lit., "order," referring herein to the festive meal on the first night of *Pesach* (also second night outside *Eretz Yisroel*) which follows the order of discussion, drinking and eating as prescribed by the *Hagadah*

Sefer Ha'bahir: book of conceptual and metaphysical explanations of the Torah by Rabbi Chanunyah ben Hakanah in the 1st c. of the common era

Sefer Hachinuch: "Book of Education," a scholarly but very readable work which describes all of the 613 mitzvos; written by an anonymous 13th century rabbi from Spain

Shabbos(os): the Sabbath(s)

Shalaim: whole, complete

Shalom zachar: "Welcome, young boy!", the name given to the reception held after the *Shabbos* evening meal during the first week of the child's birth

Shas: acronym for the Six Orders of the *Mishnah*, often referring to the entire Talmud, which comprises 63 tractates

Shavuos: the Feast of Weeks, which celebrates the giving of the Torah at *Har Sinai* in the year 2448 of the Jewish calendar

Shechinah: the Divine Presence

Shel rosh/shel yad: see *Tefillin*

Shema: lit., "Hear"; the declaration which proclaims Hashem's unity: includes three paragraphs from *Devorim* 6:4-9, *Devorim* 11: 13-21, *Bemidbar* 15:37-41

Shemini Atzeres: the eighth day of holy gathering, the holiday that immediately follows the seventh day of *Succos* and on which, in *Eretz Yisroel*, *Simchas Torah* is also celebrated

Shemitah: the Sabbatical Year

Shemonah Esreh: the eighteen (actually, nineteen) blessings said in the standing, barely audible meditation, the *Amidah*

Shemos: lit., "the names," the second book of the *Chumash*, referred to as *Exodus* in English

Shemos Rabba: a *Midrash* on the book of *Shemos*

Shewbread: a specially formed unleavened loaf of bread, twelve of which were placed on the *Shulchan* in the *Beis Hamikdosh*

Shofar: the ram's horn blown on *Rosh Hashanah*

Shofaros: the name given to the section of the *Rosh Hashanah* prayers which deals with the blowing of the shofar

Shulchan: the Golden Table in the *Beis Hamikdosh*

Shulchan Aruch: lit., "the prepared table," title of the Code of Jewish Law, which is divided into four major sections

Siddur(im): prayer book(s)

Sifrei: halachic *Midrash* on *Bemidbar* and *Devorim*, redacted at the end of 2nd c. of common era

Sifsei Chachomim: commentary on Rashi's explanation of the Chumash by Rabbi Shabsai Bass (1640-1717)

Simchas Torah: holiday upon which we finish the annual reading of the Torah and then begin it again, with joyous dancing and song; see *Shemini Atzeres*

sinas chinom: causeless hatred

Sitra Achra: lit., the "other side," i.e., the force created by Hashem that allows humans to choose not to do what their Creator instructed

Soton: lit., "the hinderer," the force that seeks to block the Jew from serving Hashem

Succos: the Feast of Tabernacles/Booths

Sulam: ladder

T

Taharas hamishpachah: the rules of family purity, i.e., the regulation of marital relations and the requirement of ritual immersion

Talmud: the discussions and explanations of the Oral Law, including legal argumentations, stories, parables and allegories; see *Shas*

Talmid(ei) chachom(im): Talmudic scholar(s)

Tamay: spiritually impure

Targum Yonason (ben Uziel): translation and explanation of the Hebrew Torah into Aramaic by Yonason ben Uziel in the 1st c. of common era

T'chias hameisim: revival of the dead

Tefillin: phylacteries; one *tefillin* is placed on the biceps muscle (*shel yad*) and one on the head (*shel rosh*)

Temple: see *Beis Hamikdosh*

Tenach: acronym for the three major sections of the Bible: Torah, *N'veim* (Prophets) and *K'suvim* (Writings)

Teshuva: lit., "return," repentance

Tiferes Yisroel: commentary on the *Mishnah* by Rabbi Yisroel Lipschutz (1782-1860)

Tikunei Zohar: additions to the *Zohar* (the mystical explanations of the Torah) from Rabbi Shimon bar Yochai (2nd c. c.e.) and his school

Torah: the five books of Moses — *Bereishis, Shemos, Vayikra, Bemidbar, Devorim* (the written part), plus the Talmud (the oral part)

Torah Judaism: the observance of Judaism according to its over 3500-year tradition of law and custom, as basically described and explained in the *Shulchan Aruch* and its commentaries

Tosefos: lit., "additions"; name given to a group of extraordinary European rabbis of the 12th to 14th centuries, whose comments were first added to Rashi's commentary on the *Gemora*, and then later both were placed on the page of the actual *Gemora*

Tosefos Yom Tov: commentary on the Mishnah by Rabbi Yom Tov Lipmann Heller (1579-1654)

Tov: good

Tur: This shortened name was given to Rabbi Yaakov ben Asher (1270-1343), who wrote a very important halachic work called the *Arba Turim* (Four Rows)

Tzaddik(im): righteous person(s)

Tzedoka: rightful due of the poor

Tzitzis: fringes on a four-cornered garment

U

Unesane-tokef: lit., "And we shall give [utterance] to the power [of this day]"; a dramatic and poignant prayer on *Rosh Hashanah* and *Yom Kippur*, reminding us of our mortality and giving advice how to avert an evil decree

V

Vayikra: lit., "And He called," the third book of the *Chumash*, referred to as *Leviticus* in English

Vayikra Rabba: a *Midrash* on the book of *Vayikra*

Vilna Gaon: see Gra

Y

Yaakov: Jacob

Yafeh To'ar: commentary on the *Midrash Rabba* by Rabbi Shmuel Yaffe Ashkenazi (16th c.)

Yalkut Shimoni: Talmudic and Midrashic anthology collected by Rabbi Shimon Ashkenazi (13th c.) from Frankfort am Main

Yehoshua: succeeded Moshe as leader of the Jewish People and led them into *Eretz Yisroel*

Yerushalayim: Jerusalem

Yeshivah: school of Torah learning

Yetzer hara: evil inclination

Yetzer hatov: good inclination

Yiras Shamayim: fear of Heaven

Yitzchak: Isaac

Yom Kippur(im): the Day of Atonement

Yom Tov: lit., "Good Day," referring to the Jewish holidays

Yoreh De'ah: lit., "instruct knowledge," the section of the *Shulchan Aruch* dealing with a whole range of subjects: *kashrus*, oaths, honoring parents, *bris milah*, *tzedoka*, *challah*

Z

Zair: rim, crown, wreath

Zichronos: Remembrances, herein referring to the section of the *Rosh Hashanah* prayers which deals with Hashem remembering the righteous deeds of the *tzaddikim*

INDEX

Note:
Page numbers in regular type: 123
Footnote numbers in bold type: **123**

Achievement, individual 170
Achieving the infinite 12, 13
Adams, John **46**
Adom
    and Chava 24
    ate of forbidden fruit 24
    challenged the Creator 166
    composite of the Jewish People 167
    death sentence commuted **246**
    first being with a human soul 136
    purpose of creation 25, 167
Adultery
    cause for First Temple's destruction 181
    give up life rather than commit 66
Aharon, the High Priest
    example of no jealousy 88
    peace-pursuing 218
    wore Breastplate 88
Akeidah
    connection to *Avodah* 16
    to prayer 16
    Yitzchak's control of instincts 19-21
Altar
    outer
        symbol of Yitzchak 19-21
        the three fires **108**
    Golden
        ketores burnt on 216, 249
        lit from one of the three fires **108**
        rim of, representing Crown of *Kehunah* 147
Angel of Death
    (see *Malach Hamoves*)
Anger
    behavior indicator 139
    connection to arrogance, glory-seeking 179
    like idolatry 179
Anti-Semitism 43, 57, 170
Arizal
    Adom and the Jewish People 167, 247
    Purim and *Yom Kippurim* 134-5, **175**
Aron
    representing the heart 218, 249
    rim of, representing Crown of Torah 147, 148

Arrogance
    basic problem 7
    Bilam, example of 140
    blessing children to avoid **225**
    connection to anger, idol worship 179
    problem began with creation 24
    Rabbi Akivah's students 112
    removes person from world 143
Assimilation
    causes 123-5, **159**
    early problem in Jewish history 82-3
    lack of Hebrew skills 88
    tendencies even among the observant 161
Avodah
    connection to *Akeidah* 16
        to prayer 16
    of the heart 111
    sacrifices (see *Karbonos*)
    three daily prayers 95-6
    three fires on the Altar **108**
    Yitzchak, model of 19-21, 11
Avos
    connection to *Shema* 81
    constructed the three pillars 11
    models of the three Pilgrimage Festivals 114
Avraham
    Egyptian bondage 185-6
    Eretz Yisroel 186
    Passover lamb 119-21, **162**
    Pesach 115
    pillar of *chesed* 16, 17-19, 11
    qualities of 140
    Shabbos, first meal 151-3
    Shacharis 95, **120**
    Shema, all our heart 71-5
    tent, symbol of 17-19

Basic dichotomies 236
Basic thesis
    abilities, full usage of **4**, 205, 226-7
    achieving the infinite **7**, 13, 143, 170-1
    basic analogy 233

beyond-self = infinite-like 12-3, 217
categories overlap 11, 93-103, **196**, **259**, 238
emulating the infinite 217
going beyond self 7-8, 92, 143, 217
individual achievement 170
purpose of world 13, 143, 165
self — beyond-self continuum 7, 231
self=finite 12, 143, 165, 233
synopsis 204-6, 224
three components of human 5-6
threefold key 9-11
Behavior
    (see Qualities of a Jew)
    person known through three traits 139
    three prime Jewish traits 26-33
Beis Hamikdosh
    (see Altar, *Avodah*)
    First, reasons for destruction 181
    rebuilding by *Mashiach* 190
    rebuilding through our effort 191-2, 218
    Second, reasons for destruction 182-3, 248
    service of the *kohanim* 144
    spiritual elevation of the people 173
    three major objects 218, 249
Berachos
    engendering humility 101-3
    extending Hashem into world **129**
Bilam 140
Birkas Hamazone
    bris/*Eretz Yisroel* 253
    prayer for peace and harmony **258**
Birth
    key in Hashem's hands 161-3
Blessings (see *Berachos*)
Bloom, Allan 209-10, 211
B'nei Yisroel
    Kohanim and *Levi'im* 144-6
Body
    controlling desires of 19-21
    necessary relaxation 122
    three parts 5-6

Breastplate
(see Aharon, the High Priest)
Bris milah
blessing given to newly-circumcised boy **116**
sign of a Jew **39-42**
Yosef, to prove identity **100**
Business practices **178**

Causeless hatred
arrogance, compared to **191**
loshon hara, connection to **276**
reason for Temple's destruction **182-3**
Challah **60-1**
Chametz **121, 156**
Chanukah **174**
Charity (see *Tzedoka*)
Chava
and Adom
(see all references under Adom)
Chesed (see lovingkindness)
Avraham **17-19, 11**
pillar of **90-1, 93-5**
Children
birth of **161-3**
blessing newborn **116**
blessing on *Shabbos* evening **225**
Chosen People **39, 113, 187-8, 190**
Clothing
different from Egyptians **85-87**
rules of modesty **86**
Competition
eliminated in the World to Come **259**
muted on *Shabbos* **39**
Converts **113**
Creation, purpose of **10-13, 143, 165, 170-1**
Crowns, the three **147-9**

Davening (see Prayer)
David, King
the fourth component **248**
Torah leader **190**

Day of Repentance (see *Yom Kippur*)
Dessler, Rabbi E.E.
givers and takers **195**
importance of *chesed* **27, 28**
Dichotomies (see Basic dichotomies)
Dispersion, generation of **24**

Eating **162-3, 199**
Education, Torah
importance for Jewish survival **87-8, 123-5**
insufficient amount **159**
lack of Hebrew skills **88**
Egyptian bondage
and Avraham **186**
assimilation into Egyptian culture **82-3, 99**
reasons for **122-5, 185-6**
volunteered labor **122-3**
Emotions
child's development **53-4**
feelings of inadequacy **206**
growth beyond self **9, 206-9**
importance of mother **53-4**
Ephraim and Menashe
blessing of **225**
Eretz Yisroel
Avraham and **186**
bris milah, connection to **253**
control of physicality **172-4, 189**
holiness of **172-3**
judges, appointed to oversee **188-9**
present from Hashem **172-4**
retaining possession **174, 186**
sexual purity **173, 254**
Shemitah **173, 180-1**
Esav
battle with Yaakov **140**
reason for eating *maror* **162**
Evil eye
Bilam **140**
compared to jealousy **191, 197**
removes us from the world **191**
Evil tongue (see *Loshon hara*)

Evolution 71, **83**, **136**
Exile
    four exiles 248
    ingathering of 190-1

Family
    Jewish People one family 146
    together on *Shabbos* 37-8
    under mother's influence 53-4
Family purity laws 58-9
Far Eastern religions **251**
Feinstein, Harav Moshe 118
Festival Holidays 114-8
Final Redemption (see Redemption)
Finite
    analogy to "self" 12, 143, 165, 233
    basic dilemma of 11-13
    challenge to achieve the infinite 12, 13, 143, 165, 170-1
Flood, Generation of the 24
Forefathers (see *Avos*)
Free will 13, 166
Fourth component
    composite of threefold key 247-9
    gifts to poor 163
    Golden Altar 249
    good name 220
    levity 177

Gan Eden 177
Gehenom 154, 177
Givers and takers 37, 195
Glory-seeking (see anger, arrogance)
Gog and *Magog*, war of 158
Golden Altar (see Altar)
Golden Calf
    levi'im withstood test of 145
    women's refusal to worship 202
Golden Table (see *Shulchan*)

Hagadah
    three categories of *mitzvos* **123**
    three topics requiring explanation 119-26
Happiness
    Jewish success 222-5
    Purim 127-36
    Shabbos 37-8, 152-3
    Shema 79
    Simchas Torah 118
Har Hamoriah 24-5
Hester panim 128
Hevel and Kayin 24
Hebrew language
    books teaching **106**
    identity indicator 87-8
    importance of learning 87-8
High Holidays 106-13
History
    Jewish analysis of 128-30
    secular analysis of 128-9
    unfolding of life's tests 24
Holidays (see Pilgrimage Festivals)
Holocaust
    connection to *Purim* 170
    Kristallnacht 170
    remnant surviving 231
Home
    atmosphere on *Shabbos* 38
    importance in Judaism 53-4
    woman's power to mold 53-62
Humility
    Avraham 140
    berachos 101-3
    Micah's dictum 141-2
    Moshe Rabbeinu 187
    Yaakov and Yosef 186-7

Identity indicators 82-9
Idolatry
    anger like idolatry **179**
    arrogance like idolatry **179**
    give up life rather than commit 66-7
    reason for First Temple's

destruction 181
Infinite
   dilemma of life 11-13
   human's natural connection **114**
   purpose of creation 13, 143, 165
   striving to achieve 170-1
Intermarriage 123-5, **159**
Israel, Land of (see *Eretz Yisroel*)
Israel, State of
   emigration from **257**
   lack of Jewish identity **160**
   Torah non-observance 173-4

Jealousy
   basic problem 7
   blessing children to avoid **225**
   eliminated in the World to Come **259**
   evil eye, comparison to **191**
   problem began with creation 24
   removes person from the world 143
Jerusalem (see Yerushalayim)
Jewish identity, signs of
   external 24-52, 82-9
   internal 16-25, 26-33
Jewish People (see Chosen People, Qualities of a Jew)
   achievements:
      economics 44
      education 47
      professions 47
      science 43, 47
      wealth 47
   assimilation (see topic)
   contribution to civilization 46
   composite of Adom 167
   choosing Hashem **113**
   guarantors for each other 146
   identity savers 82-9
   intermarriage (see topic)
   one unity 146
   three subdivisions 143-7
   wandering Jew **148**
Johnson, Paul 46

Judges (see Sanhedrin)
   appointed by redeemer 188-9
   compared to Hashem **215**
   enforcing physicality controls 188-9
Judgment
   control of physicality 141, 142
   Micah's dictum 141
   world continues because of 142

Karbonos (see also *Avodah*) **16**, **108**, **111**, 190, **293**
Kayin and Hevel **24**
Kehunah, the Crown of 147, 148
Ketores **108**, 148, 249
Keys, the three 160-8
Kishon, Ephraim 212-3
Kohain Gadol
   peacekeeping powers **218**
   perfection model **271**
Kohanim
   Levi'im and *B'nei Yisroel* 143-7
   models of restraint 199
   receiving *challah* 60, **69**
Kosel 57
Kosher food 41, 133
Kristallnacht **170**

Land of Israel (see *Eretz Yisroel*)
Leah **10**, 53-62
Levi'im
   carriers of the *Aron* 145
   Kohanim and *B'nei Yisroel* 143-7
   Levite cities 145
   never enslaved in Egypt 123
   refused to worship Golden Calf 145
Levity **177**
Loshon hara
   atoned through the *ketores* 249
   connection to causeless hatred **276**
   not speaking, cause for Exodus **100**
   reason for Second Temple's destruction **276**

Love Your Neighbor
    examples 244-6
Lovingkindness (see *Chesed*)
    greater than *tzedoka* 93-5
    love your neighbor 84-5, 97-9, 146
    Micah's dictum 141
Lust
    basic problem 7
    Bilam 140
    chametz 121
    compared to *yetzer hara* 191
    problem began with creation 24
    removes person from world 143

Ma'ariv (evening prayer) 96
Maharsha
    reproof of his generation **279**
Malach Hamoves **249**
Malchus, Crown of 147, 148-9
Maror 122-5
Marriage
    blessing for newborn child **116**
    elevating to a spiritual level 58-9
Mashiach
    composite of the *Avos* 248
    factors for his arrival 179-83, 185
    ingathering of the exiles 190
    rebuilding the Temple 190
    returning kingship of *Beis Dovid* 190
    three criteria 186-9
    travail at his coming 151-3
Matriarchs 53-62
Matzah 121-2
Meals, three (of *Shabbos*) 150-9
Measure for measure 32, 161
Meat and milk 31-2
Megillah 128-31
Men, dress code 86-7
Menashe and Ephraim
    blessing of **225**
Menorah
    lit from Altar **108**
    symbolic of intellect 218, 249

Metaphysical terms for human
    components **1**
Mezuzah 141
Micah 141
Minchah (afternoon prayer) 95-6
Mitzrayim (Egypt)
    conceptional definition 188
Mitzvos
    means to achieve the infinite 217
    three categories **123**
Modesty
    rules of proper dress 86-7
Moshe Rabbeinu
    example of humility 187
Murder
    give up life rather than commit 55
    reason First Temple destroyed 181

Names, Jewish
    identity indicator 84-5
Nezikim (damages) 97-9
New Year (see *Rosh Hashanah*)
Noahide laws 190
Non-Jews
    may convert **113**
    observing the Noahide laws 190
    refused Torah **113**

Personality types **1**
Pesach
    Avraham 115, 119-21, **162**
    Hagadah 119
    maror 122-5
    matzah 121-2
    Passover lamb 119-21
    Pilgrimage Festival 115
    Seder meal 119-25
Pillars of the world
    constructed by *Avos* 11, 90-1
    significance 91, 143
Pilgrimage Festivals
    (see *Pesach, Shavuos, Succos*)

Pirkei Avos
    introspection 99-101
Prayer
    connection to *Akeidah* 16
        to *Avodah* 16
    divestiture of physicality 18
    Ma'ariv 96
    means to avert evil decree 109-10
    Minchah 95-6
    Rosh Hashanah/Yom Kippur 106-13
    service of the heart 111
    Shacharis 95
    Unesane-tokef 108-13
Presents, the three 169-77
Purim
    connection to Holocaust 170
    festive meal 133-6
    gifts to friend 132-3
        to poor 131-2
    Megillah 128-31
Purpose of creation
    achieving the infinite 10-13, 7, 143, 165, 170-1
    becoming a *tzaddik* 10-11
    bringing Hashem into the world 12-13, 69, 91-2
    elevating physical to spiritual 165-6, 293

Qualities of a Jew (see Jewish People) 17-19
    benevolent 17-19, 27-9
    compassionate 32-3
    self-controlled 19-21
    shamefaced 29-32
    truth-seeking 21-5

Rachel 10, 53-62
Rains
    key in Hashem's hands 160-1
Redemption
    process of 185-92
    the three *Shabbosos* 271
Relaxation 122
Repentance (see *Teshuvah*)

Reproof by Maharsha 279
Revival of dead
    key in Hashem's hands 164-8
    step-by-step process 146
Rivkah 10, 53-62
Rosh Hashanah
    creation of first human 136
    Musaf, three parts of
        malchuyos 107-8
        shofaros 108
        zichronos 108
    three means to avert evil decree 109-13
    Unesane-tokef 108-9
Roth, Cecil 107

Sabbatical year (see *Shemitah*)
Sacrifices (see *Karbonos*)
Sanhedrin 188-9, 190
Sarah 10, 53-62
Seder, Pesach 119-26
Self
    going beyond self 7-8, 92, 143, 217
    its best usage 217, 227
    proper care of 4, 205, 226-7
    relaxation 122
    self=finite 12, 143, 165, 233
    self−beyond-self continuum 7, 231
Sexual desires
    directed beyond self 39-42, **240**
    Ramban's prayer 266
Shabbos
    blessing children 225
    bringing the redemption 180
    purpose of creation 151
    sign of a Jew 37-40
    three meals of 150-9
    women lighting candles 54-6
Shacharis 95
Shavuos 116-7
Shechinah 56-9
Shema
    being 75-7

heart 71-5
humble acceptance 79-80
substance (might, resources) 77-9
success of a Jew 223
unification 69-70
Shemini Atzeres 118
Shemitah
  bringing the redemption 180
  debts cancelled 181
  land open to all 181
  refraining from food production 181
  time to learn Torah 181
Shofar 108
Shulchan
  rim of 147-9
  symbolic of instincts 218, 249
Signs, of a Jew
  bris milah 36, 39-42
  Shabbos 36, 37-9
  tefillin 36, 42-52
Sinas chinom (see Causeless hatred)
Sitra achra 71, 140, 236
Simchas Torah 118
Soton 162, **249**
Success, Jewish 222-5
Succos 117-8

Talmid chachom
  bringing the redemption 180
  disrespect of 184
  humility 202
  leaders of the generation 80, 202
Tefillin
  four-headed *shin* 248
  power of 55
  shel rosh 56
  shel yad 56
  sign of a Jew 36, 42-52
  thought converted to action **243**
  Threefold Key 238
  three-twined cord 141
Temple, Holy
  (see *Beis Hamikdosh*, Altar, *Avodah*)

Teshuvah
  definition 111-2
  means to avert an evil decree 109
  Rambam's approach **141**
  Rosh Hashanah 108-9, 111-3
  Unesane-tokef 108-9
  Yom Kippur 108-9, 111-3
Thesis (see Basic thesis)
Three Crowns 147-9
Three keys 160-8
Three meals of *Shabbos* 150-9
Three pillars 90-2
Three presents 169-77
Threefold Key 5-11, 91, 238-40
Three-twined cord 141
Tolstoy, Count Leo N. **46**
Torah
  Crown of 147, 148
  education 87-8, 123-5
  learning in *Shemitah* 181
  overcomes the *Malach Hamoves* **249**
  pillar of the world 91
  present from Hashem 171
Torah Sages (see *talmid chachom*)
Traits (see Qualities of a Jew)
Truth
  definition of Hashem **140**
  world continues because of 142
Twain, Mark 47, **51**, 129, **165**
Tzaddik
  examples of **308**
  purpose of creation 10-11
  qualities of 140
  world sustained because of **220**
Tzedoka
  importance at *Rosh Hashanah* 110-11
  rightful due 93, **236**
  showing appreciation 161
  ten percent to charity **95**
  ten percent of time 118
Tzitzis 141
Unesane-tokef 108-13

Western Wall (see *Kosel*)
Women
    blessing given to newborn girl 116
    cause for Exodus from Egypt 100
    determine Jewish identity 53-4
    dress code 86
    Golden Calf, refusal to worship 202
    influence on child's development 53-4, 61-2
    Matriarchs 10, 53-62
    mitzvos of
        challah 60-1
        family purity 57-9
        Shabbos candles 54-6
    source of the home's blessing 60-1
    subtle power of 53-62
World to Come
    description of 175-7, **259**
    how to earn 174-7
    loss of 143
    present from Hashem 174-7

Yaakov
    criteria for redeemer 186
    dream of ladder 21-5
    Esav, battle with 140
    Ma'ariv 96
    maror 122-6, **162**

    pillar of Torah 11
    Shabbos, third meal 155-9
    striving for truth 21-5
Yerushalayim
    reasons for destruction 183-5
Yetzer hara
    compared to lust **191**
    equated to *soton* and *Malach Hamoves* 249
Yisroel
    Land of (see *Eretz Yisroel*)
Yitzchak
    Akeidah 19-21
    altar, symbol of 19, **16**
    Minchah 95-6
    pillar of *Avodah* 11, **16**
    Shabbos, second meal 153-4
    self-restraint 17
Yom Kippur
    day of perfection **271**
    Purim, comparison to 134-5
    three means to avert evil decree 109
    Unesane-tokef 108-13
Yosef
    criteria for redeemer 186
    revealing his identity **100**

Notes

Notes

Notes

Notes